PENGU

FESTIVE BA
GERMANY

Sarah Kelly was born in 1943 at Colorado Springs. After gaining a B.A. in Political Science and Soviet Studies, she went to Germany where she began her culinary career, her skills at that time being limited to the preparation of chili con carne. Many years later, after being tutored by chefs and, mostly, good friends in Switzerland and Germany, she moved to London. While there she attended the London Cordon Bleu School of Cookery, receiving her Chef's Diploma in 1976. Upon returning to the United States, she set up her own cooking school and also cooked for still photography and television. She began her writing career on her return to England in 1978 and worked as a freelance journalist for several American magazines, including *Food and Wine*, *Connoisseur* and *Cuisine*, and was also Food Editor for *Brides* magazine. In addition she was a consultant to the *Time/Life* Good Cook series, for which she also prepared food for photography and illustration, and wrote a weekly column syndicated in English-language newspapers worldwide. Her fluency in German and interest in baking led her to research the techniques and refinements of preparing regional specialities from the German-speaking countries. In September 1981 she presented a paper at the Oxford Food Symposium on 'Speciality Baking in Austria, Germany and Switzerland', which she later developed into this book. Sarah Kelly is now living in New York where she works for Creditanstalt-Bankverein, and is also preparing another cookbook, *Open House*.

Sarah Kelly

FESTIVE BAKING IN AUSTRIA, GERMANY AND SWITZERLAND

PENGUIN BOOKS

To Om and Op

Penguin Books Ltd, Harmondsworth, Middlesex, England
Viking Penguin Inc., 40 West 23rd Street, New York, New York 10010, U.S.A.
Penguin Books Australia Ltd, Ringwood, Victoria, Australia
Penguin Books Canada Ltd, 2801 John Street, Markham, Ontario, Canada L3R 1B4
Penguin Books (N.Z.) Ltd, 182–190 Wairau Road, Auckland 10, New Zealand

First published 1985

Copyright © Sarah Kelly 1985

All rights reserved

Made and printed in Great Britain by
Cox & Wyman, Reading
Typeset in Linotron Aldus by
Rowland Phototypesetting Ltd
Bury St Edmunds, Suffolk

CONTENTS

INTRODUCTION

The custom of baking to celebrate holidays, festivals and special occasions is an ancient one. This book explores the vast and artistic array of seasonal and speciality baked goods – biscuits, cakes, pastries and breads – which appear in shops, market stalls and homes in German-speaking countries to mark various holidays and high days throughout the year. The evolution of recipes from these countries sharing a common language, the symbolic custom of baking to communicate joy and good fortune, and the strong force of tradition are themes which recur throughout this book.

Looking back, bread is more than just sustenance; as the 'staff of life' it has served as a symbol for fruitful harvests or fertility. The sweet cakes which first appeared in the Middle Ages and which were used as tokens to mark special occasions expanded the scope of symbolic baking. Most people lived in villages at this time and baking was generally done in communal ovens or by professional bakers as fuel was limited. Bread was a necessity, and the village baker was an important figure in the community. Proud of his art, he developed designs which differentiated breads for special occasions from the daily loaves, shaping, plaiting and twisting wheat dough into different forms.

Geography played a significant role in the development of decorative bread making: northern Germany excepted, the area we are considering was a wheat-growing region. Wheat was not used generally for daily loaves, but it is the only grain that can produce a bread both soft and light enough to model and its availability allowed the baker to expand his creative skills. He was still limited, however, by the fact that yeast doughs, even when made from the finest milled wheat, are difficult to control since they expand in all directions.

Although sugar was scarce until the seventeenth century, honey was readily available. When mixed with flour and spices, it sweetened one of the earliest fancy biscuits – Lebkuchen – which were printed with elaborately carved moulds or cut in heart shapes and colourfully decorated. Besides decorative breads, other sweet cakes and biscuits were devised. Since most of these were intended for special occasions and given as tokens, the shapes were often of pagan origin or symbolic of a mythical or historical event.

Today in the German-speaking countries, there are hundreds of different biscuits, cakes, pastries and breads baked for special occasions – for the most part, based on traditional recipes. However, there are numerous contemporary factors which influence the quantity and mix of baked goods, including communications, taste, new ingredients, economics, modern equipment and life-style.

Owing to improved communications, a common language (albeit with regional variations) and the proliferation of cookery books, many of the baked goods that were local specialities are now found in the best *Konditorei* and household repertoires throughout the region. The influence of other countries is also apparent both in ingredients and imports of baked goods – though foreign cakes and pastries are generally not consumed on important holidays. Taste is another factor responsible for the evolution of recipes. Women, both as bakers and discriminating customers, keep baking standards high; bakers apply professional skills and imagination to their creations; and new ingredients and equipment are available – all these factors play a role in determining what is baked today and how.

My fascination with this subject stems from a childhood fixation for things Germanic (when I first began studying the language), a love of artistic baking and many years spent living in various cities in the three countries. In gathering material for this book, I have used old and new German-language cookery books from different regions as a documentary source from which to analyse quantities, techniques and variations. However, it is the many delicious cakes and pastries I have consumed and the many baking friends I made while living and travelling in these countries that have given me an up-to-date perspective on the subject and the necessary 'insider's' clues (the kind rarely mentioned in written recipes) on how to reproduce them professionally.

As a guideline, I have selected only recipes that I feel qualify as 'festive baking', either because they have an historical association with certain holidays or events, or because they fall outside the realm of 'everyday baking,' due to the use of unusual equipment or to the effort and skill required to produce them. While reference is made to historical recipes, I have taken contemporary taste, ingredients and equipment into account and have concentrated on documenting specialities as they are prepared today.

I have assumed that many or all of these items have not been seen or sampled by the reader, and so I have given a brief description of each in the introductions to the recipes. This includes historical facts, when applicable, personal notes, degree of difficulty, time involved in preparation, and storing capabilities. Thus you can decide, without reading through the recipe, whether or not it is something that will appeal to you and if it can be made practically in the time available and with the equipment to hand.

To provide continuity in technique, the chapters have been organized according to individual dough type. In as many instances as possible, I have given a basic dough recipe which, with additions, will provide a variety of specialities. In this way, you can make up one dough (a double recipe, if desired) and produce two or three different items – an especially useful time-saver for Christmas baking. The Baking Calendar on pp. 11–15 lists all the major holidays and special occasions, noting the appropriate specialities.

Because baking is one of the most demanding and unforgiving culinary disciplines, one which is readily affected by varying ingredients, climate, altitude and equipment, I have written the recipes to allow for these variables. Moreover, teaching in various cooking schools with other people's equipment and different brands of ingredients has made me especially sensitive to the need for providing descriptive, flexible recipes and for warning about certain types of unsuitable equipment. For a full breakdown of equipment, see pp. 16–21.

As for why I have written this book, my reasons are both personal and inspirational. Cookery books for those who write them with love are semi-autobiographical, reflecting the writer's origins and preoccupations. As for a regional cookery book written by an outsider, many writers and philosophers have noted that one observes with greater clarity in a foreign environment. It is no doubt partially due to my non-Germanic background that I have been so impressed and excited by this subject and have wanted to document it. With my outsider's account of what I've eaten, baked and loved, where these items are found and how they can be reproduced, I hope to communicate my own joy and good fortune and, in the process, to inspire in others some of the same excitement for festive baking and its traditions.

BAKING CALENDAR

The list below includes major holiday dates and those occasions for which special cakes, biscuits, breads or pastries are baked. Besides religious holidays (both Catholic and Protestant, depending on the region), a few secular holidays are also observed with festive baking.

6 January	Twelfth Night (*Dreikönigsabend*) is celebrated in many German-speaking regions with Dreikönigskuchen (p. 150) – usually a round wreath made of rich yeast dough with a single almond or trinket baked inside.
Mardi Gras (Carnival) and Shrove Tuesday	*Fasching* (in Switzerland, *Fastnacht*) and *Rosendienstag*. Several cities are famous for their *Fasching* celebrations, most notably Munich, Mainz, Cologne and Basel. However, *Fasching* – the period following Advent and preceding Lent – is observed throughout the German-speaking area with costume balls, parades, satirical skits and special food, most notably a variety of deep-fried pastries which are sold by street vendors or made at home. On Shrove Tuesday, it is traditional to eat jelly doughnuts which go by different names in different regions.
14 February	St Valentine's Day. Plaited hearts (of yeast dough – follow the directions for Osterkranz, shaping the braid into a heart rather than a wreath, p. 153) and large heart-shaped gingerbreads (see Lebkuchen-Herzen, p. 51) are made. This is an observance of recent

11

origin and special baked goods are produced in bakeries rather than in homes.

Easter
: While not celebrated to the extent that it is in the neighbouring Eastern European countries, Easter (*Ostern*) is generally observed by commercial and home bakers with special yeast breads (plaited wreaths, Easter-egg nests, fish, doves, among others), see Oster-Hefegebäck, p. 152.

Mother's Day
: *Muttertag*, of recent origin. Bakers in many areas make heart-shaped cakes, often small, for children to present to their mothers.

2 November
: All Souls' Day (*Allerseelen*). In earlier times, the Zopf (plaited bread, see p. 168) was the traditional speciality baked in Germany for this day. Nowadays, however, plaited loaves are baked throughout the year, generally for Sundays.

11 November
: Feast of St Martin (*St Martinstag*), celebrated in some Protestant areas. In the Würzburg area, bakers produce a small Martinsweck (a rich yeast bun with two 'ears' on either side and a plait across the top).

Christmas Market
: A Christmas fair (*Weihnachtsmarkt*) – generally from early December until the twenty-third of the month – is held in the marketplace of many German-speaking cities, the most famous of which is the one held in Nuremberg. Frankfurt, Munich, Rothenburg ob der Tauber, Vienna and Strasbourg are only a few of the other cities which observe this custom. In Nuremberg, market stalls feature the famous Nürnberger Elisenlebkuchen (p. 66) as well as decorated gingerbread hearts (Lebkuchen-Herzen, p. 51) and Zwetschgenmännla (figures made of prunes). In Strasbourg, gingerbread pigs (Lebkuchen Glücksschweinchen, p. 53)

symbolizing good luck are sold by vendors who write the recipient's name on each pig. Fruit breads, too, are generally a feature of the markets, including Hutzelbrot (p. 164) and Früchtebrot. Other sweets that are a standard item at these fairs include caramelized almonds (Gebrannte Mandeln), nougatine (Türkischer Honig) and chocolate-dipped marshmallow confections (Negerküsse).

6 December	St Nikolaus. In most German-speaking areas, children receive their gifts on this day rather than on Christmas Day as is customary in the English-speaking world. Something made of marzipan is traditional (see the many baked marzipan confections in Chapter 2), as is either Lebkuchen or rich yeast dough Santa Claus figures (Weihnachtsmänner, p. 143) or the Swiss figures (Grittibänzen, p. 144; similar figures are baked in Germany and called *Weckmann*) which wear neckties, and carry pipes in their mouths. Additional historical notes on St Nikolaus are given on p. 97.
24–5 December	Christmas Eve and Christmas Day (*Heiliger Abend* and *Weihnachten*). Christmas Eve is traditionally a family celebration, with the Christmas tree lit for the first time, followed by a festive dinner. The many Christmas goodies (*Weihnachtsgebäck*) that have been baked, received as gifts and purchased are finally fully displayed. Some of the most famous of these are Lebkuchen (gingerbread, p. 43), Springerle (anis-flavoured whisked egg biscuits, p. 73), and Zimtsterne (ground almond egg-white biscuits, p. 92). Most of the biscuits given in this book would be considered appropriate for Christmas baking, and those in the Lebkuchen chapter, p. 43, are generally baked only at Christmas time.

Large tangled snowballs (Rothenburger

Schneeballen) are an interesting deep-fried pastry made for Christmas.

Rich breads are also baked for the Christmas holidays. In addition to those mentioned above under Christmas Market and 6 December, there is also one of the most famous fruit and nut-filled loaves, Dresdner Christstollen (p. 160), as well as numerous different plaited loaves (see Weihnachts-Hefegebäck, p. 143).

In Austria, people also bake and exchange their finest cakes (see Chapter 5) as well as breads and biscuits.

31 December and 1 January	New Year's Eve and New Year's Day (*Silvesternacht* and *Silvester*). Various yeast breads and deep-fried pastries are prepared for the celebration on New Year's Eve, an occasion which is, in general, celebrated with the family. Yeast specialities include Speckkuchen (flat 'bacon cake', p. 166). Toggenburger Doppelfladen (a spicy pear tart on a yeast base), Neujahrs-Glücksschweinchen (yeast dough pigs filled with marzipan, p. 146) and Geflochtene Neujahrs-Brezeln (plaited yeast pretzels). A selection of deep-fried pastries would also traditionally be consumed at New Year, the selection varying in different regions. Jelly doughnuts (Berliner Pfannkuchen), which are traditionally eaten on Shrove Tuesday, are also eaten on New Year's Eve in many places.

*

First communion; Confirmation; Wedding; Birthday	On any of these occasions, a special cake is usually prepared, either home-made or purchased from the local baker. See Chapter 5 for a selection.
Local village fairs;	*Volksfeste*, *Messen*, and *Kirchweih* – for these regional fairs, local bakers and itinerant

Trade fairs; Church fairs	vendors normally prepare different deep-fried pastries, among them Apfelküchel (apple fritters), Eieröhrli (deep-fried pastry rounds), Schlupfküchlein (pastry knots).
Sundays	Because Sunday is the baker's day off, Sunday bread is often baked at home. Two such traditional loaves are Zopf (a rich yeast braided loaf, p. 168), and Kugelhopf (an unmoulded rich yeast round studded with raisins, p. 169). In addition, the coffee hour on Sunday is a special focal point, when either a special home-made cake or pastry is consumed when the family makes an outing (an *Ausflug*) to a charming country inn or a popular café with a pause for *Kaffee* and *Kuchen*.

EQUIPMENT

Most of the recipes in this book can be made using the standard baking equipment which I have listed below (excluding knives and saucepans). A number of recipes, however, call for special equipment which I have described separately. In case you are buying new equipment I have, whenever possible, stated preference for various models or materials and the reasons for my choice.

STANDARD BAKING EQUIPMENT

FOR PASTRY AND DOUGH MAKING

Cutters. A useful investment is a nest of fluted or plain round *biscuit cutters* in various sizes. Small *aspic cutters* are suggested in several recipes but a thimble or small bottle lid can be substituted. *Pastry wheels*, zig-zag or plain, are used for decorative pastry work such as cutting out free-form flowers and leaves or for cutting out printed biscuits.

Dredgers. These are not essential but are useful if you bake often. Have three – one for flour, one for icing sugar and the third for granulated sugar. (I also keep a fourth filled with cocoa powder.) Most important is the one filled with flour which can be used to dust sparingly the pastry board and rolling pin when rolling out dough.

Mixing bowls. You will need several in various sizes, including one medium-sized crockery or glass bowl (for making whisked sponge cakes and whisked egg biscuits) and one large non-aluminum bowl in crockery or plastic (for beating egg whites).

Palette knives. A large palette knife or *metal spatula* is used for spreading icing and removing biscuits from baking sheets. If you have two that match, they are especially good for cutting butter into flour when making butter pastry or butter biscuit dough. A *small palette knife* is not essential but it is useful for removing small biscuits from baking sheets and doing touching-up work on icing and decorations.

Piping bags. Ideally you should have one medium sized and one large. I prefer piping bags that are made of a thin, flexible, plastic material as they are easier to wash, dry more quickly, and don't absorb flavours like some that are made of heavy plasticized cotton. For more information see Baking Tips, p. 31.

Pastry boards. These can be made of marble or wood or a synthetic material. A marble slab is especially suitable for butter-rich pastry and biscuit doughs because of its constant cool temperature and glassy surface. Almost as good are the new synthetic white boards which have the added advantage of being light, relatively non-stick and dishwasher-proof. If using a wooden pastry board, reserve it for pastry only as wood absorbs flavours from other foods.

Pastry brushes. Keep one always dry for brushing excess flour from dough.

Pastry scraper. This is a thin metal rectangle with wooden handle (now also made in tough plastic) used to scrape sticking dough from a pastry board. A palette knife (metal spatula) can also be used for this. The scraper is also used to work chocolate and icing mixtures on a marble slab.

Rolling pin. I prefer a long cylindrical rolling pin for general use (mine is approximately 1¾ inches/4·5cm in diameter), the same diameter throughout, without handles. This gives much better control for pastry making than one with handles, though the latter is fine for biscuit doughs. The French-style rolling pin with tapered ends is useful for rolling out very firm doughs since you get added leverage.

Rubber spatula

Wire or plastic sieves. Small and large sieves are used for sifting flour and icing sugar, and for straining.

FOR WHISKING AND MIXING

Beaters. Use an *electric beater* – in some recipes I have specified a hand-held model – or a *rotary beater*.

Food processor. I don't recommend using a food processor for the biscuit and pastry doughs in this book, since it makes them too greasy and the end results are inferior. However, food processors are useful for sifting icing sugar – just pour it in and turn on the machine – puréeing both thick and thin mixtures, softening butter that has just come out of the refrigerator, and grinding quantities of nuts and breadcrumbs. However, if the nuts need to be very finely ground, as in marzipan, a liquidizer must be used.

Liquidizer (blender). This is especially useful for grinding nuts very fine.

Spoons. A *large metal spoon* is better than a rubber spatula for folding in beaten egg white or flour, since the sharp edge of the spoon cuts more efficiently through the mixture. You will also need two or three *wooden spoons*.

Wire whisks. Small and large whisks are useful.

FOR CUTTING AND GRATING, ETC.

Cheese grater. Use for grating chocolate and lemon rind, and for flaking the butter in pastry and biscuit doughs using my method.

Lemon squeezer. Not essential because you can squeeze lemon juice through your closed hand into a bowl.

Scissors

FOR MEASURING

Kitchen scales

Measuring cups or **jug**

Measuring spoons

Ruler. Especially useful for measuring biscuits.

FOIL AND PAPER

Aluminium foil. This is useful for wrapping food before freezing.

Greaseproof paper. This is especially useful when sifting dry ingredients.

Heavy paper. Used for cutting out paper stencils.

Non-stick baking paper. This is available in department stores and specialist shops and is especially recommended for soft whisked-egg biscuits and for delicate egg white biscuits such as meringues and macaroons, though it is not an essential item if you follow the instructions given in the recipes about lining baking sheets. It can be wiped off and reused.

Parchment paper. This is my preference for lining cake tins and baking sheets. It is heavier and more durable than greaseproof paper and fairly resistant to sticking. Unlike aluminium foil which insulates and alters baking times, parchment paper allows both heat and steam, should it build up, to pass through its pores.

Plastic wrap or **cling film**. This is especially good for wrapping dough, since it sticks directly to the surface and prevents it from drying out when refrigerated – something that often happens when using greaseproof paper or aluminium foil.

FOR BAKING

Baking sheets. Ideally, you should have three if you are making biscuits. Black steel baking sheets which are sold in some specialist shops are good for pastry but are not suitable for most of the delicate and sugar-rich items in this book, since the black metal conducts the heat more rapidly than light-coloured or non-stick baking sheets and has a tendency to burn the bottom of the biscuits or cakes before they are baked through.

Cake tins. Use 8 and 9 inch (20 and 23cm) tins. Hinged tins, the kind with sides that can be removed by releasing a clamp, are especially versatile. They are deeper than most, and thus can be used in all cake recipes. The base makes a handy stencil for cutting out or marking circles and is useful for putting under cakes that are being decorated. The cake can then be moved easily to a serving plate, either by lifting it with a large spatula or by sliding it carefully on to the plate.

Tart tins. These should be 10 or 11 inches (25 or 28cm), preferably made of tin (which conducts the heat better than ceramic), with a fluted edge and removable bottom. When removing the sides, place the baked tart on top of a slightly smaller casserole or on top of a large tin. Carefully release the outside rim from the pastry. It will fall down on the work surface leaving the pastry exposed.

Thermometers. An *oven thermometer* is helpful when checking oven temperatures. A *jam thermometer* is needed for certain meringues, nut brittles and deep-fried pastries.

Airtight tins, with lids. Use these for storing biscuits at room temperature. For refrigerator storage, use plastic containers with lids.

SPECIAL BAKING EQUIPMENT

MOULDS AND TINS

Wooden or *ceramic moulds*, decoratively carved or imprinted, and carved wooden rolling pins are required for many of the traditional biscuits in this book. See individual recipes for notes on traditional moulds and where substitutions are possible. While old moulds are increasingly difficult to find in any of the German-speaking countries, since they have become collector's items, contemporary moulds are being produced and have been exported. They are available usually only in large, well stocked specialist cookware shops. Small *decorative tin moulds* are generally used for confections.

Bundt tin is the trade name for a round tin with a perpendicular decorative fluted design, generally shallower than a Kugelhopf mould, for which it can be substituted.

Kugelhopf mould is a deep round tin with decorative flutes that generally twist around the outside. It is used to bake Kugelhopf. A plain savarin mould or Bundt tin can be substituted.

Rehrücken tin is a metal baking tin shaped in a half cylinder with parallel ridges on either side, usually about 12 inches (30cm) long. It is used to bake a special Austrian cake that resembles a roast rack of venison.

Savarin mould is a plain round tin called for in Frankfurterkranz.

Stollen moulds are hinged iron moulds in a traditional Stollen shape. Such moulds are used by professional bakers to give their Stollen loaves a uniform shape and to keep them from browning.

Home bakers, however, rarely use such moulds. The recipe for Dresdner Christstollen (p. 160) gives a technique for baking without a mould.

INGREDIENTS

The following section covers the major ingredients used in this book and tips on how to process them.

BUTTER

I always use unsalted butter which is generally made from a higher quality cream than is salted butter, and which imparts a much richer, fresher flavour to all baked goods. In recipes where softened butter is called for, you can accelerate this process by cutting it in pieces and spinning it for several minutes in a food processor. You will have to turn the food processor on and off several times to scrape down the sides, but eventually you'll have soft butter.

CHOCOLATE

All but one recipe calls for dark, semi-sweet chocolate. Buy a good-quality chocolate such as Menier. It is best not to melt chocolate over direct heat: use a double boiler, if you have one, filling it with several inches of water kept at simmering point. The method I prefer is to place a shallow heatproof soup plate or bowl over a pan filled with several inches of simmering water. This makes it particularly easy to scrape out every bit of chocolate, using a rubber spatula; if you need the chocolate just for glazing or dipping, the shallow container is also suitable for this purpose. Avoid melting chocolate near a pan of simmering or boiling water or in a dish or pan that is not completely dry. A drop or two of water will cause it to 'seize', to become dry and grainy. If this should happen, stir a teaspoon or so of vegetable oil into the chocolate until it is smooth. Chocolate can be melted with a large quantity of liquid (in several recipes it is melted with an equal weight of cream), but small amounts of liquid should be avoided.

CREAM

The cream used in all these recipes is whipping cream or, if that is unavailable, double cream. Single cream is not rich enough.

Cream can be whipped with a large wire whisk, a rotary beater or an electric beater. For the best results, chill the beater and the mixing bowl in the freezer for about 15 minutes and make sure the cream is well chilled also. I prefer to use a large whisk because I find I can beat more air into the cream than with a rotary beater, giving it a lighter consistency. This way I can see and feel the consistency of the cream as I beat, stopping before it curdles. Electric beaters are quick and efficient but you must watch the cream very carefully to avoid curdling. Or you can use an electric beater until the cream is quite thick, and simply finish it off with a whisk. A few electric mixers come with very thin beaters specially designed for beating cream. If the weather or the kitchen is extremely hot, put the chilled mixing bowl in another bowl filled with ice.

Whipping cream served with cakes or tarts is usually not sweetened in the German-speaking countries. However, if you wish to sweeten or flavour it, add 1 to 2 tbsp sifted icing sugar or 1 tsp of vanilla extract per half pint (275ml) before you begin beating. It can be either loosely whipped so it falls in cloud-like dollops (which I prefer), or whipped until it is stiff.

I usually avoid whipping cream for dinner parties at the last minute by whipping it fairly stiffly two to three hours in advance, refrigerating it, covered. Just before serving, I whip it again. It thickens in a few seconds.

EGGS

The eggs used in these recipes are large, weighing approximately 2 oz (50g) each. If you have larger or smaller eggs, multiply the number of eggs required in the recipe by two, which will give you the number of ounces required, i.e., four eggs would mean that the recipe calls for 8 oz (225g) of eggs. Then use kitchen scales to weigh out the correct amount.

To bring refrigerated eggs to room temperature place them in a bowl, cover them with hot tap water for two minutes and drain. This should warm them sufficiently.

Lightly beaten egg is often used to glaze baked goods. The white alone gives a clear, shiny glaze; a whole egg produces a medium brown glaze; and the yolk, usually beaten with a tablespoon of cream, produces a rich brown glaze. Bread is usually glazed twice: once after it has shaped but before it has gone through the proving stage, and then again just before it is baked.

EGG WHITES

Although eggs are easier to separate when they are cold, the whites beat to greater volume when they are at room temperature. Because most of the egg whites in this book are eventually beaten together with sugar to produce a stiff meringue, I recommend using an electric beater since beating with a whisk or rotary beater is too tiring. Make sure the mixing bowl is perfectly clean, with no traces of fat, and completely dry. A speck of water or fat in the bowl will prevent the egg whites from thickening properly. If a speck of yolk falls into the whites when you are separating the eggs, scoop it out with a half egg-shell to which it will adhere naturally. The least bit of fat from an egg yolk will also keep the whites from thickening properly. Separate the whites one at a time, first into a small bowl then pour it into a mixing bowl. In this way you don't run the risk of ruining an entire bowl of egg whites by breaking a complete yolk into it just at the end.

When beating egg whites, never stop half-way through. Use stiffly beaten egg whites immediately as they will deflate if you let them rest and then beat them a second time.

Egg whites keep very well for up to a month in the refrigerator. I usually keep a small covered container just for that purpose, labelling it with the date when the first white went in. Or I freeze them, two at a time, in small freezer bags. When thawed to room temperature they can be beaten as if they were fresh.

FLOUR

With a few exceptions, the flour used in all but the yeast recipes is plain flour. I prefer unbleached flour, which more closely resembles the flour used in central Europe, but bleached flour can also be used. For yeast breads and strudel dough, however, bread flour – strong wheat flour – is generally called for because of its high gluten content. Gluten, a protein substance, becomes elastic when worked and activated by moisture, and this elasticity helps the bread to expand as carbon dioxide is liberated from the yeast. It also helps the bread to keep its shape in baking.

While whole wheat and rye flours are used a great deal in Germany and Switzerland for everyday baking, white flour, which was a luxury in the past, is still generally preferred for festive baking.

LEAVENING AGENTS

Besides stiffly beaten egg white and alcohol, which causes a leavening reaction when heated, the other standard leavening agents called for in this book include the following:

YEAST

Yeast, which comes both fresh and in dried granular form, is a living organism, activated by warmth (as low as 50°F/10°C) but killed by heat (130°F/54°C). Cold, on the other hand, simply retards its growth without killing it, so that unbaked bread dough can be frozen. Brought back to room temperature, the yeast will reactivate. Sugar, which is added to yeast to activate it, serves as its food. However, too large an amount will inhibit its growth. For this reason, only a small amount of sugar is first combined with the yeast in the two basic sweet yeast dough recipes, with the remainder added after the yeast has had a chance to develop in the 'sponge'.

Salt also has a retarding effect and kills the yeast when placed in direct contact with it. Because of this, salt is added after the initial 'sponging'.

I prefer to use fresh yeast and I have usually called for it in these recipes. It should be light in colour and crumble easily. When old it shrivels at the edges and turns brown, in which case it should be thrown out. Fresh yeast is usually creamed with a small amount of sugar which turns it to a liquid. Any additional liquid in the recipe should be hand-warm (75 to 80°F/23·5 to 27°C).

Dry yeast is activated by being mixed with a small amount of sugar and hand-hot water (90 to 110°F/32 to 44°C), or heated according to the manufacturer's directions. If it doesn't rise in ten minutes, the yeast is bad and a new packet should be used.

To substitute dry yeast for fresh yeast, use 1 tbsp (⅜ oz/10g) of dry yeast for 1 oz (25g) of fresh yeast and use some of the liquid given in the recipe to dilute it, warming it as described above.

When yeast is activated, it produces alcohol and carbon dioxide – the gas which causes the dough to rise. Punching and kneading help to distribute the gas through the dough to produce a finer, more even texture. If yeast is allowed to expand too much, it can use up its energy so that little power is left to make the bread rise during baking. On the other hand, if the dough isn't left to mature fully, the loaves will be small and dense. In general, bread that has risen slowly has a better texture and flavour.

BAKING POWDER AND BAKING SODA

In many contemporary German-language cookery books, one or both of these powders in combination have replaced traditional leavening agents. In order to neutralize an acidic factor such as honey or spice, I have combined baking soda with baking powder (mainly in the Lebkuchen chapter). The main leavening action is left to the baking powder.

TRADITIONAL LEAVENING AGENTS

These are the chief traditional leavening agents found in German-language cookery books:

Backpulver (baking powder) is made up of baking soda, an acidic substance such as cream of tartar, and starch.

Hirschhornsalz (powdered ammonium carbonate, formerly made of powdered deer horn). This is used only in thin, flat baked goods (traditionally in Lebkuchen) and imparts a very crisp texture. However, it must be heated to an inner temperature of 150°F (60°C) for the strong flavoured ammonia gas to be released. It is generally sold in glass tubes and must be kept tightly sealed.

Pottasche (today, a chemical preparation of potassium carbonate). When heated, it releases carbon dioxide and remains odourless. It is usually dissolved in liquid before being used, at which point the dough should be used right away. After baking, it has the property of absorbing moisture, helping to keep baked goods moist (see

Pfeffernüsse, p. 49). It is generally sold in glass tubes and must be kept tightly sealed.

Natron (bicarbonate of soda). This works the same way as *Pottasche*. If not used with something acidic, it has an unpleasant odour.

NUTS

Many of the recipes call for various kinds of ground nuts. Once they have been shelled and blanched (skinned) as directed, they can be ground in a liquidizer (blender), food processor or nut grinder. To grind nuts in a liquidizer, run the machine at high speed before dropping the nuts into the machine through the hole at the top one at a time. They will grind very fine in a matter of seconds and stick to the sides of the container. Grind only 3 oz (75g) at once. Empty the container completely before grinding more nuts. For recipes such as marzipan which require that the almonds be ground as fine as dust, a liquidizer is the only household appliance that will grind them fine enough. With a food processor, place up to 6 oz (175g) of nuts in the container of the machine. Turn the machine on and off repeatedly until the nuts are chopped or ground to the desired consistency. For most recipes, unless specifically stated, a food processor can be used for grinding the nuts. Nut grinders come in different models though, generally speaking, the nuts are simply put through a slot at the top and the handle is turned to grind them. Regardless of what method you use, grinding nuts freshly makes a big difference to the flavour of your biscuits, cake or tart and is worth doing if you have the time (even though almonds, in particular, can be bought already ground).

ALMONDS

To blanch almonds (to remove their skins), place them in a bowl and cover with boiling water. After two to three minutes, the skins should slip off easily.

To split almonds, first blanch them as described. While they are still soft, insert the point of a small sharp knife along the side of each, then carefully cut through. This will produce two perfect almond shapes with a flat side where they were cut. Work quickly. Once the almonds have dried, they will generally break when you try to split them. For decoration, unless otherwise stated, place them rounded side up.

To grind almonds that have just been blanched, they must first be completely dried out. Dry them on paper towels and then either leave them in a dry place (not, ideally, a steamy kitchen) for several hours, or place them in one layer on a baking sheet in a 250°F (120°C/gas 1/2) oven for fifteen to twenty minutes, being careful not to leave them too long and let them brown. Grind as described above.

When chopping almonds or any other rounded nut by hand, first sprinkle the board with a little granulated sugar as this will keep them from slipping off so easily.

HAZELNUTS

To remove the skins from hazelnuts, place them in one layer on a baking sheet in the middle of a preheated 425°F (220°C/gas 7) oven for five to seven minutes, watching them closely. The hazelnuts are ready when they have begun to give off an aroma and the skins are darkened, shrivelled and beginning to flake off. Remove the baking sheet from the oven. When the hazelnuts are cool enough to handle, place them in a large wire sieve, about 3 oz (75g) at a time, and roll them back and forth, pressing them in well with your hand as you roll them. The mesh of the wire should grate the loose skins from the nuts. If the skins do not remove easily, return the nuts to the oven for several minutes longer and try again. When one batch is finished (you can remove any small clinging bits of skin with your fingers), place the skinned hazelnuts in a bowl and proceed with the rest.

NOTE: When hazelnuts are moderately fresh, the skins are much tighter on the nuts. These generally take slightly longer in the oven and because the skins are so tight, it may not be possible to remove all the skin. However, the skin is more nut-like than dry and flaky, so it will not hurt if a little remains on hazelnuts that are to be ground. Green cob nuts still in their shells cannot be used.

SPICES

For Christmas baking in particular, the standard spices called for in this book include:

allspice
anis (ground and whole)
cardamom
cinnamon
clove
coriander
mace
nutmeg
poppy seed
sandalwood, powdered (an unusual spice used in
   Swiss baking to flavour and colour red)
vanilla

SWEETENING

The following are used to sweeten baked goods in this book.

HONEY

The oldest sweetener for biscuits and cakes, honey is a traditional ingredient in Lebkuchen and is especially good for baking that is done in advance since it has very good keeping properties. For best results, buy pure honey. When warming it, do not allow to boil as this will make biscuits, especially, hard and brittle.

TREACLE

This is the traditional sweetener for the north German version of Lebkuchen – Braune Kuchen – which gives them their distinctive dark brown colour.

SUGAR

In most of the recipes in this book I have specified castor sugar because it is more refined than granulated sugar and takes far less beating time to break down. In older German recipes, it is common to find directions for beating the sugar and eggs for thirty to forty minutes. With the very refined sugars we have today, such lengthy beating is no longer necessary. Icing sugar which is used for icing and dusting cakes and biscuits should always be sifted before use (see pp. 36–7). Decorating sugar, which can be procured from a bakery supply or specialist shop, is suggested in only a few recipes, and granulated sugar given as a substitute. It has a much coarser grain than granulated sugar and makes an attractive finish to certain biscuits and breads.

BAKING TIPS

GENERAL RULES

1. Read the recipe through first and have all ingredients pre-weighed, utensils ready and baking sheets or tins prepared as directed.
2. Preheat the oven approximately fifteen minutes before you are ready to bake.
3. When baking something for the first time and always when baking biscuits, watch closely so as not to overcook. Rely on the description for doneness given in each recipe, since baking times are approximate, varying according to different ovens, baking equipment and density of baked goods.
4. Allow all baked goods to cool to room temperature, usually on a rack unless otherwise directed, before storing in tins, refrigerating or freezing.

ROLLING OUT PASTRY AND BISCUIT DOUGHS

Biscuit dough which is rolled out and cut out into small shapes is more forgiving than pastry which is rolled out in a round and transferred to a cake or tart tin. Even if the biscuit dough sticks to the board (which ideally it shouldn't), small biscuits can easily be loosened from the board with a sharp palette knife. A round of pastry, on the other hand, will generally tear if it has stuck to the board and you try to move it.

So, while you need not be such a perfectionist with biscuit dough, it offers you a good chance to practise proper rolling-out techniques which will aid you immeasurably when rolling out pastry.

As I mentioned in the Equipment section above, I prefer a long cylindrical rolling pin, the same diameter throughout, without handles. The 'quick, short turns' referred to below when describing the best method for rolling out would not apply when using a rolling pin with handles as this rolls in one continuous movement.

1. Make sure the dough has chilled long enough to firm it before rolling it out.

2. When rolling out, flour only the pastry board and rolling pin, never the dough itself. Excess flour will make the dough dry and tough.

3. Before rolling a round of dough straight from the refrigerator, hit it forcefully with the side of your rolling pin in two or three places to help flatten it out. Do this repeatedly if the dough has been refrigerated for a long period and is extremely hard. Make several gentle rolls forward. Then use your hands to force the ragged edges which will have appeared back into a smooth round. In the early stages of rolling out, when the dough is still fairly thick, continue this process.

4. Always roll in quick, short turns away from you in the beginning. Lift the pastry after each roll and give it a quarter turn. This will ensure that it rolls out evenly and doesn't stick to the board. Re-flour the board or rolling pin as needed.

NOTE: A flour dredger is ideal for this purpose since it dusts only a small amount of flour on to the board or rolling pin and sifts it at the same time.

5. Work as quickly as possible so the dough doesn't get too warm and greasy.

6. If the dough sticks to the board, lift it up immediately, scrape away the sticky dough with a palette knife or pastry scraper and re-flour the board lightly, working as quickly as possible. Do the same for a sticky rolling pin.

7. Try to roll your dough out as evenly as possible. For biscuits, this will ensure that they are all the same thickness (which looks nicer) and that they all bake in the same amount of time. For pastry rounds, this means you won't have an overcooked or undercooked spot on one side of the pastry.

LINING TART TINS, FLAN RINGS AND PIE TINS

To transfer a round of dough to a tart tin, flan ring or pie tin, use the following method. Place a plain rolling pin (without handles) in the middle of the pastry. Fold one-half of the round over it and carry the dough to the tin draped over the rolling pin. Lay the pastry round bottom side up (the side that was facing the board originally) in the tin or flan ring. Brush off any excess flour with a dry pastry brush. This will help keep the pastry as light and flaky as possible.

To line a tin or flan ring, the pastry round should be about 4 inches (10cm) larger than the tin or ring; for a pie tin, it will need to be slightly larger to account for the deeper sides. Ease the pastry gently into the corners of the tin and smooth out the bottom. For a tart tin or flan ring, flour the back of your index finger, press the pastry well into the corners, at the same time pulling extra pastry down into the side areas so that the sides are slightly thicker than the base. Go around a second time, pressing the pastry well against the side of the tin or ring. For flan rings, push a small ridge of pastry up with your right index finger, at the same time pressing on the upper outside edge with your left index finger. This will produce a narrow lip or rim at the top of the flan ring. Go around and neaten the rim so that it is all the same width. For both tart tins and flan rings, run your rolling pin right across the top of the tin or ring which will press against the pastry and cut off the excess neatly. For a flan ring, reshape the narrow rim once again, pressing it slightly towards the centre so that after baking, the ring may be removed easily.

For a pie tin, once the pastry round has been laid in the tin and smoothed, use a pair of scissors to cut off the excess pastry, leaving about a ¾ inch (2cm) overlap. Tuck the overlap under to produce a thick rim. To produce a decorative scalloped edge: with your right thumb and index finger ½ inch (1·5cm) apart and on the inside of the pie tin, press them against the thick pastry rim, at the same time inserting your left index finger in between them on the outside of the pastry rim and pulling the centre bit in. Place your right index finger where your thumb was, moving slightly to the left, and repeat. Continue around until the entire rim is scalloped. Alternatively, crimp the edge with a pastry crimper made for this purpose.

BAKING PASTRY AND BISCUIT DOUGH

Tarts and pies made of a rich shortcrust (in this book, Mürbeteig) are generally baked either just above or in the centre of an oven heated to 375°F (190°C/gas 5). Biscuits are generally baked on buttered and floured baking sheets in the middle of a slightly cooler oven, generally about 350°F (180°C/gas 4), unless otherwise directed. Thick, shaped biscuits such as pretzels spread slightly less if baked on unbuttered baking sheets. However, this is the exception.

PREPARING TINS, MOULDS AND BAKING SHEETS

For plain round cake tins and baking sheets with rims that are being lined for sheet cakes, put softened butter on a crumpled piece of paper towel and rub it generously around the bottom and sides of the tin. Then place the tin or baking sheet on top of a piece of greaseproof or parchment paper. I prefer parchment paper because it is especially durable and is, to a certain extent, non-stick. Aluminium foil is unsuitable because it tends to wrinkle slightly in the bottom of the pan, and the wrinkles then bake into the cake. It also insulates the cake from heat, and will alter the baking time and bottom texture of the cake. Using a pencil, trace around the bottom of the cake tin or baking sheet on to the paper. For hinged tins, it is easiest to remove the bottom of the tin to get the most accurate measure. In all but the latter case, cut the paper liner out a fraction of an inch inside your tracing, to make up for the fact that you were tracing on the outside of the tin, which adds about ⅜ inch (1cm). Place the lining in the bottom of the tin, smoothing it to the edges. It is important to have the paper liner exactly the right size so that when the cake is unmoulded, the edges, too, unmould straight and even. If the paper is slightly short, some of the edge will be left in the pan. If it is too large, the edge will be slightly rounded but generally uneven. For cakes that are to be heavily iced, this is not an important point. However, it's a good discipline to learn since many cakes are simply dusted with icing sugar, an instance when a well-executed cake will be especially appreciated. After the tin or baking sheet has been lined, butter the piece of paper well. Then dust the entire tin or baking sheet with flour. A flour dredger is especially useful for this. For cake tins and square or rectangular baking tins with high sides, rotate the tins to spread the flour evenly. Turn them over and tap out the excess flour. For lining a baking sheet with a very low rim, see the directions given in the recipe for Maroniobersschnitten (p. 189).

Round tins such as Kugelhopf, savarin, Rehrücken, or Bundt tins are best coated with butter by being first placed in the freezer for fifteen minutes or the refrigerator for twenty minutes. While the tins are chilling, melt and cool about 2 oz (50g) of butter. Using a pastry brush, coat the chilled tins generously with melted butter, getting well into the crevices. Chill again. Coat a second time with butter. At this point, some recipes call for first sugaring the tins and then flouring them. In other instances, where an extra coating of flour is not needed, I instruct you to chill the tin again until it is needed, which will firm the butter coating.

PIPING BAGS

I have already mentioned my preference for thin, flexible plastic piping bags. If they are not available, the next best are plastic lined canvas bags, though they are much stiffer to use. Use them with the plastic lining on the inside.

To fill a piping bag, first fit it with the appropriate nozzle, as specified in the recipe. Some nozzles must be placed inside the bag. Others are fitted on the outside of the bag and screwed into a mount which is placed inside the bag. With this type, you can change nozzles easily without removing the filling. With most bags, you have to cut the bag with scissors so that the nozzle protrudes. However, if the hole is cut too large, pressure on the bag will force the entire nozzle (as well as the filling) out of the bag. Be cautious when you are cutting.

To fill a piping bag once it has been fitted with a nozzle, twist the end with the tip several times to prevent anything flowing out while you are filling the bag. Turn down a 3 to 4 inch (8 to 10cm) collar all around the bag. Place your left hand under the collar, holding the bag with the palm of your hand and your thumb wrapped around the side underneath the collar. Using a rubber spatula, scoop up the mixture and scrape it off into the bag by pushing the rubber spatula against your thumb which supports the bag from the outside. Continue in this fashion until the bag is filled nearly to the collar. Don't fill it too full or it will squeeze out of the top when you are using it. Pull the collar up and twist the top securely around the filling. Hold the bag at the top with your right hand which is also grasping the twisted top. If you are holding it correctly, you should be able to use the bag with one hand so that the other hand is free to guide it. Apply pressure by pressing your right hand against the bag, always keeping the top twisted tight with your thumb and index finger, and pipe the mixture as described in the recipe. For piping thick fingers, rounds or ovals, hold the bag upright to produce the best shape. If you've never worked with a piping bag, a good way to practise is to make up a batch of instant mashed potatoes and try out different shapes and tips.

It is useful to have two or three different sized bags. A large bag is specially helpful for piping large amounts, such as when making

Preiselbeerenschaumtorte, where a heated meringue texture must be piped, ideally, in an uninterrupted spiral over the top of the cake.

THE FOLDING-IN TECHNIQUE

For mixtures that have stiffly beaten egg white added at the end, or for whisked egg or creamed mixtures that have flour and sometimes melted butter added at the end, the instructions call for folding in the final ingredients. I prefer a large metal spoon – the really large kind that comes in sets with a few other matching kitchen tools. The sharp edge of the spoon is especially efficient at cutting through the mixture while its rounded edge fits the sides of the bowl to pull up any unfolded mixture lurking at the bottom. If you don't have a large metal spoon, then you can substitute a rubber spatula.

To fold, cut the spoon or rubber spatula straight through the final ingredient on the top (stiffly beaten egg whites, flour or melted butter) to the bottom of the bowl. Lift up as much mixture as you can from the bottom, bring it up to the surface, and turn the spoon or spatula completely over so the mixture falls off on top. Turn the bowl a quarter turn and repeat the process. This is known as cutting and folding. Continue to turn the bowl in quarter turns, cutting and folding until everything is mixed in. Flour is mixed in when you no longer see any clumps or pockets as you turn the mixture up and over. Egg whites are mixed in when you no longer see any large clumps or distinct streaks of white. At this point, it is important to stop folding. The cutting and folding process is meant to preserve as much air as possible in the whisked eggs or beaten egg whites. You must therefore be careful not to beat the mixture when the recipe calls for 'folding' and not to over-fold.

SIFTING FLOUR, ICING SUGAR AND OTHER DRY INGREDIENTS

While there are large cups with a spring action made especially for this purpose, the easiest way to sift dry ingredients is through a sieve, about half full. Hold the sieve over your mixing bowl and simply tap the side of the sieve. The dry ingredients will pass through easily. In a recipe with spices, salt and baking powder, I usually suggest that you sift them together with the flour to mix them well and break up any clumps.

Icing sugar that has been on the shelf for some time often

hardens. I find a food processor excellent for breaking up all the lumps and reducing the sugar back to a powder. Simply weigh out the amount that you need, put it in the food processor, and turn the machine off and on several times until the sugar is smooth.

PLAITING

There are many plaiting techniques for bread used in the German-speaking countries, particularly for rich bread. The simplest method is a plain three-strand braid, plaited in the normal fashion. For long loaves of bread (as in the case of Weihnachtszopf), the plaiting process is begun in the middle of the three strands, then plaited out to the ends to make a tight braid. With any plait, it is important to tuck the ends well under the loaf. Brush them with a little lightly beaten egg to make them stick. This will ensure that the loaf doesn't unravel during the proving or baking stages.

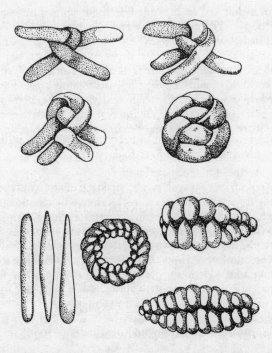

For a plain Zopf (one without fruit and nuts, see p. 168), you can use a plain three-stranded plait or one of the other braids illustrated above, remembering to tuck the ends under at the end before putting it on a buttered baking sheet.

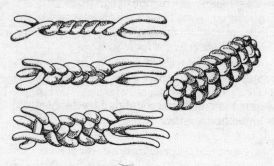

STORING

For biscuits that are to be stored at room temperature (such as Lebkuchen, whisked egg biscuits and meringues), store different types of biscuits separately so the flavours don't mix. Separate each layer with a piece of greaseproof paper or aluminium foil so they won't roll around in the container. Ideally, use an airtight tin with a lid. Lebkuchen or whisked egg biscuits that get too hard after prolonged storage can be softened in two ways: either place a slice of apple or potato in the container for two days which will produce some moisture, or leave the tin open in a steamy kitchen for several hours. In general, this category of biscuits has especially good keeping properties, in many cases, up to three months or more See individual recipes for specific reference.

Butter biscuits in general, can be stored in a jar or tin with lid at room temperature for at least a week. They will keep longer but I find they begin to loose their fresh butter taste after that time. They will keep fresher in the refrigerator, ten days or longer, and can be stored in a plastic container with a lid. For longer storage, however, I find it is best to freeze them. If they are flat, I simply stack them neatly and package them tightly in a length of aluminium foil. For more delicate, decorated biscuits, it is necessary to put a piece of foil or greaseproof paper in between before wrapping.

Breads can usually be frozen extremely well. I always bake the shape first, allow it to cool completely, then wrap it tightly in several thicknesses of aluminium foil before freezing. It can be frozen for up to three months, unless otherwise directed in a specific recipe.

Most cakes and tarts have fairly good keeping properties and can generally be frozen successfully, though it is important to consult each recipe for specific instructions. For cakes that are heavily decorated with butter cream I find it is usually easiest to freeze them for several hours first, so the butter cream is quite firm, before attempting to cover them with a loose wrapping.

A NOTE ON MEASUREMENTS

Where quantities are given in spoonfuls a **level** spoonful should be used unless otherwise specified.

THE RECIPES

1

LEBKUCHEN

Lebkuchen – the honey-sweetened gingerbread of central Europe – are very popular for special occasions, are very versatile and have a long history. They are cut out as hearts and pigs and candle-holders; joined together to make a gingerbread house (Hexenhäuschen); sandwiched with fruit and nuts (Honigkuchenwürfel); and filled with marzipan (Biberli). Best of all, they can be shaped in traditional wooden moulds with a symbolic motif (see Gedrückter Lebkuchen and Alte Züri-Tirggel, p. 47).

It was not until the Middle Ages that sweet cakes and biscuits came into existence. Sugar was scarce until the seventeenth century, but honey was readily available, generally from monasteries, which kept bees to provide the candle wax. In Germany – where they are first recorded in correspondence dated 1320 – Lebkuchen were originally made in monasteries; eventually special guilds were formed for the bakers. The *Lebküchner* or *Lebzelter* (Austrian), as the guild bakers were called, were given special privileges, practising their highly respected craft in many cities from Vienna and Basel to Leipzig and Aachen. Eventually, however, Nuremberg became the most prominent and productive, owing to its position as a distribution centre for oriental spices and as the centre of Bavarian honey production.

The earliest recorded German recipe for Lebkuchen, from the sixteenth century, now in the Germanisches Nationalmuseum in Nuremberg, calls for honey, sugar, cinnamon, nutmeg, ginger, pepper, and flour. None of the eggs, butter or leavening agents which one generally finds in recipes today was used; nor were chopped nuts or minced mixed peel a part of the mix. This recipe, like most, has been refined and enriched over time.

Today, there are many variations under many names: Lebkuchenzelten (simple Lebkuchen); Honigkuchen (honey biscuits –

which can be spiced or not); Pfefferkuchen (heavily spiced ginger-bread); Leckerli (Swiss gingerbread with mixed peel and nuts), to name a few. All of these contain honey and are made according to a standard formula: the honey is heated with the sugar (if called for) and butter or lard (if called for), before being mixed with the dry ingredients and then the eggs. The one exception is Nürnberger Elisenlebkuchen – perhaps the most famous Lebkuchen – which has been included in this chapter but is actually made according to the 'whisked egg' method (see p. 66).

In earlier times, Lebkuchen were made in both a simple form – plain flat biscuits, sold in bundles or wrapped in coloured paper – and in more elaborate forms, generally printed with moulds made of carved wood, or occasionally ceramic or metal ones. Sold at fairs, carnivals and markets and given on special occasions – to celebrate birthdays, marriages, saints' days or to show special affection – the embossed pictures depicted an appropriate scene: a biblical or historic subject; decorative hearts; lords and ladies; stags and hounds. In time, Lebkuchen developed aesthetically to reflect both the artistic styles of the time, classic or romantic, and the Germanic love of folklore. In addition to using moulds, bakers during the Romantic period decorated their Lebkuchen with colourful pictures, or drew on them hearts and flowers, names and sayings in coloured sugar icing. This tradition is still alive, and large decorated Lebkuchen hearts are an expected offering at regional fairs (see Oktoberfest Lebkuchenherzen) and Christmas markets.

While most of the recipes in this chapter require no special equipment, I have given directions for mould Lebkuchen because the effect is so beautiful and the technique is rarely discussed in modern cookery books. Both wooden and ceramic moulds are now sold in specialist cookery shops and can be used in many different recipes in this book.

Because honey has especially good keeping properties, Lebkuchen can be baked well in advance and stored in an airtight tin at room temperature for up to three months or more. Commercial and home bakers use this to special advantage at Christmas time, baking their biscuits and small cakes in October. For the best flavour, Lebkuchen should be stored for at least two weeks before they are eaten as the spices ripen with time. If Lebkuchen become too hard once they are stored, which is often the case, they can be softened by leaving the tin open in a steamy kitchen or by placing a slice of raw apple or potato in the closed tin for a few days.

BASIC LEBKUCHEN DOUGH
Lebkuchenteig

It is important to heat the fat, sugar and honey sufficiently to allow the sugar to dissolve, but at the same time not to let the mixture come to the boil as this adversely affects the honey and makes the gingerbread brittle. Because different brands of honey have different degrees of concentration and because humidity varies, the amount of flour required will also vary slightly. When all the ingredients have been kneaded together and the dough is still warm, it will be soft and look somewhat moist and sticky, but will not stick to your hands. Once the dough cools and has rested for a time, it becomes quite firm.

For the best flavour, make any biscuits or cakes using this dough several weeks or even several months before they are needed.

1 lb (450g) plain flour	½ tsp grated nutmeg
1 tsp baking soda	½ tsp ground ginger
1 tsp baking powder	8 oz (225g) honey
1 tbsp cinnamon	7 oz (200g) sugar
1 tsp ground cardamom	4 oz (125g) butter
½ tsp powdered cloves	1 large egg, lightly beaten
½ tsp powdered anis	

Sift the flour on to one sheet of paper and the other dry ingredients on to another. Heat the honey, sugar, and butter together over a low flame, stirring all the time until the butter has melted and the sugar dissolved. Do not allow the mixture to boil. Remove the pan from the heat. Stir in the sifted spices. Gradually beat in the sifted flour, adding as much as is needed to make the dough, when stirred, pull away from the sides of the pan. You will need most of the amount given. Allow the dough to cool for 5 minutes. If the pan is still very hot, remove the warm dough to a bowl. Beat in the lightly beaten egg and then knead the dough with your hands first in the pan or bowl, then briefly on a flat surface. If the dough is too sticky to handle, knead in a little more flour until it no longer sticks to your hands.

If not using it immediately, wrap the warm dough in plastic cling film and leave at room temperature until required.

VARIATIONS

In some of the plainer recipes, additional texture and flavour is imparted by adding, for the quantity of basic dough given above:

4 oz (125g) mixed peel, finely chopped
6 oz (175g) blanched almonds, finely ground

Add the mixed peel and/or ground almonds to the basic Lebkuchen dough just before adding the flour to the butter, sugar and honey mixture.

VERZIERTER LEBKUCHEN

Decorated Lebkuchen

Basic Lebkuchen dough, once it has been made up and rested overnight, can be rolled out ⅛ inch (3mm) thick and cut out with decorative cutters before being baked. However, more traditionally, it is rolled out slightly thicker – ¼ inch (6mm) – and cut out in simple 3 inch (8cm) stars, hearts or rectangles, which are decorated with split almonds in the corners and a halved glacé cherry in the centre. For puffier biscuits, it can be rolled out, cut and baked as soon as the dough is made, while it is still warm. They can be left unglazed or brushed with a lightly beaten egg before they are baked. If you don't have a large biscuit cutter, you can make a stencil from a piece of heavy paper and use it as a pattern, cutting out hearts or stars with a knife.

Bake, one sheet at a time, in the middle of a preheated 350°C (180°C/gas 4) oven until lightly coloured and puffed, approximately 15 minutes. Loosen with a metal spatula and leave on the baking sheet for 2 minutes to firm slightly. Remove to wire racks to finish cooling. When cool, store in an airtight tin for three months or longer.

NOTE: Lebkuchen shapes can be used for Christmas tree decorations if a small hole is pierced in each with a skewer before they are baked. When they come out of the oven, enlarge the holes with the skewer, since they have a tendency to close up during baking. A narrow length of red ribbon or string can then be threaded through them once they have cooled, to hang them from the tree.

GEDRÜCKTER LEBKUCHEN

Moulded Lebkuchen

Though seen less frequently today, from the Middle Ages on Lebkuchen were traditionally printed with decorative wooden moulds, as described on p. 44. Any decorative mould can be used to make Lebkuchen as described below. One traditional type which is still made is the Berner Honiglebkuchen from Bern, in Switzerland. They are distinguished by a small bear (the symbol of Berne) embossed in the centre, and are cut into rectangles. Once they have cooled, the bear only is brushed with a glaze to make it shine.

For moulded Lebkuchen, use the basic Lebkuchen dough (p. 45). While it is still soft and warm, break off a piece of dough and flatten it with your hands in a round or oval almost as large as your mould. Place a damp cloth under the mould to prevent it slipping. Brush the mould lightly with oil and place the flattened piece of dough on it. Roll your rolling pin (ideally one without handles) back and forth over the mould, pressing the soft dough into the carved indentations and over the surface of the mould. Carefully pull the piece of dough away, place it on a lightly buttered and floured baking sheet and trim the edges with a sharp knife.

They can be baked right away, making puffier Lebkuchen. Otherwise, they can be left to dry out overnight, uncovered, at room temperature which will help to set the pattern. The next day, bake them in the middle of a preheated 350°F (180°C/gas 4) oven until they colour – the time varies with the size of the biscuits, approximately 15 minutes. Remove small biscuits to a wire rack to cool. Larger biscuits should be loosened with a metal spatula and allowed to cool for several minutes on the baking sheet to firm them before being removed to wire racks.

ALTE ZÜRI-TIRGGEL

Old-fashioned Zurich Moulded Wafers

Makes about 50

At Christmastime in the famous Zurich pastry shop, Sprüngli, and in all the gourmet food shops scattered to the right and left of the glittery Bahnhofstrasse, Zurich's main shopping street, thin round flat Tirggel – spicy honey biscuits delicately embossed with scenes or designs – are fancifully displayed, generally piled in pyramids of graduating sizes.

Tirggel differ from most other Lebkuchen in that they are paper-thin and light in colour, with only the embossed pattern being allowed to brown.

The method traditionally used is to roll out a small piece of dough on an oiled carved mould. Because the dough is soft, it sinks into the crevices of the mould, picking up all the details of the carving. This method is suitable if your moulds are shallow. For deeply carved moulds, however, it is best to roll out the dough very thin and then, using a plain pastry wheel or knife, cut out a piece of dough the right size and press it into the oiled mould. Traditional Tirggel moulds are round, but you can use any shape or size mould to print the Tirggel dough.

Depending on the moulds you are using you may have to vary the oven temperature. For shallow relief, a very hot oven will be best; for higher relief, you might have to lower the temperature slightly. Bake the Tirggel on the top rack in the oven – this is important since only the pattern is supposed to brown. This will ensure that Tirggel with a high relief are cooked right through.

When cooled, they can be stored in an airtight tin at room temperature for three months or more.

NOTE: This recipe produces a very brittle Lebkuchen which takes a pattern better than the basic Lebkuchen dough recipe. However, most people nowadays are used to a certain amount of butter or lard in their Lebkuchen and will prefer the basic recipe, p. 45, for flavour. For patterned Christmas-tree ornaments or wall hangings, however, this dough produces the most beautiful results. Make a small hole in each biscuit before browning so that they can be hung.

1 lb (450g) honey
1 tbsp ground ginger
1 tbsp ground cinnamon
¼ tsp ground clove
¼ tsp ground nutmeg
1 lb (450g) plain flour, sifted
Vegetable oil for the moulds

Equipment
carved wooden moulds of any size

Preheat the oven to 475°F (240°C/gas 9). Heat the honey with the spices, stirring constantly over a medium low heat, until the honey is very hot to the touch but not boiling. Remove the pan from the heat. Gradually beat in the sifted flour while the mixture is still hot, adding as much as is needed to make the dough pull away from the sides of the pan when stirred. The amount will vary slightly according to the concentration of the honey used and the humidity. When the dough is well blended and still warm, but cool enough to handle, knead it for 1 to 2 minutes on a lightly floured board. According to the type of mould you are using (see above) roll out small pieces of the dough directly on to the mould, which should first be brushed with oil, or roll out the dough ⅛ inch (3mm) thick and cut out pieces the size of your moulds, pressing the pieces into the oiled moulds and then removing them.

Place the biscuits on lightly buttered and floured baking sheets. Bake on a high shelf in the oven until the relief is well coloured and the underside is still uncoloured. (Watch them closely.) Allow to cool on the baking sheet for 2 minutes, then remove to a rack to cool completely.

Store in airtight tins when cooled.

PFEFFERNÜSSE

Pepper Nuts

Pfeffernüsse, one of the older traditional German Christmas biscuits from several regions, come in almost as many variations as Lebkuchen. Two things, however, they all have in common: a large amount of spice and a small and very thick shape. Pfeffer or pepper refers not to pepper itself (though it is called for in some recipes, but to the Pfefferländer ('pepper countries'), the name given in earlier times to the areas of the Orient from which spices came.

The majority of Pfeffernüsse, like Lebkuchen, are made with honey, using the warming method to heat the honey, sugar and fat, if any is called for. However, there is also a handful of Pfeffernuss recipes based on the whisked-egg method (see p. 80) which are sweetened with sugar and are particularly moist inside.

Pottasche, today a chemical preparation of potassium carbonate, is the leavening agent found in older recipes for Pfeffernüsse. After baking, it has the property of absorbing moisture, helping to keep them moist. Since most Pfeffernuss recipes have no fat the biscuits have a tendency to become hard when stored for any length of time. Baking powder, which is used in the recipe that follows, is substituted more and more in modern German cookery books because it makes a lighter biscuit (see notes on leavening agents, p. 25). It is also more readily available and keeps better. For storage, see p. 38.

The following recipe is a version from Brunswick.

BRAUNSCHWEIGER PFEFFERNÜSSE
Brunswick Pepper Nuts

Makes about 60

8 oz (225g) plain flour
2 tbsp ground cinnamon
¾ tsp powdered cloves
1 tsp baking powder
8 oz (225g) honey
extra flour as needed

Icing

4 tbsp water or lemon juice
7 oz (200g) icing sugar, sifted

Sift the dry ingredients together on to a piece of paper and set aside. Heat the honey almost to boiling point, but do not let it boil. Add 8 fl oz (230ml) water. While the mixture is still warm, add the sifted dry ingredients and as much extra flour as is necessary to keep the dough from being sticky. The dough will naturally be soft but will firm up once it is cooled. Wrap the dough in plastic cling film and leave overnight at room temperature.

The next day, preheat the oven to 400°F (200°C/gas 6). Cut the dough into four pieces. Roll each piece of dough back and forth on a board to make an even sized roll approximately ¾ inch (2cm) in diameter. Cut off rounds ½ inch (1·5cm) thick. Place them on buttered and floured baking sheets, leaving 1 inch (2·5cm) between them to allow for expansion. To level the tops, run your rolling pin lightly over the biscuits on each baking sheet.

Bake, one sheet at a time, in the middle of the oven until the biscuits are firm to the touch and light brown – approximately 10 to 12 minutes.

While they are baking, make the icing in a deep bowl. Beat the sifted icing sugar into the water or lemon juice, adding additional sugar or liquid to make a thin icing. Beat for 8 minutes to dissolve the sugar.

When they are done, remove the biscuits from the baking sheet and brush off any flour that might have stuck to them from the baking sheet. While still warm, place a few at a time in the bowl of icing. Using a wooden spoon, turn them around in the icing to coat well. Remove with a slotted spoon to a wire rack so the excess icing can drip off and the biscuits can dry. Place a piece of aluminium foil directly on the icing in the bowl when not in use. Continue icing the remaining batches in the same fashion, making more icing if necessary. Allow to dry completely before storing in an airtight tin for up to two months.

NOTE: If the icing dries out too much, place the bowl of icing in a pan of water that has just boiled. Beat the icing until it is smooth, adding a teaspoon of water, if necessary, to thin it.

LEBKUCHEN-HERZEN

Lebkuchen Hearts

Lebkuchen hearts are traditionally seen all over Germany, both at Christmas markets and at regional fairs, such as the Oktoberfest in Munich. In earlier times, they were shaped in decorative wooden moulds (see p. 44). Today, they are generally iced with chocolate and decorated with hearts, flowers and nostalgic sayings in sugar icing. They hang from satin ribbons in fair booths to be bought by a friend or lover and hung around one's neck. Besides the more '*kitschig*' (showy) fair renderings, bakers at Christmas time often produce smaller, more refined versions, decorated with simple split almonds and a halved glacé cherry (see Verzierter Lebkuchen, p. 46), or plainly iced with a simple sugar icing or chocolate.

Whether intricately or simply decorated, Lebkuchen hearts make charming presents for Christmas, birthday, Mother's Day or St Valentine's day.

OKTOBERFEST LEBKUCHENHERZEN
Oktoberfest Lebkuchen Hearts

Makes about 6

1 recipe basic Lebkuchen dough
(p. 45), increasing both the

baking soda and baking powder
to 1½ tsps

Chocolate icing

10½ oz (315g) icing sugar, sifted
4½ oz (140g) dark semi-sweet
chocolate, broken in pieces
1 tsp vegetable oil

Royal icing

2 egg whites
8½ oz (240g) icing sugar, sifted
food colouring (optional)

Equipment

narrow satin ribbon for hanging
piping bag with a fine writing
nozzle
heavy paper for stencil

Preheat the oven to 350°F (180°C/gas 4).

Fold a piece of heavy paper in half and cut out a heart 7 to 10 inches (18 to 25cm) high to be used as a stencil. Set aside.

Make up the basic Lebkuchen dough and, dividing the dough in two, roll out while still warm in a rectangle ¼ inch (6mm) thick. Place the stencil on the rolled-out dough and cut out the hearts with a knife, re-kneading the scraps and rolling them out once more. Use a skewer to make two holes, ½ inch (1·5cm) apart, in the top middle of each where the heart comes to a point. Lay the hearts on buttered and floured baking sheets, leaving at least 1½ inches (4cm) between each.

Bake them, one sheet at a time, in the middle of the oven until they are lightly coloured and puffed – approximately 15 to 20 minutes. Loosen them from the baking sheet with a metal spatula and allow them to cool and firm on the sheet for several minutes before removing them to wire racks to finish cooling. If the holes at the top have closed up during baking, enlarge with a skewer while the hearts are still warm.

While the hearts are baking, make the chocolate icing. Melt the broken chocolate pieces with the vegetable oil in a double boiler, or rest a heatproof soup plate or shallow bowl over a saucepan filled with 2 inches (5cm) of simmering water. Stir the chocolate occasionally until it has melted. Remove from the heat and allow to cool.

Put 7 tbsp water into a large mixing bowl. Gradually beat in the sifted icing sugar using an electric mixer or a wooden spoon, beating for at least 7 to 8 minutes until the sugar has completely dissolved. Add the melted chocolate and beat for another minute or two, scraping down the sides of the bowl so that the chocolate gets thoroughly blended. Add enough extra water, one teaspoon at a time, or additional sugar to make an icing that will pour or brush easily but still be thick enough to leave a smooth, opaque coating. When not using it, keep a piece of aluminium foil pressed against the surface of the icing so it doesn't dry out.

When the hearts are cooked and cooling on wire racks but still warm, brush them evenly with the chocolate icing using a pastry brush. Allow the chocolate icing to dry completely.

While they are drying, make the royal icing. Using an electric mixer, beat the egg whites until they are frothy and beginning to thicken. Gradually beat in the sifted icing sugar. Beat for at least 8 minutes to dissolve the sugar, adding additional water or sugar as needed to make a thick icing which will hold its shape when piped. Fit a piping bag with a fine writing nozzle. If desired, you can divide the icing and colour each part differently to make multi-coloured hearts and flowers. Pipe a scalloped border around the edge of the heart. In the centre, you can pipe a name, hearts and flowers, or a saying such as '*Du allein*' (Only you) or '*Ich liebe Dich*' (I love you). Once decorated, allow the hearts to dry completely. Lace a thin, long strand of satin ribbon through the two holes at the top of each heart and tie the ends in a knot. Traditionally, the ribbon should be long enough so the heart can be hung around someone's neck.

LEBKUCHEN GLÜCKSSCHWEINCHEN
Lebkuchen 'Good Luck' Pigs

In German-speaking countries, the pig motif is used on biscuits, marzipan sweets, wooden tree ornaments and greeting cards to symbolize good luck. While no longer a part of Germany, the city of Strasbourg in French Alsace reverts to German tradition at its annual Christmas market (*Weihnachtsmarkt*) where Lebkuchen pigs, 7 inches (18cm) in length, are lined up by the score, awaiting customers whose names will be piped on them in white icing. Small and large pig cutters are available in specialist cookware shops. However, a simple pig stencil can also be cut from heavy paper. Pigs etched with names make amusing decorations or place cards on the Christmas dinner table. If a small hole is pierced in the pigs before they are baked, they can be hung on the Christmas tree with a thin piece of red ribbon. They can also be decorated before baking with split blanched almonds and halved glacé cherries.

Make up one recipe of basic Lebkuchen dough (p. 45), with or without the additions of finely minced mixed peel and ground almonds. While the dough is still warm, roll it out ¼ inch (6mm) thick on a lightly floured board. Using a special cutter or a 5 to 8 inch (12·5 to 20cm) stencil and a sharp knife, cut out the pigs. If they are not to be iced after baking, decorate them with split blanched almonds at either end and a halved glacé cherry in the centre. If they are to be hung, make a hole in the top centre with a skewer. Place on buttered and floured baking sheets, leaving 1 inch (5cm) between each. Allow to rest for 1 hour at room temperature.

Preheat the oven to 350°F (180°C/gas 4). Bake, one sheet at a time, in the middle of the oven until lightly coloured – approximately 12 to 15 minutes. Loosen them carefully with a metal spatula and leave for 2 minutes on the baking sheet to help firm them. Remove to a wire rack to finish cooling. If they have a hole at the top which has closed in baking, reopen it using a skewer while they are still hot.

If they are to be decorated with icing, use the recipe for royal icing under Oktoberfest Lebkuchenherzen (p. 52). Place the icing in a piping bag fitted with a fine writing nozzle. Pipe a line around the edge of the pig to frame it. Pipe a face. In the centre, pipe a name or a decorative design of hearts and/or flowers. Allow to dry completely, approximately 30 minutes, before storing.

LEBKUCHEN STERNE MIT KERZEN

Lebkuchen Star Candle-Holders

Lebkuchen move from the biscuit tin to the mantelpiece in the form of candle-holders. Made from a pyramid of three graduated stars, the candle-holders are charmingly decorated with split blanched almonds. The icing serves as 'cement' so make sure it is thick enough to hold the stars securely, adding additional sugar to thicken it if necessary. Use a minimum amount of icing – just in the centre of the stars, so that when they are assembled it doesn't show. These make charming gifts for Christmas and are a good project for children.

1 recipe basic Lebkuchen dough (p. 45)
split blanched almonds (p. 27)
1 egg, lightly beaten

Icing

1 egg white
4½ oz (140g) icing sugar, sifted

Equipment

3 paper star stencils
1 small round aspic cutter,
  thimble or small bottle lid
  (½ inch/1·5 cm diameter)
small red, white or green candles

Using heavy paper folded in half, cut out three 6-pointed stars – 4, 3 and 2 inches (10, 8 and 5cm) across. Set the paper stencils aside.

Make the Lebkuchen dough and divide it in two. While still warm, roll it out 3/8 inch (1cm) thick. Using a sharp knife, cut out one of each sized star for every candle-holder, re-kneading the scraps and rolling them out again. Use a small round aspic cutter (or thimble or small bottle lid) to cut out a small circle from the centre of the two smaller stars. Place a split blanched almond on each point of the two larger sized stars, the almonds pointing away from the centre. Brush all the stars with lightly beaten egg. Allow to rest for 1 hour, uncovered, at room temperature.

Preheat the oven to 350°F (180°C/gas 4). Bake, one sheet at a time, on buttered and floured baking sheets in the middle of the oven until lightly coloured and puffed – approximately 15 to 20 minutes.

While the stars are baking, make the icing. Beat the egg white with an electric mixer until frothy and starting to thicken. Gradually beat in the sifted icing sugar, beating for at least 8 minutes to dissolve the sugar. If necessary, add a bit more sugar, a tablespoon at a time, to make the mixture thick enough to be used as 'cement'. Keep a piece of aluminium foil pressed on the surface of the icing when not using it.

When the stars are done, loosen them with a metal spatula, leaving them on the baking sheet for several minutes to help firm them before moving them to a wire rack to cool. If the holes have closed up too much, enlarge them with a small knife while the stars are still hot.

Using a small spoon or pastry brush, place a 1 inch (2·5cm) circle of icing in the middle of the largest star and a rim of icing around the hole of the second largest star. Stack the stars on top of each other with the points lined up in different planes, ending with the smallest star. Press the stars together well, applying more icing if necessary to make them stick, but not so much that it shows.

Allow them to dry for at least 30 minutes. Choose a small candle – red, white or green – the size of the hole and place one in each holder.

LEBKUCHEN HEXENHÄUSCHEN

Gingerbread House

The gingerbread house – a traditional Christmas project for patient German mothers and professional bakers – is familiar to us from the charming fairytale of Hänsel and Gretel. The German name, Hexenhäuschen, actually means 'witch's house', referring to the fantastic gingerbread house where the children were locked up by the wicked witch. Having seen some of the whimsical baked creations in shop windows and homes, one can easily understand why the children were lured inside. Part of the charm of these houses – in addition to the heavenly aroma of spice from the Lebkuchen and the enticing bits of sweets and biscuits decorating the roof and walls – is the imagination that the baker puts into making them. With all the illustrations that have appeared in magazines and cookery books, it is rare to find anyone who would want to copy someone else's model from a photograph. Each house seems to have its own character and coaxes its maker into the world of fantasy from whence it came.

So long as you have a large enough selection of different shaped and coloured sweets, some extra biscuits and lots of royal icing and patience, you will end up with a house that can't help but charm.

Gingerbread houses can be small, medium or large – it is simply a matter of personal preference. For my taste, the smaller houses are the most charming, since the sweets and biscuits that decorate them seem oversized, emphasizing the fantastic nature of the creation. The proportions for the house given in the diagram, therefore, are based on elements which will produce a relatively small house approximately 9 inches (23cm) long (measuring the overhanging roof which expands slightly in baking) and 7 inches (18cm) wide, (the roof measurement from eave to eave).

While some books suggest baking the dough in large sheets, then cutting out the shapes once the dough is baked, I prefer the method given below which requires the pieces be cut out carefully first, using heavy paper models, then baked. The roof generally loses a perfect edge; the windows close up a bit; the door expands or the base loses its tidy edge. It isn't perfect. The dough somehow takes over and comes to life to create a house with a preordained spirit. It isn't tempting fate, however, because the pieces always fit. And should a roof piece that perhaps was rolled out thicker in one spot than another expand disproportionately when baked, or should the doorway close up too much, you can simply cut off the extra bit or widen the doorway by cutting it with a sharp knife while the baked dough is still warm. Even if you discover a problem once the dough has cooled, you can warm it again for several minutes in the oven and it will cut neatly without breaking. Otherwise, I let the house develop as it wants. The one thing you will want, using this system, is extra interior supports. Any join that isn't perfect is sandwiched with lots of icing, then reinforced with several supports. They don't show, so it doesn't matter how many you use. But they do ensure that the walls stand up straight and solid with more than sufficient strength to support the weight of the heavy roof.

For decorative piping on the walls, you can do as little or as much as you like. I use a fine writing nozzle to etch subtle scrolls, scallops or whatever takes my fancy. I recently piped a flower garden at the back of the house, then later 'planted' two candy sticks arching in opposite directions, using icing to cement them against the wall.

Since the houses are intended as fantasies, they take well to asymmetrical decorating. You needn't worry about matching a heart shape on one side with a mate on the other. Feel free to be spontaneous.

For decoration, I assemble an assortment of sweets and biscuits. The sweets I find that work especially well are fruit gums in assorted colours; small flat boiled sweets; flat red and white peppermint drops; small candy sticks; smarties; dolly mixtures; and jelly dots. For biscuits, I bake extra Lebkuchen dough into large and very small rounds – some fluted, some with the centres cut out – and hearts, stars and pretzels. I then ice some in melted chocolate diluted with a few drops of vegetable oil. Any other Christmas biscuits or small cakes you have baked can be used as well. The Bahlsen brand of

Pfeffernüsse, available in delicatessens at Christmas time, make wonderful roof tiles.

Those of you who aren't purists and who don't feel like making gingerbread can use a packaged gingerbread mix, following the directions for biscuit dough rather than cake mixture (you won't need the milk called for in the cake instructions). Using this quick method, three boxes is sufficient for the house plan below.

The houses will keep for years, stored in several plastic bin-liners in a cool dry room.

You will need at least one other person to help when you are assembling the house, at least 3½ hours of time and a great deal of patience. But, once completed, the house will give everyone such pleasure, produce a marvellous aroma wherever it is displayed and, something to keep reminding yourself, it won't have to be made again next year – unless, that is, you become addicted to building gingerbread houses in the process.

BASIC LEBKUCHEN DOUGH FOR HEXENHÄUSCHEN

This is simply a larger quantity of basic Lebkuchen dough (p. 45), with a slightly larger proportion of baking powder and baking soda. It is sufficient to make the gingerbread house and base as illustrated.

1½ lbs (675g) plain flour
2 tsp baking powder
2 tsp baking soda
1½ tbsp ground cinnamon
2 tsp ground cardamom
¾ tsp powdered cloves
¾ tsp powdered aniseed
¾ tsp grated nutmeg
¾ tsp ground ginger

12 oz (350g) honey
10 oz (300g) sugar
6 oz (175g) butter
1 large egg, lightly beaten

Equipment

large tray, piece of heavy
   cardboard, or baking sheet on
   which to place house
piping bag with plain writing
   nozzle

Combine the ingredients following the instructions for basic Lebkuchen dough (p. 45). Once the dough is made, wrap it in plastic cling film and leave at room temperature while making the stencils.

Using a ruler, make heavy paper stencils for the structural elements of the house; the dimensions are given in the diagram.

Divide the dough in three even portions. Roll out two rectangles with a cutting space measuring 9 by 13 inches (23 by 33cm) and one measuring 10 by 13 inches (25 by 33cm). If you don't have enough baking sheets, roll out one portion at a time. Cut out the various elements for the house shown in the diagram, using your cardboard stencils. The windows cut out of the side walls can be cut in half lengthwise and used as window shutters. Likewise, save the door which you cut out from the front of the house. It can be baked and propped open with icing later on. Cut out at least eight inner support

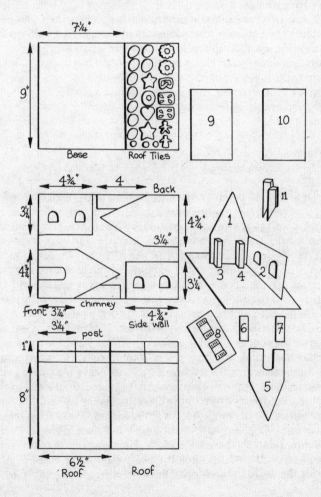

posts. From the remaining dough, cut out various shapes for roof tiles and decorations. If desired, you can cut out a witch or two gingerbread figures or a tree to place in front of the house. Place the pieces 1½ inches (4cm) apart on buttered, floured baking sheets. Leave uncovered at room temperature for 1 hour.

Preheat the oven to 350°F (180°C/gas 4). Bake the pre-cut pieces, one sheet at a time, in the middle of the oven until golden – approximately 15 to 20 minutes. When done, remove the baking sheet from the oven and loosen the pieces carefully with a metal spatula, leaving them to cool on the baking sheet. At this point, if you feel the need to enlarge a doorway or straighten a wall, cut the dough with a sharp knife while it is still warm.

When all the pieces have been baked, make the royal icing and assemble the decorations.

Royal icing

6 large egg whites
1 lb 10 oz (750g) icing sugar, sifted plus up to 2 oz (50g) additional sugar

Decorations

assorted sweets and biscuits

In a large mixing bowl, beat the egg whites with an electric mixer until frothy and slightly thickened. Beat the icing sugar into the egg whites, 2 oz (50g) at a time, beating well between each addition. When all the sugar has been added, beat the icing for another 5 minutes. To test the consistency of the icing, dip a wooden spoon into it. The icing should be thick enough to form an icicle which will not drop off the spoon. If necessary, add more sugar until the mixture is thick enough. Cover the icing completely with a wet towel or aluminium foil whenever it is not being used. Scoop a large cupful of icing into a piping bag fitted with a plain writing nozzle. Decorate the shutters, door, doorways, windows and front and back of the house. Allow the icing to dry completely before proceeding. Place the base on an attractive tray or piece of heavy cardboard so the house can be moved with ease. Assemble the structural elements on the base in the order given in the diagram, beginning with the back of the house. To assemble, pipe a generous amount of icing on the bottom and side of the back of the house and place it several inches from the edge of the base, centring it. Pipe icing on the bottom and sides of one side piece and join the two pieces on the base. To help support the walls and reinforce the seam where they join, lavishly ice one or two support posts and place them inside the house near the corner seams. Allow each section to dry for at least 5 minutes, holding it, before proceeding. When all the wall pieces are standing and well supported from the inside, allow the house to rest for 15 minutes before you decorate it. Meanwhile pipe a large amount of icing on one chimney piece and sandwich the two pieces together, allowing some of the icing to protrude. If you like, you can pipe icicles to drip off the top. Ice some of your biscuit decorations with the white icing. For chocolate icing, you can simply add a bit of melted chocolate or cocoa powder to a small amount of the white icing, diluting it with a teaspoon or more of water so it will spread.

After 15 minutes, decorate the sides and front of the house with sweets and biscuits. To apply them, first squirt a large blob of icing where you want to place the sweet, then press it into the middle of the icing. It should stick easily. However, heavier pieces have a tendency to slip at first so you might have to hold them for a minute. Place the shutters on either side of the windows. Allow the decorations to dry for 10 minutes.

To roof the house, pipe a generous amount of icing on all the exposed top edges of the house walls and the top edge of each roof piece. Have someone else hold one roof piece standing opposite you on the other side of the house. Join your two roof pieces, making sure they are lined up so the overhang in the front and back is approximately the same and the roof pieces are touching the house walls. Pipe more icing into any cracks where the roof doesn't quite touch and additional icing down the seam at the top. Hold the roof carefully for about 10 minutes or place props underneath it to free your hands.

Ideally, wait 30 minutes before decorating the roof to make sure it is well secure. You can leave the props in place while decorating. Using a metal spatula, spread the roof pieces generously with icing. In the front and back, you can drip bits of icing over the edges to resemble icicles. Place the chimney piece – now sandwiched – on the roof. Press biscuits into the icing for roof tiles – they can be big and small. You can further decorate some of the biscuits with small sweets or run a row of sweets down the top seam where the roof pieces join, to simulate tiles.

In the front of the house, you can ice and decorate the door and prop it open. A tree or figures can be made to stand on the base in the front of the house.

Some people ice the base, then sprinkle it with sugar to look like snow. However, I usually leave the base gingerbread colour. Once it is decorated, allow the house to dry overnight before moving it.

BASLER LECKERLI

Basel Spiced Biscuits

Makes about 120

The word *lecker*, which in high German means 'delicious', becomes a noun in Switzerland where it is applied to a wide variety of finger-length and rectangular biscuits that are baked for holidays. While many cities, including Bern and Zurich, have their own versions – each quite different and not necessarily spicy – the honey and spice version from Basel is certainly the most famous. In fact, one bakery in Basel produces nothing but Leckerli which are shipped all over the world in charming tin drum containers, symbolizing the Basel *Fastnacht* (carnival), a three-day pre-Lenten celebration, when the haunting music of pipes and drums, played by costumed Baselers, fills the air. Though this bakery now lies in the centre of town, most Baselers know the narrow, stepped passage – the Imbergässlein – in the hilly periphery of the old city to be the original home of the city's early Lebkuchen bakers. The 'Imbergässlein' got its name from the many spices, including ginger (*Ingwer*), used by the guild bakers. Basler Leckerli are made with a high proportion of honey and sugar, enriched with mixed fruit and nuts, iced, and cut into short, thick, narrow rectangles.

Heated ingredients	*Dry ingredients*
1 lb (450g) honey	1 lb 2 oz (500g) plain flour, sifted
10 oz (300g) sugar	¾ tsp baking soda
1½ tbsp cinnamon	¾ tsp baking powder
¼ tsp powdered cloves	
½ tsp grated nutmeg	

Additions

7 oz (200g) mixed peel,
  finely minced
7 oz (200g) unblanched almonds,
  coarsely chopped
grated rind
  of 1 lemon
3 fl oz (100ml) Kirsch
  (if unavailable, use rum)

Icing

8 oz (225g) icing sugar, sifted

Equipment

2 buttered, floured rimless baking
  sheets, or turn a baking sheet with
  rim upside down and use
  the underside

Preheat the oven to 350°F (180°C/gas 4). In a heavy-bottomed saucepan, heat the first five ingredients over a low flame, stirring until the sugar has dissolved. Do not allow the mixture to boil. Stir in the additions. Sift the dry ingredients together and add to the other ingredients while the mixture is still warm. Beat well to form a cohesive dough. If the dough is too sticky to handle (because of the different concentrations in different honeys), add just enough additional flour to keep it from sticking. When it reaches the proper consistency, it will be very soft but can be handled.

While still warm, divide the dough in two and roll out rectangles approximately 10 by 12 inches (25 by 30cm) on each of two baking sheets prepared as instructed above. Bake, one sheet at a time, in the middle of the oven until golden brown – approximately 30 minutes.

When both cakes have been baked, prepare the icing. Heat the icing sugar with 4 fl oz (125ml) water in a saucepan, stirring until the mixture comes to a boil. Allow the syrup to boil until it spins a thread, i.e. when a jam thermometer registers 230°F (110°C). Place the saucepan in a pan of cold water to stop the cooking. Pour half of the sugar syrup over each cake while it is still warm. Spread it with a metal spatula or pastry brush to cover the cakes evenly but thinly. Allow the icing to set completely, ideally overnight, as it will cut more neatly. If the icing becomes too thick, reheat it briefly with 2 tsp of water.

Using a long, sharp knife, trim off the crusty outer edges. Cut the Leckerli into narrow bars, ⅞ inch (2·1cm) wide and 2 inches (5cm) long. For the best flavour, store for several weeks in an airtight tin at room temperature. Leckerli keep for three to four months and improve with age.

HONIGKUCHENWÜRFEL

Honey Cake Squares

❧

Makes about 55

This delicious sheet cake cut into bite-sized squares is made with two layers of iced Lebkuchen sandwiched with a fruity apricot/raisin/almond filling which keeps it moist. A favourite Christmas treat of mine for many years, this recipe came from a friend in Frankfurt. I once forgot a tin which I had purposely put out of my own reach high on a cupboard shelf. When I discovered it eight months later, the little cakes were better than ever – proof that they can be made long in advance and keep well.

1 basic Lebkuchen recipe (p. 45)

Filling

9 oz (250g) unblanched almonds,
    coarsely chopped
5 oz (150g) raisins
1 lb 4 oz (575g) apricot jam
3 tbsp lemon juice
4 oz (125g) mixed peel, finely diced

Icing

3 tbsp lemon juice
5 oz (150g) icing sugar, sifted

Equipment

1 rimless baking sheet 15 by
    11 inches (37·5 by 28cm), or
    reverse a baking sheet with
    sides and use the underside

Butter and flour the baking sheet and set aside. Make up the basic Lebkuchen dough and while still warm, divide the dough in two. Roll out one piece directly on to the buttered and floured rimless baking sheet, making a rectangle approximately 13 by 8½ inches (33 by 21·5cm). There should be at least a 1 inch (2·5cm) rim left free on the baking sheet to allow for expansion. Roll out the second piece the same size as the first on a piece of parchment paper. Set aside.

Preheat the oven to 350°F (180°C/gas 4). Make the filling. Mix all the ingredients for the filling together in a bowl, adding additional lemon juice if the mixture is too thick to spread. Distribute the filling evenly over the dough on the baking sheet leaving a ½ inch (1·5cm) rim around the edges. Reverse the other half of the dough quickly on top of the filling, peeling off the paper. Press the edges together well and trim evenly. Bake until golden – approximately 25 to 30 minutes.

While the cake is baking, make the icing. Put the lemon juice in a large mixing bowl. Gradually beat in the sifted icing sugar, beating for at least 8 minutes to dissolve the sugar completely. Add enough extra lemon juice or water or additional sugar to make an icing of thin pouring consistency. While the cake is still warm, pour the icing over it, brushing it evenly with a pastry brush to cover. Allow to set overnight at room temperature. The following day, cut off the coarse outer edges. Cut the cake in 1¼ inch (3cm) squares. For the best flavour, store in an airtight tin for several weeks before eating.

BIBERLI

Marzipan Lebkuchen Rounds

Makes about 25 to 30

These sweet rounds of Lebkuchen are filled with marzipan which, when baked in a hot oven, bubbles up and browns to a shiny mahogany. While these biscuits are found elsewhere in the German-speaking world, they originate from Switzerland, where they are always diminutive, making them look particularly refined and enticing. Because of the high oven temperature, use aluminium, non-stick or light coloured steel baking sheets – not black steel, which conducts the heat too rapidly and tends to overcook the bottoms.

½ recipe basic Lebkuchen dough (p. 45)
9 oz (250g) block marzipan
1 whole egg, lightly beaten

Make up the basic Lebkuchen dough and allow to rest, well wrapped, overnight at room temperature.

The next day, preheat the oven to 400°F (200°C/gas 6). Roll out the dough on a lightly floured board in a long, narrow rectangle, approximately 5½ to 6 inches (14–16cm) wide and ⅜ inch (1cm) thick. Trim the edges evenly and cut the rectangle in half, length-wise. You should have two strips approximately 2½ inches (6cm) wide. Roll the marzipan back and forth into a long log ¾ inch (2cm) in diameter. The log should be twice the length of the Lebkuchen strips. Cut the log in two. Lay a marzipan log down the centre of each Lebkuchen strip. Wrap the dough around the marzipan, allowing ¼ inch (6mm) overlap. If the overlap is greater, trim off the excess. Moisten the edge of the dough with water and press the seam together to seal. Slice each roll in ½ inch (1·5cm) slices. Using a small metal palette knife or table knife, plump the slices back into a neat circular shape and pat the surface of each to flatten. Brush the tops of each round with lightly beaten egg. Place on a buttered and floured baking sheet. Bake one sheet at a time, in the upper third of the oven until the marzipan is mahogany and bubbling out of the centre – approximately 10 minutes. Watch carefully since they burn easily. Remove to a wire rack to cool. Store in an airtight tin for two to three months.

NÜRNBERGER ELISENLEBKUCHEN
Nuremberg Lebkuchen

Makes about 22 2½ inch (6cm) biscuits

One of the most unglamorous Lebkuchen biscuits, as well as one of the most delicious and famous – the Elisenlebkuchen from Nuremberg – defies the original definition of Lebkuchen given in the introduction to this chapter. It is not made with honey. The best Elisenlebkuchen, furthermore, are not made with flour. In fact, to be called 'Elisenlebkuchen', the biscuits must, by law, contain no more than one-tenth their weight in flour, with a third to half their weight made up of ground nuts (almonds or a mixture of almonds and hazelnuts). With the exception of spices, Elisenlebkuchen have little in common with the original model, and they are made by a completely different technique based on whisked egg and sugar. They are, however, the Lebkuchen most exported and are the basis for one of the major industries of Bavaria. Traditionally mounded on *Oblatten* (rounds or rectangles of edible rice paper), the nut-rich dough is sometimes decorated before baking with blanched almonds, and afterwards usually glazed with sugar icing or chocolate. The mixture must be of the right consistency to prevent it from spreading too much, and at the same time loose enough to produce a biscuit with a moist interior. Elisenlebkuchen are sold in many delicatessens around Christmas time. If you wish to try your hand at baking them at home, the following recipe uses ingredients found in an ordinary grocery shop.

If you are able to obtain *Oblatten*, use the recipe below and spoon the mixture on to the round or square rice paper shapes. If you have a sheet of rice paper, spoon the mixture in mounds on to the sheet – leaving 1½ inches (4cm) in between each for expansion. When the biscuits have baked and cooled, break the rice paper away, discarding the pieces in between the biscuits.

However, it may not be easy to obtain either pre-cut *Oblatten* or rice paper. The temperatures and technique below produce the same delicious biscuit without using a base. The instructions for icing the bottoms apply to those which have not been baked on a base. They can be made in rounds, measuring from 3 inches (8cm) in diameter to as large as 6 inches (16cm). Decorate larger Elisenlebkuchen, with a blanched almond in the centre, and several others placed near the edge. Those decorated with almonds can be left plain or iced in sugar icing. Chocolate icing will not show off the almonds so should be used on plain biscuits. Biscuits iced in white will look somewhat transparent at first. By the next day, however, they will have turned a rippled opaque white – their traditional appearance.

The amount of ground almonds used varies somewhat depending on how finely ground and how oily or dry they are. A liquidizer is recommended for grinding the nuts (see p. 27).

It is necessary to insulate the baking sheets as much as possible from bottom heat. To do this, cover two baking sheets with a double layer of aluminium foil. Butter the top layer of foil (to make the paper stick) and cover it with a piece of parchment or non-stick baking paper. Butter and flour the piece of paper and set the baking sheets aside. (If you are using *Oblatten*, simply place it directly on the baking sheet.)

3 large eggs
10½ oz (315g) castor sugar
¼ tsp ground cloves
1 tsp ground cinnamon
½ tsp baking powder
grated rind of 1 lemon
2½ oz (65g) mixed peel,
   finely minced
12–14 oz (350–400g) unblanched
   almonds, finely ground

Icing
12 oz (350g) icing sugar, sifted

If you are not using *Oblatten* or edible rice paper, prepare several baking sheets as instructed above.

Choose a heatproof crockery mixing bowl that will fit into a saucepan with its base resting well above the bottom of the pan. Bring 2 inches (5cm) of water to the boil in the saucepan and remove from the heat. Set the bowl in the pan, put the eggs and sugar in the bowl and, with an electric mixer or whisk, beat the mixture rapidly until it is thick and mousse-like – about 4 minutes. To test the consistency, use the beater to lift a little of the mixture and trail the shape of the letter M over the mixture in the bowl. If the shape of the letter holds for 3 seconds, the mixture is sufficiently beaten. If the shape dissolves, beat longer, then test again.

Remove the bowl from the pan of water and continue to beat for a further 3 minutes. Add the spices and grated lemon rind and fold several times. Then add the finely minced mixed peel (this can be minced in a food processor or by hand) and the minimum amount of ground almonds. Blend the mixture well. Allow it to rest for 5 minutes. If you are using *Oblatten*, place the paper on top of the prepared baking sheets.

Now, test the Elisenlebkuchen mixture. Place 2 tbsp (or more for very large biscuits) in a mound on the prepared baking sheets. Wait for 3 minutes. Within that time, it will have spread and flattened just slightly, but should not have flattened completely. If it looks like a flat pancake and has spread as much as 1 inch (2·5cm), return the mixture to the bowl. Add some of the remaining 2 oz (50g) of almonds. Allow the mixture to rest for several minutes and test again. At this point it should hold its shape sufficiently. Add more ground almonds only if the mixture doesn't pass the test.

Once the mixture has reached the proper consistency, spoon it on to the baking sheets, using 2 tablespoons, leaving 2 inches (5cm) between mounds. They can be medium sized (2 heaped tbsp) or large (4 tbsp). Allow to set for 3 minutes. Dip your index finger in water and smooth the sides and tops of the mounds. If desired, decorate with blanched split almonds for large biscuits, following the instructions above. Leave to dry out for 4 to 6 hours (or overnight if the weather is somewhat moist or the kitchen slightly steamy).

Preheat the oven to 325°F (170°C/gas 3). Bake, one sheet at a time, in the middle of the oven until golden and lightly risen – approximately 20 to 25 minutes. Check several times so that the biscuits don't dry out. When done, they should be easy to remove from the paper. Remove from the oven. Carefully loosen the bottoms and allow to cool on a wire rack. If they have not been based on *Oblatten*, when cool, turn them upside down and return to the oven for 4 to 5 minutes – just long enough to dry the bottoms. Though dry on the outside, the biscuits should be slightly soft and moist inside. Remove to a wire rack to cool and proceed with the next tray in the same fashion.

To make the icing, place 6 tbsp water in a large mixing bowl. Gradually beat in the sifted icing sugar, beating for 5 minutes. Place the bowl in a pan filled with water that has just boiled. Beat for another 5 minutes to dissolve the sugar completely. Add enough extra water or additional sugar to make an icing of thin pouring consistency. Using a pastry brush, brush the bottoms of each biscuit, if not based on *Oblatten*. When the bottoms have dried, turn them over and brush the tops. Press a piece of aluminium foil over the icing when not using it. For chocolate icing, beat 3–4 oz (75–125g) of melted dark, semi-sweet chocolate into the sugar icing, adding a bit of extra water to thin it. Brush the tops with the chocolate icing and allow them to dry completely before storing them. Store for up to three weeks, well wrapped in the airtight tin in a cool place. They need not be refrigerated.

BRAUNEKUCHEN

'Brown' Biscuits

These thin, cut-out biscuits from northern Germany – the Lebkuchen of the north – differ from variations further south in that they are made with treacle rather than honey, which accounts for their dark colour, and with a high proportion of fat, some of which is lard which adds flavour and body.

This family recipe comes from a good friend in Schleswig-Holstein who advises that the dough should be rolled out as thin as possible to make especially crisp biscuits. For the best results, bake them several weeks in advance and store in airtight tins.

Heated Ingredients

2½ oz (65g) butter
2½ oz (65g) lard
4 oz (125g) treacle
4 oz (125g) sugar

Dry ingredients

8 oz (225g) plain flour
2 oz (50g) cornflour
1 tsp cinnamon
¼ tsp ground cloves
⅛ tsp grated nutmeg
⅛ tsp ground cardamom
½ tsp baking powder
½ tsp baking soda

Additions

grated rind of 1 lemon
1 tbsp candied orange peel, finely
    chopped
1½ oz (40g) blanched almonds,
    finely chopped

Equipment

decorative biscuit cutters

Warm the butter, lard, treacle and sugar over a low heat, stirring until hot and the sugar and fat have dissolved. Allow to cool for several minutes. Sift the dry ingredients together on to a piece of greasproof paper. Add them gradually to the heated ingredients, beating well with a wooden spoon. Add the remaining additions and stir in well. The dough will be very soft but should not stick when handled. If it is sticky, add just enough flour to keep it from sticking. If it is too crumbly, add a teaspoon or more of warm water. Wrap well in plastic cling film and leave at room temperature overnight – do not refrigerate.

The next day, preheat the oven to 350°F (180°C/gas 4). Divide the dough into two pieces. Roll out each piece on a lightly floured board until ⅛ inch (3mm) thick, i.e., very thin. Use cutters to cut out decorative shapes, traditionally hearts, stars, pretzels, rounds and crescents, but any decorative cutter can be used. Place on buttered and floured baking sheets.

Bake in the oven for about 15 minutes or until the edges have shrunk and the biscuits have begun to change colour. Because of the high sugar content, they are baked at a moderate temperature so they won't burn. However, they must be watched carefully since they colour rapidly once done.

Remove to a wire rack to cool. Though not traditional, they can be piped with royal icing, see p. 52, in decorative patterns if desired.

2

WHOLE-EGG AND EGG-WHITE BISCUITS AND CONFECTIONS

Eierschaum- und Eiweissgebäck

Whole-egg biscuits – made by the 'whisked-egg method' (as used for fatless sponge) – are much in evidence in German-speaking countries at Christmas time. Butterless biscuits, they are generally leavened with a small amount of baking powder and first shaped, or rolled out and printed, then left on a baking sheet to dry out overnight. This is important. The drying ensures that the biscuits keep their shape when baked, that no fissures develop – due to moisture escaping during baking – and that the biscuits rise evenly and develop the characteristic *Fuss* (foot), or base, which is of a darker, more grainy consistency than the smooth surface.

From an aesthetic standpoint, two of the most beautiful biscuits in the book are found in this chapter: printed Springerle and leaf-shaped Chräbeli. The smooth, pristine white of these biscuits gives them an especially regal character.

Another interesting printed biscuit found in this chapter is the Swiss Wygützli which makes lovely Christmas tree decorations. Flavoured with nutmeg and clove, this biscuit is unusual in that it is coloured with red wine and, traditionally, powdered sandalwood – the natural red spice colouring found exclusively in old Swiss recipes which I have replaced with red food colouring.

Butterless whole-egg biscuits have especially good keeping properties and can be stored for at least two or three months in an airtight tin at room temperature. These biscuits have a tendency to become quite hard, however, and can be softened in one of two ways: either leave the tin open in a steamy kitchen, or place a slice of raw apple or potato in the closed tin for a few days.

The egg-white biscuit recipes contain a representative selection of meringues (*Baisers*), macaroons (*Makronen*) and ground nut confections, including marzipan. Generally flourless, these contain a large proportion of sugar which gives body to the egg whites.

Zimtsterne (cinnamon stars) and the many forms of marzipan given to children on St Nikolaus Day, 6 December, are part of the traditional Christmas repertoire; other biscuits and confections in this group are eaten at Christmas and throughout the year.

Meringues and macaroons, unless coated with chocolate, keep well for two to three months in an airtight tin at room temperature. Baked marzipan, on the other hand, has a tendency to get hard and dry in a short period of time. I have therefore recommended it be stored in an airtight container in the refrigerator to help keep it fresh.

BASIC WHISKED-EGG DOUGH

Eierschaummasse

Although butterless biscuits made with eggs, sugar and flour are relatively unknown in English-speaking countries, they are traditional favourites in German-speaking countries and in Italy.

For heating the eggs and sugar, use a crockery or glass mixing bowl that will rest on the rim of a saucepan with its base well above the bottom of the pan which has been filled with several inches of simmering water. Neither stainless steel nor plastic mixing bowls are satisfactory for this purpose: stainless steel conducts the heat too rapidly, 'cooking' the egg mixture on the sides of the bowl, and gives a slightly greyish tinge to the eggs, while plastic does not conduct heat sufficiently to accelerate the thickening process.

BASIC WHISKED-EGG TECHNIQUE

Choose a crockery or glass mixing bowl and saucepan as in the guidelines given above. Set aside the ingredients for the recipe you have chosen. Bring 2 inches (5cm) of water to the boil in the saucepan and remove the pan from the heat. Set the bowl in the pan, put the eggs and sugar in the bowl and, with an electric hand mixer or whisk, beat the mixture rapidly until it is thick and mousse-like – about 4 minutes. To test the consistency, use the beater to lift a little of the mixture and trail the shape of the letter M over the mixture in the bowl. If the shape of the letter holds for 3 seconds, the mixture is sufficiently beaten. If the shape dissolves, beat longer, then test again.

Remove the bowl from the pan of water when ready and continue to beat for a further 3 minutes. Continue with the instructions in the recipe.

SPRINGERLE

Moulded Anise Biscuits

Makes about 38 1¾ inch (4·5cm) biscuits

The brittle egg-shell white whisked egg biscuit called Springerle which originated in Swabia in the fifteenth century is traditionally flavoured with anise – whole or powdered – and shaped with wooden moulds like Lebkuchen. In the ancient German duchy of Franconia (Franken), the same biscuit or similar versions go by different names: Würzburger Marzipan from Würzburg (not, as you might expect, almond paste); Reiterle from Rothenburg ob der Tauber (the same dough stamped with old wooden moulds depicting mounted riders or grand ladies, traditionally given to children on St Nikolaus Day, 6 December); and Eierzucker from Nuremberg, the same dough, flavoured with Arrak and made with traditional moulds. In Switzerland, Springerle often go by the name of Anisbrötli.

There are several theories about the origin of the name, Springerle: one is that it could mean a small jumping horse, referring to the many moulds carved with a horse or mounted rider. However, perhaps the simplest explanation is that the biscuits, when baked, do in fact 'spring' or rise to double or triple their height, forming the characteristic *Fuss* (foot), or base, which is of a slightly more grainy consistency, and the smooth, egg-shell white 'heads'.

Now a favourite at Christmas time, these biscuits were originally baked for other celebrations as well, as attested to by old moulds featuring Easter lambs, rabbits and religious motifs depicting various holy days.

At the beginning of the nineteenth century, it was the fashion to paint every detail of the relief in different colours. Though this is rarely done today, the baker Edmund Prezel, in Rothenburg ob der Tauber, is an exception, stamping his Springerle and Eierzucker with 200-year-old moulds and painting many of the biscuits after they are baked.

While few home recipes for Springerle or Eierzucker contain a commercial leavening agent, those purchased from bakeries all contain a small amount, generally of ammonium bicarbonate (ABC-Trieb, used commercially). So, baked at home, the biscuits barely rise and are never as attractive as their purchased counterparts. Therefore I have followed the baker's example and added a small amount of baking powder to the recipe.

It is important to follow the instructions and allow the biscuits to dry out overnight (or even longer if it is extremely humid). This sets the pattern which has been printed. If not sufficiently dried, steam will escape through the surface of the biscuits and fissures will develop.

It has been my experience that this is not everyone's favourite biscuit if they haven't grown up with a taste for it. However, few people will deny that this is one of the most aesthetically pleasing from the traditional repertoire. The whisked egg-dough, more than any other (Lebkuchen or butter biscuit doughs) picks up every detail of the moulds that are pressed into it. Provided the biscuits are sufficiently dried, they lose none of this detail in baking. The combination of a beautifully ornate picture embossed on a pristine creamy-white biscuit is truly impressive. I have therefore never worried whether or not anyone would want to eat them: they make beautiful presents to hang on the wall or Christmas tree (with a tiny hole pierced in the top before baking).

As for transforming them to suit other tastes, I once presented an eccentric Irish friend in London with an elaborate mounted knight brought from Herr Prezel's shop in Rothenburg. My friend sampled the hard biscuit without great pleasure, then whisked it away to the kitchen. A few minutes later, he returned with the now rather soggy knight on a plate – well soaked in sherry, the solution used for revitalizing dried sponge cake. Within minutes, it had disappeared. While this would not be to everyone's taste, I tell the story simply to illustrate that any resourceful recipient of one of these beautiful biscuits will no doubt find a way of adapting it to his or her palate.

2 large eggs
8½ oz (240g) castor sugar
1 tbsp rum, or as needed
8 oz (225g) plain flour, or more
  if needed
1 tsp baking powder
1 tbsp powdered aniseed

Equipment

decorative wooden moulds in any
  shape or size or decorative wooden
  rolling pin

Whisk the eggs and sugar together in a mixing bowl over steaming water as in the instructions for basic whisked-egg technique (p. 72). Proceed, adding the rum and beating the mixture for a further 30 seconds.

Sift the flour and baking powder together with the powdered aniseed. Add to the egg mixture and blend well with a spoon. Remove the dough to a lightly floured board and knead it until smooth and cohesive – about 3 minutes. The dough should be quite soft. However, if it is sticky, add a small amount of flour, 1 tbsp at a time, until the dough can be handled. If it seems too dry and liable to crack when rolled out, knead in an additional teaspoonful of rum until the dough is soft but not sticky. Wrap the dough tightly in plastic cling film and leave at room temperature for 1 hour before using.

Roll out the dough ¼ inch (6mm) thick on a lightly floured board. Dust the wooden moulds (or decorative wooden rolling pin) and the dough itself with flour, brushing off the excess. Press the moulds or rolling pin firmly into the dough, then lift off carefully. Cut them apart with a sharp knife or a plain pastry wheel.

NOTE: If the detail on the moulds is quite deep, it will be necessary first to cut out an oval or rectangle of dough approximately the same size as the mould. After dusting the mould and dough with flour, press the thin piece of dough well into the mould to pick up all the detail. Tap the mould firmly on the table several times to release the dough. Then use a sharp knife or plain pastry wheel to cut out the shape neatly.

If there is any flour left on the biscuits once they have been moulded, brush it off with a dry pastry brush. Place the biscuits 1 inch (2·5cm) apart on buttered and floured baking sheets. Leave to dry out, uncovered, at room temperature for 15 to 24 hours.

Preheat the oven to 300°F (160°C/gas 2). Bake one sheet at a time, in the lower third of the oven, with the handle of a wooden spoon propped inside the oven door to keep it slightly ajar. Bake the biscuits until firm, risen and barely egg-shell in colour – about 20 to 25 minutes. Do not allow them to colour.

Allow to cool completely on a rack before storing. Store in an airtight tin at room temperature for up to three months.

CHRÄBELI

Leaf-shaped Anise Biscuits

❦

Makes about 38

A speciality from Baden in Switzerland, traditionally baked at Christmas time, these attractive white biscuits flavoured with anise are first rolled into short, narrow logs, then cut in three places and curved to produce the characteristic fanned leaf shape. Like Springerle (for which the dough is the same), the Chräbeli must be left out overnight to dry. When cooled, they can be stored in an airtight tin for up to three months. See p. 38, for further advice on storing.

Prepare the Springerle dough as described on p. 73, rolling it into a log 1½ inches (4cm) in diameter while it is still warm. Wrap in plastic cling film and allow to rest at room temperature for 1 hour.

Butter and flour several baking sheets and set them aside. Slice the log into ⅓ inch (8mm) rounds. Press each round into a log shape, then roll it back and forth on the board until it is 3 inches (8cm) long and approximately ⅝ inch (1·8cm) in diameter. Cut 3 short diagonal gashes on one side of each log, about half-way into the log. Bend the logs in a semicircle so that the 'leaves' fan out. (The gashes will be on the outside.) Place them on the prepared baking sheets, about 1 inch (2·5cm) apart, and allow to dry out uncovered at room temperature for 15 to 24 hours.

Preheat the oven to 300°F (160°C/gas 2). Bake one sheet at a time in the lower third of the oven. Insert the handle of a wooden spoon inside the oven door to keep it slightly ajar. If the biscuits start to colour or crack, lower the oven temperature. They should be a pale egg-shell colour when done, firm, and well risen with the characteristic *Fuss* (foot), a grainy-textured base. Baking time will be approximately 20 to 30 minutes. Remove to wire racks to cool before storing.

WYGÜTZLI

Moulded Red Christmas Biscuits

❧

Makes about 50 1¾ by 2 inch (4·5 by 5cm) biscuits

Switzerland (where Gützli or Gützle means biscuits, especially those baked at Christmas) is unique in the German-speaking countries in using an unusual spice – powdered sandalwood. While it has a delicate flavour, it is particularly favoured for the natural red colour it imparts to baked goods. Because powdered sandalwood is not readily available, I have substituted red food colouring in this old family recipe. The biscuits are further coloured by red wine. A hard biscuit made like Springerle, Wygützli also make lovely Christmas decorations (with a hole pierced in the top of each before baking).

For moulding, you will need decorative wooden moulds or a carved rolling pin, like those used for Springerle. Once moulded they must be dried overnight before baking. After cooling, they can be stored in an airtight container at room temperature for up to three months or more.

12½ oz (365g) castor sugar
2 large eggs
2 fl oz (60ml) dry red wine, slightly warmed
1 tbsp kirsch, or lemon juice
3–4 drops red food colouring
grated rind of 1 lemon
12 oz (350g) plain flour

1 tsp baking powder
¼ tsp grated nutmeg
¼ tsp ground cloves
pinch salt

Equipment

carved wooden moulds or carved rolling pin

Whisk the eggs and sugar together in a mixing bowl over steaming water as in the instructions for basic whisked-egg technique (p. 72). Proceed, adding the warmed red wine, Kirsch (or lemon juice), food colouring and lemon rind and beat for a further 30 seconds, adding more food colouring if necessary to produce a light red/pink mixture. Sift the flour together with the baking powder, nutmeg, cloves and salt on to greaseproof paper. Using a large metal spoon, fold the dry ingredients into the egg mixture and knead with your hands until the mixture forms a cohesive mass. Remove the dough to a lightly floured board and knead for another minute. The dough should be quite soft but not sticky. If it is, add a small amount of flour, 1 tbsp at a time, until the dough can be handled. If it seems too dry and liable to crack when rolled out, knead in an additional teaspoonful of Kirsch or lemon juice, or as much as is needed, until the dough is soft but not sticky. Wrap the dough tightly in plastic cling film and leave at room temperature for 1 hour before using.

Roll out the dough ¼ inch (6mm) thick on a lightly floured board. Dust the wooden moulds or carved wooden rolling pin and the dough itself with flour, brushing off the excess. Press the moulds or rolling pin firmly into the dough, then lift off carefully. Cut the biscuits apart with a sharp knife or a plain pastry wheel.

NOTE: If the detail on the moulds is quite deep, it will be necessary first to cut out an oval or rectangle of dough approximately the same size as the mould. After dusting the mould and dough with flour, press the thin piece of dough well into the mould to pick up all the detail. Tap the mould firmly on the counter several times to release the dough. Then use a sharp knife or plain pastry wheel to cut out the shape neatly.

If there is any flour left on the biscuits once they have been printed, brush it off with a dry pastry brush. Place the biscuits 1 inch (2·5cm) apart on buttered and floured baking sheets. Leave to dry out, uncovered, at room temperature for 15 to 24 hours. If using for Christmas ornaments, make a hole with a skewer in the top of each biscuit before they are left to dry.

Preheat the oven to 300°F (160°C/gas 2). Bake a sheet at a time, in the lower third of the oven, with the handle of a wooden spoon propped inside the oven door to keep it slightly ajar. Bake the biscuits until firm, risen and barely coloured – about 20 to 25 minutes. Cool them completely on a rack before storing in an airtight tin.

POMERANZENNÜSSE
OR POMERANZENBRÖTCHEN

Orange Nuts

Makes about 48

Many biscuit recipes from the traditional German Christmas repertoire call for Pomeranzenschale – the rind of Seville oranges (the kind used for marmalade) which was both grated and candied, producing a strong bitter orange flavour. Because candied orange peel, not specifically from Seville oranges, is now readily available throughout the year, contemporary recipes no longer specify Seville oranges. 'Pomeranzen', however, continues to be used in the name of some of these old-fashioned biscuits, generally shaped into balls, called -*nüsse* or -*brötchen*.

3 large eggs, lightly beaten
8½ oz (240g) castor sugar
8 oz (225g) candied orange peel, finely minced
grated rind of 1 lemon
8½ oz (240g) plain flour, plus more as needed
1 tsp baking powder

Whisk the eggs and sugar together in a mixing bowl over steaming water as in the instructions for basic whisked-egg technique (p. 72). Proceed, adding the finely minced candied orange peel and grated lemon rind, mixing them in well to break up any clumps. Add the flour and baking powder and mix together well.

Remove the dough to a lightly floured board and knead it until smooth and cohesive – about 3 minutes. The dough should be quite soft. If it is sticky, however, add a small amount of flour, 1 tbsp at a time, until the dough can be handled. If you have added too much flour and the dough seems dry and liable to crack when rolled out, knead in a teaspoonful of water (or rum), or as much as is needed, until the dough is soft but not sticky.

Form the dough into balls 1 inch (2·5cm) in diameter, rolling them under your palm on a pastry board. Arrange them 1 inch (2·5cm) apart on buttered and floured baking sheets. Leave them to dry out at room temperature, uncovered, for 15 to 24 hours.

Preheat the oven to 300°F (160°C/gas 2). Bake in the middle of the oven until they have risen and coloured lightly – approximately 20 to 25 minutes. They should still be moist inside but firm on the outside. Transfer to racks to cool before storing.

PFEFFERNÜSSE

'Pepper Nuts' (made by the whisked-egg method)

Makes about 40

For notes on the origins and storing of Pfeffernüsse, see p. 49.

2 large eggs
8½ oz (240g) castor sugar
1 tbsp rum, or as needed
1 tbsp ground cinnamon
¼ tsp ground cloves
¼ tsp grated nutmeg
¼ tsp ground ginger
1 tsp baking powder

7½ oz (215g) plain flour
3 oz (75g) unblanched almonds,
  finely ground (see p. 27)
1 tbsp mixed peel, finely minced

Icing

5 oz (150g) icing sugar, sifted
3 tbsps lemon juice

Whisk the eggs and sugar together in a mixing bowl over steaming water as in the instructions for basic whisked-egg technique (p. 72). Proceed, adding the rum, and beat for a few seconds longer. Sift the spices, baking powder and flour together on to the egg mixture. Add the ground almonds and finely minced mixed peel. Mix well with a spoon. Remove the dough to a lightly floured board and knead it until smooth and cohesive – about 3 minutes. The dough should be quite soft. If it is sticky, however, add a small amount of flour, 1 tbsp at a time, until the dough can be handled. If you have added too much flour and the dough seems too dry and liable to crack when rolled out, knead in an additional teaspoonful of rum, or as much as is needed, until the dough is soft but not sticky.

Form the dough into balls 1 inch (2·5cm) in diameter, rolling them under your palm on a pastry board. Arrange them 1 inch (2·5cm) apart on buttered and floured baking sheets. Leave them uncovered to dry out for 15 to 24 hours.

Preheat the oven to 375°F (190°C/gas 5). Bake, one sheet at a time, in the centre of the oven until firm and light brown in colour – approximately 12 to 14 minutes. During baking, the balls will 'burst' slightly as moisture escapes from the centre, forming cracked patterns on the surface. Transfer them to racks to cool.

For the icing, gradually beat the icing sugar into the lemon juice and beat for 8 to 10 minutes until the sugar has dissolved completely. The icing should be thin enough to brush on using a pastry brush. If it is too thin or too thick, adjust the consistency with more sugar or lemon juice.

While the Pfeffernüsse are still warm, brush them evenly with the icing. If they have cooled completely, reheat them in the oven for 2 or 3 minutes. Allow the icing to set firmly before storing. Store in an airtight tin at room temperature for up to three months.

MERINGUES

(Baisers) – Basic Method

Makes about 28 small or 6 to 8 large meringues

Snowy plain white meringues – as well as those lightly coloured and flavoured – are a favourite year-round treat in all German-speaking countries, though they are especially popular at Christmas when they are piped in small wreaths or arabesques and hung on the tree or served with coffee and a selection of other Christmas goodies.

There are various techniques used in making meringues. In one method, approximately two-thirds of the sugar – preferably castor sugar which dissolves quickly – is gradually beaten into egg whites that have been beaten 'half stiff', with the remainder carefully folded in at the end. This method produces a very light, delicate meringue. In the other similar method, all the sugar is gradually beaten into the 'half stiff' egg whites, producing a slightly stiffer meringue. Both these methods produce what are known as Swiss meringues.

Italian meringues, on the other hand, are warmed first before baking. There are two basic techniques for warming: either a hot sugar syrup is beaten into stiffly beaten egg whites (which may or may not have had some of the sugar beaten in); or a stiffly beaten meringue mixture, with all the sugar already added, is beaten in a bowl over a pan of simmering water until warm, then beaten off the heat until cool. This method produces the stiffest meringue which is especially suitable for dry nut- or fruit-filled meringues that will hold a perfect shape, whether piped or spooned.

Baking sheets

For both plain and nut-filled meringues or macaroons, I have found one method of dealing with baking sheets or liners to be superior. If you have a large plain wood chopping or pastry board, wrap it twice with aluminium foil. Put a small dab of the meringue mixture in the corners and cover it with a piece of non-stick baking or parchment paper. Place the board on a baking sheet so it isn't in direct contact with the oven rack. Pipe or spoon your mixture on the paper and proceed according to recipe directions. By using a board, you protect the meringue mixture from bottom heat which not only keeps the finished product perfectly white, but also keeps heat from building up inside and producing cracks in the meringue and/or spreading. If you don't have a suitable board, then simply use parchment or non-stick baking paper on a baking sheet. Buttered aluminium foil can be used for plain and stiff nut-filled meringues. Avoid using black metal baking sheets which conduct the heat too rapidly through the bottom of the meringues. If you use the lined baking sheet method, as opposed to the lined wooden board, and your meringues have stuck slightly to the paper when they are done, simply turn the entire sheet of paper, with meringues still attached, upside down on the baking sheet. Moisten the paper with water. Return the meringues to the oven for a few minutes. The paper should peel off easily.

Baking tips

The meringues should all be baked at one time once they are shaped. If you do not have enough oven space to bake them all on the same rack, you will have to swop the position of the baking sheets once during baking. This isn't the ideal solution as the upper baking sheet conducts added top heat to the meringues below. However, it's the only solution under the circumstances. I have baked meringues in this way on numerous occasions without difficulty.

To keep them from colouring, meringues should be baked in the bottom third of the oven in a very low heat. They are meant to be no more than egg-shell in colour. If you find your oven seems a little too warm (they are colouring or cracking before they are done), insert the handle of a wooden spoon inside the door to keep it slightly ajar and prevent the heat from building up too much. Alternatively, turn the oven down or off for a period of time. For the dryest plain meringues, leave them in the turned-off oven over-night once they have baked. This will keep them dry even with prolonged storage.

Storing

Plain meringues (i.e. without chocolate coating) keep well for two or three months in an airtight jar or tin at room temperature. They should not be refrigerated or frozen, however, as this causes them to lose their dry crisp texture.

In Switzerland, plain Swiss meringue is frequently seen piped in large 3½ to 4 inch (9–10cm) arabesques which, when baked, are placed on their sides in pairs, flat bottoms facing in, and used to sandwich vanilla ice-cream accompanied by a dollop of whipped cream (meringue glacé) or, more simply, to sandwich whipped cream which is piped in a decorative frill.

The basic recipe that follows can be used for large arabesques, nests (to hold a cream filling or berries and ice-cream), wreaths, to hang on the Christmas tree, or any shape you wish.

3 large egg whites, at room temperature
pinch of salt
pinch of cream of tartar
6½ oz (190g) castor sugar

Preheat the oven to 225°F (105°C/gas ¼). Line a large board or baking sheet as described on p. 81. Using an electric mixer, beat the egg whites in a non-aluminium mixing bowl (aluminium will turn them grey) with a pinch of salt. Begin with the mixer on a low speed. When the egg whites are foamy, increase the speed to moderately fast, add the cream of tartar, and beat until the egg whites stand in soft peaks. They should hold their shape but not be dry. Add the sugar by the tablespoonful, beating 20 seconds between each addition, until it is used up. Beat for a further 3 minutes or longer, until the meringue is thick and glossy. Use in one of the following shapes.

ARABESKEN

Meringue Arabesques

For large meringue arabesques (to be sandwiched with ice-cream or plain whipped cream as described) use a piping bag fitted with a large star nozzle. An arabesque is made by piping an S-shaped figure with no spaces left in between. Pipe 3½ to 4 inch (9 to 10cm) arabesques on the prepared baking sheet or board, leaving 1¼ inch (3cm) space between them. Bake in the lower third of the oven for 1¾ to 2 hours, or until the meringues are completely dry and remove easily from the paper. Turn off the oven and leave them to dry out overnight. Use immediately or store in an airtight container.

BAISERBAUMBEHANG

Meringue Christmas Tree Wreath Ornaments

Using the basic meringue recipe, 2½ inch (6cm) wreaths can be made plain white or coloured. For cocoa-coloured wreaths, beat 3 to 4 tsp of cocoa powder into the meringue mixture just before folding in the final addition of sugar. For pale pink or pale green, beat several drops of red or green food colouring into the meringue before folding in the final addition of sugar.

Pipe the meringues in 2½ inch (6cm) wreaths on a board or baking sheet lined with parchment or non-stick baking paper (see p. 81) using a piping bag fitted with a medium star nozzle. If desired, the wreaths can be decorated with a small rosette of meringue and then left plain; or they can be sprinkled with granulated sugar, hundreds and thousands or silver balls; or garnished with a sliver of glacé cherry.

Bake for 1 to 1¼ hours, or until the meringues are dry and remove easily from the paper. Turn off the oven and leave them to dry out overnight. Use a narrow ribbon, a piece of yarn or cord to suspend the wreaths from the tree branches.

If you don't feel like using these for ornaments, they are of course equally nice to eat.

MANDELKÜSSE

Almond Meringue Kisses

Makes about 36

This recipe for snow-white firm little mouthfuls of almond meringue is made according to the Italian meringue method, i.e., the meringue mixture is warmed before it is baked. Using this basic recipe, you can substitute the same amount of finely ground walnuts or shelled, skinned ground hazelnuts (see p. 28), if desired, garnishing the meringues with the appropriate nut.

Meringue mixture

3 large egg whites, at room
    temperature
pinch of salt
pinch of cream of tartar
6½ oz (190g) castor sugar

6½ oz (190g) blanched almonds,
    finely ground (p. 27)
1 tbsp cornflour

split blanched almonds to
    garnish (optional)
icing sugar

Equipment

piping bag fitted with plain
    ¾ inch (2cm) nozzle

Preheat the oven to 225°F (105°C/gas ¼). Line a large baking sheet or board as described on p. 81. Set aside.

Use a heatproof crockery bowl that will rest on the rim of a saucepan with its base well above the bottom of the pan. Bring 3 inches (8cm) of water to the boil in the saucepan, cover the pan and turn the heat off.

Using the quantities of egg white and sugar above, prepare the meringue according to the technique for basic meringue (p. 81). Bring the water in the saucepan back to a simmer. Rest the bowl in the saucepan and, still using the electric mixer, beat the meringue, scraping down the sides of the bowl frequently, until the mixture is warm – about 5 minutes. Remove the bowl from the pan and continue beating until the meringue and bowl are cool – approximately another 5 minutes.

Mix the ground nuts together with the cornflour (the cornflour will help to separate the granules). Using a large metal spoon, fold in the nuts until they are evenly distributed. Scoop the mixture into a piping bag fitted with a plain ¾ inch (2cm) nozzle. Holding the bag up straight, perpendicular to the prepared baking sheet or board, pipe small ¾ inch (2cm) rounds, leaving at least ¾ inch (2cm) between each. When all the meringue mixture has been used up, lightly moisten your finger and smooth the tops and sides (if necessary) of each meringue so it has a perfectly smooth surface. If desired, garnish the top of each with a split blanched almond (see p. 27). Bake in the lower third of the oven for approximately 1 hour, or until the meringues are completely dry and remove easily from the paper. If desired, dust them with sifted icing sugar. When cool, store in an airtight tin or jar.

VARIATION

Pipe especially low rounds of meringue and omit the final nut garnish. Save a small amount of the uncooked meringue mixture, covering it with a damp cloth until needed. When the meringues have finished baking, sandwich two together by spreading a small amount of the moist meringue mixture on the bottom of one. Leave on a lined baking sheet in a turned-off oven for several hours to dry out.

FRÜCHTEMAKRONEN

Fruit-covered Almond Macaroons

Makes about 30

In this Viennese recipe, small almond meringues (Mandelküsse) are prettily garnished with apricot glaze, topped with rum-soaked fruit, then glazed overall with a thin sugar icing.

1 recipe Mandelküsse (p. 84),
    omitting the garnish
6 oz (175g) mixed peel, coarsely
    chopped
3 tbsp rum
12 oz (350g) apricot jam
glacé cherries, to garnish

Icing
3+ tbsp lemon juice
5 oz (150g) icing sugar, sifted

Make and bake the Mandelküsse as directed, eliminating the split almond garnish and icing sugar at the end. When smoothing the little rounds with your finger, flatten the tops a little so that after baking they can be turned upside down and rest fairly flat.

The day before or up to 4 hours before finishing the macaroons, soak the coarsely chopped mixed peel in 3 tbsp of rum. If you warm the rum lightly, without boiling, it will penetrate the fruit more quickly. After the fruit has steeped for at least 4 hours, strain. Boil the apricot jam, stirring, with 1 tbsp water. Strain the hot jam into another saucepan, pressing well against the fruit. Reserve the apricot pulp and add to the rum-soaked fruit.

Turn all the macaroons upside down so the flat bottoms are facing up. (Pare a small slice off the bottom if they wobble.) Brush the bottom of each macaroon with the warm jam, reheating it briefly if it becomes too thick. Mix about 2 tbsp of jam with the drained fruit – enough to bind it. Spoon a small amount of fruit on each macaroon, dividing it evenly among them. Use a half or a quarter of a red glacé cherry (depending on size) to garnish the top of each.

For the icing, beat the sifted icing sugar into 3 tbsp lemon juice for 8 to 10 minutes until the sugar has dissolved completely to make a smooth icing. The icing should be of a thin consistency so that when it is used, it will be somewhat transparent. Add an additional teaspoon or more of lemon juice, if necessary, to make a thin icing.

Place the fruit-covered macaroons on a wire rack. Spoon a little icing over each, to cover the fruit. Using a pastry brush, glaze the sides of each to cover. Allow the macaroons to dry completely before storing carefully in an airtight tin. Although they will taste delicious for a longer period, they begin to look a little tired after a week to 10 days.

MARONIBAISERS

Chestnut Meringues

Makes about 14

In both Switzerland and Austria, sweetened chestnut purée is a favourite dessert. Called *Vermicelles* in Switzerland, it is put through a mincer, a small piping bag with a plain nozzle, or a special multi-holed press made just for this purpose, to produce long tangled strands resembling wholewheat spaghetti. They are served with a mound of whipped cream. In Austria, the favourite variation – Kastanienreis (sieved chestnut purée) – is pressed through a coarse wire sieve over a mound of whipped cream. In one of its most luxurious presentations, Maronibaisers, small meringue shells are glazed inside with melted chocolate, embellished with a spoonful of morello cherry jam, piped high with whipped cream, and covered all over with sieved chestnut purée. If you can't find morello cherry (or any kind of cherry) jam, raspberry jam would also be good.

The meringues can be made in advance and stored in an airtight container, while the Kastanienreis can be made in advance and frozen. Only the sieving and final assembly with filling and cream need be done on the same day.

For another luxurious Austrian Kastanienreis dessert, see Maroniobersschnitten (p. 189), made with layered chocolate cake.

Meringue

5½ oz (190g) sugar
4 large egg whites, at room
  temperature
1½ oz (40g) sugar

To finish

3 oz (75g) dark, semi-sweet
  chocolate, broken in pieces
12 oz (350g) morello cherry jam with
  whole cherries, or raspberry jam
1 pint (575ml) whipping cream

3 tbsp icing sugar, sifted
¾ pint (425ml) sieved Kastanienreis
  (see p. 87), weighed after it is sieved
glacé cherries, halved, to garnish

Equipment

large pastry bag with large star
nozzle coarse wire sieve for
Kastanienreis jam thermometer

Preheat the oven to 225°F (105°C/gas ¼). Line a large board or several baking sheets as described on p. 81. Set aside.

Place the sugar and 4 fl oz (125ml) water in a heavy saucepan and set aside.

To make the meringue, beat the egg whites in a large non-aluminium mixing bowl with an electric mixer until they are half stiff. They should hold their shape but not be dry. Increase the speed and begin adding 1½ oz (40g) sugar by the tablespoon, beating for at least 20 seconds between additions. When all the sugar has been added, beat a few minutes longer until the meringue is smooth, thick and glossy. Immediately heat the sugar and water over a low heat until the sugar has dissolved. Bring to the boil and boil without stirring until the syrup reaches the hard ball stage, 248°F (120°C) on a jam thermometer. While boiling, wash down any sugar crystals from the sides of the pan with a pastry brush dipped in water. Remove the syrup from the heat when it has reached the required temperature and gradually pour it on to the meringue mixture, beating at high speed with an electric mixer. Scrape down the sides of the bowl frequently and continue beating until the meringue is cool.

Fit a large piping bag with a large star nozzle. Have the baking sheets ready. Pipe the meringue in a spiralling motion, beginning in the centre, to form a 2½ inch (6cm) circle. Without stopping the flow of meringue, pipe a second ring of meringue on top of the outside edge to make a tiny nest. Continue until all the meringue has been used, leaving at least ¾ inch (2cm) between each.

NOTE: If the hole in the centre is too small, moisten your thumb with water and rotate it around in the centre of the nest to increase the size of the opening.

Dust the nests with sifted icing sugar. Bake in the lower part of the oven for 1½ to 2 hours, or until dry, with the handle of a wooden spoon propped inside the oven door to keep it slightly ajar. This helps keep the oven temperature moderate. If the meringues start to colour too rapidly, remove them from the oven and lower the heat. When done, they should be a light egg-shell colour and come away easily from the paper. If the bottoms are still slightly moist, turn the meringues upside down and leave them in the oven until they are dry, or simply turn off the oven and leave them upside down for several hours to dry them out completely. Allow to cool to room temperature before continuing with the filling, or store in an airtight container until needed.

For the filling, melt the chocolate pieces in a double boiler or in a shallow heatproof soup plate or bowl over a pan filled with 2 inches (5cm) of simmering water. When melted, remove the bowl from the heat. Brush the inside of each meringue with melted chocolate. Allow the chocolate to set while beating the cream. When the cream has begun to hold its shape, add the sifted icing sugar gradually by the tablespoon. Beat until the cream is stiff. Place 1 tsp of cream on top of the chocolate, topping it with a spoonful of jam. Place the remaining whipped cream in a piping bag fitted with a plain or star nozzle. Pipe a high mound of cream on each filled meringue, saving a little for garnish.

Sprinkle Kastanienreis lavishly all over the cream and each meringue. Pipe a small swirl of cream on top. Finish with a halved glacé cherry. Chill until needed. Maronibaisers are best if served on the day they are filled.

STAMBUL MERINGEN

Istanbul Meringues

Makes 9 large or 27 small meringues

At Konditorei Frei in Rothenburg ob der Tauber, Germany, large snow-white meringues filled with chopped walnuts and coated underneath with chocolate are a speciality. While proprietor Hans

Karl Frei has kept the recipe for his Stambul Meringen a secret, I've worked out the following method to produce a similar melt-in-your-mouth meringue.

Meringue mixture

3 large egg whites, at room
   temperature
pinch of salt
⅛ tsp cream of tartar
6½ oz (190g) castor sugar

6 oz (175g) walnuts, coarsely chopped
3 oz (75g) dark, semi-sweet chocolate,
   broken in pieces
1 tsp butter
few drops of vegetable oil (optional)

Preheat the oven to 225°F (105°C/gas ¼). Line a large board or baking sheet as described on p. 81.

Prepare the meringue mixture using the above quantities following the technique for basic meringue (p. 81). When the meringue is well beaten, carefully fold in the chopped walnuts using a large spoon.

Using two spoons, place high, round mounds approximately 2 inches (5cm) in diameter (about 3 heaped tbsp each) on the prepared board or baking sheet 1½ inches (4cm) apart.

Smooth the mounds to remove any protruding points or edges. Bake on the next to lowest shelf of the oven for approximately 2½ hours, checking occasionally to make sure the meringues are not colouring. If they start to colour or crack, lower the oven temperature or turn the oven off. When done, the meringues can be removed easily from the baking sheet. At the end of the baking time, turn the meringues on their sides, turn off the oven and return the baking sheet to the oven leaving them to dry out with the door closed overnight.

The next day, remove the meringues from the baking sheet. Heat the broken chocolate and butter in a heatproof soup plate or shallow bowl placed over a saucepan filled with 2 inches (5cm) of simmering water, stirring the chocolate occasionally until it is melted. The chocolate should be of spreading consistency. If it is too thick, add a few drops of vegetable oil. Using a pastry brush, brush the bottoms of the meringues with melted chocolate. Place the meringues upside down on a wire rack to allow the chocolate to dry until almost set. With the prongs of a fork, make a wavy pattern in the soft chocolate on each meringue. Allow the chocolate to dry completely.

Store the meringues in an airtight container at a cool room temperature (not in the refrigerator, which will cause the meringues to soften). If packing in layers, separate each layer with greaseproof paper or aluminium foil so that the chocolate will not smudge the layer of meringues beneath. If properly stored they will keep from two weeks to a month or longer, provided the room temperature remains constant so the chocolate doesn't discolour.

NOTE: If desired, you can make smaller meringues, though the baking time given must be decreased in proportion to the size.

DATTELMAKRONEN

Date Macaroons

Makes about 30

Chopped dates and ground almonds are combined with a meringue mixture in this German recipe to produce date-shaped biscuits glazed with chocolate – a delicious treat with after-dinner coffee or as part of your Christmas baking selection.

2 large egg whites, at room
   temperature
pinch of salt
3¼ oz (85g) castor sugar
grated rind of 1 lemon
juice of ½ lemon
4 oz (125g) dates, finely chopped
2 oz (50g) blanched almonds, finely
   ground

Chocolate glaze
3½ oz (100g) dark semi-sweet
   chocolate, broken in pieces
1 tsp vegetable oil

Preheat the oven to 275°F (140°C/gas 1). Line a large board or baking sheet as described on p. 81.

Make a meringue mixture with the egg whites, salt and sugar, following the technique for basic meringue (p. 81). When the meringue is thick and glossy, beat in the grated lemon rind and lemon juice for several seconds. Using a large metal spoon, carefully fold in the dates and ground almonds until well mixed.

Spoon the mixture on to the prepared board or baking sheets in 2 inch (5cm) lengths. Moisten your finger lightly with water and smooth the mixture into a date shape. Bake all of the dates at once in the bottom third of the oven until firm and lightly coloured – approximately 1 hour. Remove carefully to a wire rack to cool.

For the chocolate glaze, heat the broken chocolate and vegetable oil in a double boiler or in a heatproof soup plate or shallow bowl over a saucepan filled with 2 inches (5cm) of simmering water. Stir occasionally until the chocolate is melted. Brush each cooled date with chocolate. If the chocolate is too thick, add a few more drops of oil. Allow to set completely before storing in an airtight tin in a cool place for up to ten days.

ZIMTSTERNE

Cinnamon Stars

Makes about 35 ⅜ inch (1cm) stars

White-glazed cinnamon stars appear, with slight variations, in all the German-speaking countries at Christmas time. Made from a flourless dough – a combination of ground almonds, sugar, egg white and cinnamon – they are flavoured in Switzerland with kirsch, and in other places often with lemon juice. They vary in size and thickness in different cities.

Household cookery books always instruct you to cut out the biscuits first and then apply the traditional meringue glaze. When made in this manner, however, the glaze is rarely even. I finally learned a secret from a Basel baker: first brush the meringue glaze over the entire surface of the rolled-out dough, then cut out the stars with a cutter dipped in hot water (to make a clean even cut). In order to re-knead the scraps and roll them out again, you will need some extra ground almond since the additional egg glaze on the scraps will make this mixture more moist than the first. Remember to reserve some of the meringue glaze to coat stars produced from subsequent batches.

I am accustomed to thick stars (about ⅜ inch/1cm) as they are made in Switzerland. However, the dough can also be rolled out thinner, to approximately ¼ inch (6mm), thus increasing your yield of biscuits.

Traditionally, a small star cutter is generally used. If your cutter is more than 1½ inches (4cm), cut a small circle out of the centre of each star using an aspic cutter or a thimble so that the biscuits are not overly moist in the centre and fall apart.

The biscuits are dried out rather than baked in a cool oven for approximately 20 to 25 minutes, depending on size. They must be watched carefully so that the glaze doesn't colour. When cooled, they will be quite firm and the glaze well set.

They can be stored in an airtight tin at room temperature for up to three months. Zimtsterne improve with age.

12 oz (350g) unblanched almonds,
   finely ground, plus 2–3 oz
   (50–75g) more as needed
1½ tbsp ground cinnamon
4 large egg whites
14 oz (400g) icing sugar, sifted
1 tbsp kirsch, or more as needed,
   or lemon juice
granulated sugar, for rolling out

Equipment
5- or 6-point star cutter

Butter and flour several baking sheets and set them aside.

Combine the 12 oz (350g) of ground almonds with the cinnamon in a mixing bowl. Using an electric mixer, beat the egg whites until frothy and slightly thickened. Beat the icing sugar into the egg whites, 3½ oz (100g) at a time, beating well between each addition. When all the sugar has been added, beat the mixture for a further 5 minutes.

Remove approximately two-thirds of the egg-white mixture and blend it together with the ground almonds. Cover the remaining egg-white mixture with a clean damp cloth – a J-cloth will do. Add the kirsch to the almond mixture and use your hand to blend all the ingredients together to form a cohesive mass. Allow the mixture to rest for 10 minutes. To test the consistency, try rolling out a small piece on a board dusted with granulated sugar (the dough itself can also be sprinkled with a small amount of sugar). If it is too sticky to handle, add more ground almonds, by the tablespoon, until it is manageable. If the dough crumbles or falls apart, add a few extra drops of kirsch or lemon juice and 1 tbsp of the reserved egg-white glaze.

When the dough has reached the proper consistency, dust a pastry board lightly with granulated sugar. Shape the dough into a flat round and dust the surface lightly with sugar. Roll the dough out into a rectangle ⅜ inch (1cm) thick (or slightly thinner, if you prefer). Remove the cloth from the reserved egg-white glaze. Use a metal spatula to smooth an even coating of the glaze over the entire surface of the rectangle, just enough to cover it completely with white. To smooth the surface further, dip the spatula in hot water and run it across the glaze. Make sure you have not used up all the glaze as you will need a small amount to glaze the scraps after they have been re-rolled. Cover the remaining glaze again with the damp cloth to keep it from drying out.

Fill a cup with hot tap water. Dip your star cutter into the hot water each time you cut, leaving as little space between stars as possible. Place the stars on the prepared baking sheets, leaving ¾ inch (2cm) between each. Knead the scraps together, adding additional ground almonds so that the dough can be rolled out. Roll out, glaze, and cut out as before. Allow to dry at room temperature for 2 hours.

Preheat the oven to 275°F (140°C/gas 1). Bake, one sheet at a time, in the middle of the oven for 20 to 30 minutes, or until the stars are firm and the glaze has dried out. Do not allow them to colour. Remove to wire racks to cool completely before storing in an airtight tin.

BASLER BRUNSLI

Basel 'Browns'

A traditional favourite from Basel in Switzerland, Basler Brunsli – part biscuit, part sweet – are as delicious as they are pretty. A flourless dough, composed basically of ground almonds, chocolate, spices, egg white and sugar, is pressed into tiny decorative moulds to give the Brunsli their charming fluted flower-like shapes. Unmoulded and left to dry for several hours, they are barely baked at a low temperature for just long enough to firm the outside and set the design. They should remain quite moist inside, giving them their confection-like texture.

If you don't have any decorative metal moulds, you can simply roll the dough into small walnut-sized balls, approximately ¾ inch (2cm) in diameter, and then roll the balls lightly in granulated sugar to give them some texture. Alternatively, the dough can be rolled out on a board dusted with granulated sugar, then cut out with small cutters. After that, they can be treated in the same way as the moulded Brunsli. Increase the baking time by 5 or 10 minutes for balls, and decrease slightly for thinner Brunsli.

Once cooled, they can be stored in an airtight tin at room temperature for up to three months.

8 oz (225g) unblanched almonds, finely ground, plus more as needed
8 oz (225g) castor sugar
½ tsp ground cloves
4 oz (125g) dark, unsweetened chocolate; if unavailable, substitute dark,
   semi-sweet chocolate and decrease the sugar by 1½ oz (40g)
2 egg whites, lightly beaten
2–3 tbsp kirsch or rum
granulated sugar, for the moulds

Equipment

small, decorative metal confection moulds, approximately 1 to 1¼ inches
   (2·5 to 3cm) in size (they can be any shape) or use the methods given
   above

Mix the ground almonds, sugar and cloves together in a mixing
bowl. Grate the chocolate on the finest blades of a cheese grater and
add to the other dry ingredients. Beat the egg whites lightly and add
to the other ingredients, along with 2 to 3 tbsp of kirsch. Knead the
mixture well with your hand to form a cohesive mass. If you can roll
the dough into balls between the palms of your hand without
difficulty, the mixture is the correct consistency. If it is too sticky to
handle, add ground almonds by the tablespoon until it is no longer
sticky. If it crumbles, add more kirsch. Allow the dough to rest for
30 minutes.

Line several baking sheets with buttered aluminium foil or
unbuttered non-stick baking paper and set aside.

For moulded biscuits, pinch off a small piece of dough just large
enough to fit into the mould. Press it into the mould. Then tap the
mould firmly on a counter to release the biscuit. After the first one
the mould will be moist so sprinkle the inside with granulated sugar
before you mould each biscuit. Place them on the prepared baking
sheets with 1 inch (2·5cm) between them. Allow to dry out at room
temperature for up to 2 hours. If making balls or cut-out biscuits,
follow the instructions in the introduction.

Preheat the oven to 300°F (160°C/gas 2). Bake, one sheet at a
time, in the middle of the oven, lowering the temperature to 225°F
(105°C/gas ¼) as soon as you place them in the oven. Bake for
approximately 15 minutes or a little longer, so that they are firm on
the outside but moist inside. Remove to wire racks to cool before
storing in an airtight tin.

BERNER HASELNUSSLECKERLI

Bern Hazelnut Spice Biscuits

Makes about 15 2 inch (5cm) square biscuits

This favourite recipe is a Christmas speciality from Bern in Switzerland. Traditionally stamped with small decorative wooden moulds or a carved wooden rolling pin, these crunchy biscuits are made with ground almonds, hazelnuts and sugar. The dough is first allowed to dry out overnight before the biscuits are cut out, dried another 2 hours, and baked. The low heat allows them to cook through without browning too quickly, the somewhat lengthy baking time varying slightly according to the size of the moulds used and the thickness of the dough. Though still slightly soft after they have browned, they should become crisp when they cool. If not, return them to the oven for another 5 to 10 minutes. Store in airtight tins. They keep well for up to three months.

NOTE: Though not traditional, if you don't have wooden moulds, the biscuits can be made using small round or decorative cutters to give them interesting shapes.

12 oz (350g) hazelnuts, roasted, skins removed, and finely ground (p. 28)
12 oz (350g) blanched almonds, finely ground (p. 27)
1 lb (450g) sugar
3½ oz (100g) mixed peel, finely minced
1 tsp cinnamon
grated rind of 1 lemon
2 tbsp apricot jam
4 egg whites, lightly beaten

Equipment

carved wooden moulds or, if unavailable, decorative biscuit cutters

Combine the ground hazelnuts and almonds with the other ingredients in a mixing bowl. Mix together well. The dough will be very moist and soft but should hold together. Wrap in plastic cling film and leave at room temperature overnight.

The next day, roll out the dough on a board sprinkled lightly with granulated sugar until ⅜ inch (1cm) thick. Dust a decorative wooden mould and the dough lightly with icing sugar. Press the mould repeatedly into the dough. Brush off the excess sugar.

Separate the biscuits with a sharp knife. If using biscuit cutters, cut out decorative shapes as desired. Place on a buttered and floured baking sheet. Allow to dry for several hours at room temperature.

Preheat the oven to 300°F (160°C/gas 2). Bake, one sheet at a time, in the middle of the oven for 20 to 30 minutes or until golden and relatively dry. Loosen the biscuits from the baking sheet with a metal spatula as soon as you have taken them out of the oven. Allow to cool on the baking sheet for several minutes before removing them to a wire rack. When cool, store in airtight tins.

BASIC MARZIPAN

Makes about 1½ lb (675g)

Marzipan – sweet almond paste flavoured with rose water – has a special place in German tradition. A favourite sweet in the Middle East, it followed trade routes to the West, appearing first in Italy. From Venice it made its way to German ports such as Lübeck and Königsberg. It was in these cities that marzipan became associated with the Christmas season. Because St Nikolaus, as the protector of seafarers as well as children, was particularly venerated in these northern ports, it became the custom for children to receive marzipan as a gift from him on his feast day, 6 December. Then, it might appear in its simplest form, plain or chocolate-dipped loaves, or in one of many colourful shapes: potatoes, sausages, pigs for good luck, decorative hearts, fruit, flowers and hedgehogs, to name a few.

Today, it is found in all German-speaking countries, either shaped as above, used as a filling in biscuits, cakes and breads such as Stollen, or shaped into confections or biscuits which are glazed and baked, such as Königsberger Herz (Königsberg heart), Züri Leckerli (Zurich marzipan biscuits), or Frankfurter Bethmännchen (Frankfurt marzipan pyramids).

While it can be purchased in many grocery shops and most delicatessens, it is best if freshly made. However, it is important to grind the almonds to a very fine dust; you will therefore need a good liquidizer.

10 oz (300g) blanched almonds
10 oz (300g) granulated sugar
2 large egg whites, lightly beaten
1 tsp rose water
2 tbsp icing sugar, or more as needed, sifted

Grind the nuts, in batches, to a very fine powder in a liquidizer. Some of the mixture may become oily, which is perfectly acceptable. Reserve.

Combine the granulated sugar with 4 fl oz (125ml) water in a heavy medium saucepan. Stir constantly over a medium heat until the sugar has melted and the syrup begins to boil. At this point, stop stirring and attach a jam thermometer to the side of the saucepan. Boil the syrup until the thermometer registers 240°F (116°C). Remove the pan from the heat. Stir in the ground almonds until thoroughly blended. Stir in the egg whites until well mixed.

Return the saucepan to a medium heat. Cook, stirring constantly, until the mixture is smooth and well combined – about 3 minutes. Add the rose water and mix well. Pour the marzipan out on to a work surface that has been lightly dusted with icing sugar. Let it cool.

When cool enough to handle, knead the marzipan until smooth and pliable. If it is too moist and sticky, knead in icing sugar, a little at a time. Use extra icing sugar sparingly. Too much will result in a dry marzipan that will crack easily. If it becomes too dry, add a little extra rose water. Wrap the marzipan well in plastic cling film and refrigerate overnight. Use as directed in the recipe.

Baking sheets

In some of the recipes that follow, marzipan is cut out or shaped and baked. In recipes where the marzipan is baked in an oven 300°F (160°C/gas 2) or lower – as opposed to those where the marzipan is baked in a hot oven or under the grill – the marzipan will stay more moist if you use a large wooden board. Wrap the board twice in aluminium foil to cover it completely. Butter the foil and cover it with a piece of non-stick baking or parchment paper (the butter will help it to stick). Place the board on a baking sheet so that it won't be in direct contact with the hot oven racks. Then place the marzipan on the paper-covered board. If you have more marzipan than will fit on the board at one time, place the rest on another piece of non-stick baking or parchment paper and set aside. When one batch has finished, remove the sheet of paper with the baked marzipan and carefully replace it with the fresh piece of paper holding the unbaked marzipan.

The advantage of the board is that it prevents bottom heat from passing through the marzipan, wood being a poor conductor of heat, and thus allows them to colour or dry out on the top without drying out inside.

If you don't have a board, first line your baking sheets with two layers of aluminium foil (since foil is an insulator rather than a conductor of heat). Butter the aluminium foil and cover with a piece of non-stick baking or parchment paper. Then bake as directed.

NOTE: Avoid using black steel baking sheets (I'm not referring to the black-coated non-stick baking sheets) since they conduct heat more rapidly than light coloured or non-stick baking sheets.

MARZIPANFIGUREN

Marzipan Figures

Marzipan can be formed into any shape you can think of, though traditional figures at Christmas time include small pink pigs (for good luck), fruits (strawberries, apricots, bananas, oranges), vegetables (potatoes, cabbages, leeks) and loaves 3½ inches (9cm) long, resembling bread.

Use professional paste food colours to colour the marzipan, so that you don't dye your hands as well. These are available in some delicatessens or in bakers' supply shops.

A simple marzipan shape that requires no special colouring is the potato. Roll small pieces of marzipan in various-sized small balls. Distort their shape slightly to look like real potatoes. Use the tip of a sharp knife or a skewer to mark a few 'eyes' on each. Roll in ground cinnamon or cocoa powder, smudging it away in a few places. For a Christmas gift, the potatoes can be placed in a small bag (you can make one out of a coarse cotton) with a draw-string; or they can be placed in a small basket and covered with plastic cling film.

For other shapes that need to be coloured, pour about 2 tbsp of water into each of several small cups, depending on how many colours you are using. Dip a fine-tipped brush into each jar of colour, using a clean brush for each. Mix the small amount of colour that adheres to the brush with the water. Adjust the intensity of colour – they are subtler if the shades are kept pastel. Let the marzipan shape dry, uncovered, overnight.

Plain loaves can be coated with chocolate if desired. For the chocolate glaze, break 3½ oz/100g (or as much as is needed) chocolate into pieces. Place it in a double boiler or in a heatproof soup plate or shallow bowl with 1 tsp of vegetable oil over a saucepan filled with 2 inches (5cm) of simmering water. Stir the chocolate occasionally until melted. Using a pastry brush, first brush the bottoms of the loaves and leave them in a cool place (not the refrigerator), chocolate side up, to dry. If the chocolate is too thick to coat easily, add a few more drops of vegetable oil. When the bottoms are dry, coat the tops and sides evenly and leave them to dry before storing in an airtight tin in a cool place.

PISTAZIENKUGELN

Pistachio Confections

Finely ground pistachios mixed with ground blanched almonds turn this marzipan-type dough a lovely green.

1 recipe basic marzipan (p. 97) substituting 6 oz (175g) shelled, skinned
    pistachios for 5 oz (150g) blanched almonds
1 egg white
icing sugar
1½ oz (40g) shelled, skinned pistachios, split, for decoration

Follow the recipe for basic marzipan, substituting shelled, skinned pistachios for blanched almonds in the quantities given above.

Pistachio skins can be removed by covering the pistachios with 2 inches (5cm) of hot water and leaving them for about 5 minutes. The skins should then slip off easily. For those to be used as decoration, split them while moist. Dry them out in a 325°F (170°C/gas 3) oven on a baking sheet for 5 to 10 minutes (do not let them brown) before grinding in a liquidizer all except those to be used for decoration. Proceed as directed in the master recipe.

Wrap the marzipan well and refrigerate it overnight. The next day, knead briefly, then break off small pieces and roll them in nut-sized balls between the palms of your hands. Beat an egg white until frothy. Brush each ball with the egg white, then roll it in sifted icing sugar. Place on a piece of parchment or greaseproof paper. Garnish each with a half pistachio. Leave at room temperature for at least 24 hours to dry out.

When completely dry, store in an airtight container in the refrigerator.

ZÜRI LECKERLI

Zurich Marzipan Biscuits

While the Leckerli from Basel – spicy and honey-based – are the most famous, Zurichers are proud of their own variation made either solely with ground blanched almonds, like marzipan, or with almonds and hazelnuts, mixed with sugar and egg white. Traditionally printed with small, rectangular wooden moulds, the Leckerli are made in four different flavours, each of which has a different tint: white, flavoured only with rose water; pale beige, spiced with cinnamon; cocoa, sweetened with chocolate; and rose, scented and coloured with powdered sandalwood (red food colouring has been substituted in the recipe that follows).

A visit to Zurich at holiday time should include a stop at the famous bakery, Sprüngli, where diminutive four-coloured Leckerli are exquisitely produced and packaged for gifts or on-the-spot consumption.

If you have the time, make the marzipan yourself from the recipe on p. 97. If you are buying the marzipan, make sure it is very fresh, off-white and soft. You can make only one colour of marzipan, or divide the marzipan into four and colour it as described below. If you are making the marzipan, do so at least 1 day before the biscuits are to be baked so that it can rest overnight. The baking is meant just to firm and finish drying the Leckerli, leaving them moist inside. The sugar icing glaze which they receive at the end gives them a soft tint.

When finished, store in an airtight container, refrigerated or at room temperature, for two weeks or longer.

WISSI LECKERLI

White Zurich Leckerli

1 recipe basic marzipan (p. 97), or 1½ lbs (675g) fresh, ready-made
   marzipan

Glaze	*Equipment*
½ large egg white	small rectangular carved wooden
7 oz (200g) icing sugar, sifted	moulds,
2–3 tbsp orange water, rose water,	if available, or decorative
or tap water	biscuit cutters

Make the marzipan as directed in the basic recipe, wrapping and refrigerating it overnight. The next day, preheat the oven to 300°F (160°C/gas 2). Roll out the prepared marzipan ⅜ inch (1cm) thick on a board lightly dusted with icing sugar. Dust the marzipan and the wooden moulds lightly with icing sugar and press the moulds into the dough. Using a knife or a plain pastry wheel, separate the biscuits, trimming the edges neatly. Prepare a board or baking sheets as described on p. 98. Bake one batch at a time, in the upper third of the oven, until the outside crust is firm but the inside still soft – approximately 15 minutes. Do not allow the marzipan to colour.

Beat the egg white with a wooden spoon or a whisk until it is frothy and begins to thicken. Gradually beat in the sifted icing sugar alternately with the liquid. Beat for at least 8 minutes to dissolve the sugar completely. The glaze is meant to be a thin icing of pouring consistency. If necessary, add a few drops of additional liquid or spoonsful of sugar to correct the consistency.

When the biscuits are done, remove the baking sheet from the oven. Allow them to rest for 1 minute before removing them carefully to a wire rack. While they are still warm, brush them evenly but sparingly with the glaze. If there are other biscuits being baked, place a damp cloth directly on the surface of the icing to keep it from drying out. Allow the icing to set before storing the biscuits.

Variation

Replace half of the ground blanched almonds with skinned ground hazelnuts, following the instructions for skinning them on p. 28 and grinding them in a liquidizer.

ROTE LECKERLI

Red Zurich Leckerli

Because the traditional flavouring and colouring ingredient – powdered sandalwood – is not readily available, tint the marzipan mixture in the above recipe with several drops of red and a tiny drop of yellow food colouring to produce a pale rose tint. Proceed as for Wissi Leckerli.

BRAUNE LECKERLI

Brown Zurich Leckerli

Make the marzipan mixture, adding 6 oz (175g) of melted dark, semi-sweet chocolate and 1–2 tbsp rum if needed. To melt the chocolate, break it into pieces and place it in a double boiler or in a shallow heatproof soup plate or bowl over a pan filled with 2 inches (5cm) of simmering water. Stir occasionally until melted. Remove the chocolate from the heat and allow it to cool. Knead the cooled chocolate into the prepared marzipan when the marzipan goes through the kneading process before being wrapped and stored. If using prepared marzipan, simply knead the chocolate into the marzipan on a board lightly dusted with icing sugar. Add just enough extra icing sugar or rum to make the marzipan malleable. Proceed as for Wissi Leckerli.

ZIMMETLECKERLI

Cinnamon Zurich Leckerli

Add 1 tbsp of cinnamon to the marzipan mixture in the master recipe for white Leckerli and proceed, making the biscuits in the usual way.

KÖNIGSBERGER MARZIPAN

Königsberg Hearts

These pretty marzipan hearts framed with a notched rim of browned marzipan and decorated with candied fruit are sold in delicatessens in many countries in and outside Germany during the Christmas season.

Only the outside rim of the hearts (not the underside) is meant to brown when they are baked, so it is best to use only top heat, browning them under a low grill. You will need to test one of the finished hearts under the flame before proceeding. If you can regulate your grill so that the flame is medium rather than high, do so. Otherwise, place your rack at least 8 inches (20cm) from the flame.

1 lb (450g) basic marzipan (p. 97),
   or fresh ready-made marzipan
icing sugar as needed

Glaze

1 egg yolk
1 tbsp cream

Icing

1 egg white
5 oz (150g) icing sugar, sifted
1–2 tsp lemon juice, as needed

Decoration

halved glacé cherries
strips of angelica or candied peel

Equipment

a 2–3in (5–8cm) heart-shaped
   cutter

If your marzipan is especially moist, knead up to 1½ oz (40g) sifted icing sugar into the dough to make it firm enough to roll out and cut easily. Test a piece first by rolling it out on a board lightly dusted with sifted icing sugar. If it is quite sticky, it will need more sugar.

Once the marzipan has been tested, roll the entire mass out ¼ inch (6mm) thick on a board lightly dusted with sifted icing sugar. Cut out hearts with a heart-shaped cutter. Using the scraps, cut out strips ⅜ inch (1cm) wide. These will be used for the rims. Brush the edges of the hearts lightly with water. Using one strip for each side of the heart, joining at the bottom and top points, measure one to establish the correct length. Then trim the other strips you have cut to the correct length, making sure you have double the number of hearts that have been cut out. Press the rims on well, smoothing the joining seam with your finger. Using the back of a knife, score parallel lines all around the rim for a decorative effect.

For the glaze, mix the egg yolk and cream together with a fork. Using a pastry brush, brush the rim only with the glaze, being careful not to let any of the glaze drip into the centre of the heart, since it is meant to remain white.

Place on a buttered baking sheet. Brown under a low grill (see the instructions above) until the rim is golden. Remove from the grill and allow to cool on the baking sheet.

Meanwhile, make the icing. Beat the egg white until frothy. Gradually beat in the sifted icing sugar, beating for 8 to 10 minutes to produce a smooth icing. It should be thin enough to be applied smoothly with a pastry brush, but thick enough to produce an opaque white. If necessary, adjust the consistency with a little lemon juice or additional sugar. Brush the centre of each heart with the icing. While the icing is still moist, decorate the hearts. If the hearts are small, quarter the cherries or cut off slivers. Place a piece of cherry at the bottom point of each heart, just inside the rim. Cut two thin slivers of angelica or citron, approximately ¾ inch (2cm) long and fan them out from the cherry towards the top of the heart.

If desired, place a smaller sliver in the centre, extending up from the cherry. Allow the icing to set before storing the hearts in an airtight tin. They will keep moist slightly longer if refrigerated.

FRANKFURTER BETHMÄNNCHEN
Marzipan Bethmanns

Makes 40

Named after the famous Frankfurt banking family Bethmann, these charming baked marzipan confections, small triangular shapes elegantly propped by three split almonds, are a speciality of Frankfurt, found in all the best bakeries and confectioners at Christmas. They are quick to make, once you have your marzipan, and make an elegant gift for marzipan-loving friends. If making them for a gift, you could mix them with another baked marzipan speciality from Frankfurt – Frankfurter Brenten (p. 107).

1 lb (450g) basic marzipan (p. 97), or fresh, ready-made marzipan
3½ oz (100g) icing sugar, sifted
rose water, as needed
3½ oz (100g) whole blanched almonds, split

Glaze

1 egg, lightly beaten

Line a board or baking sheets as instructed on p. 98. Set aside.

Break the marzipan into pieces in a mixing bowl. Add most of the sifted icing sugar and 1 tbsp of rose water and knead the mixture together well, adding more rose water or sugar as needed, so the marzipan holds together in a firm mass that can be shaped. Divide the mixture into four. Roll each into logs ¾ inch (2cm) in diameter.

Cut each log into ten even-sized pieces. Roll each piece into a ball on a pastry board dusted with icing sugar using the palm of your hand. Press each ball down firmly to flatten the base. If your almonds are not already split, cover them with 2 inches (5cm) of water that has just boiled and leave them for 3 to 4 minutes. Drain off the water and dry the almonds on paper towels. Using a sharp knife, split the almonds in half lengthwise while they are still soft. Brush each ball lightly with beaten egg. Press three split almonds into the sides so that the points almost meet in the centre and the bottoms are at the base. Pressure against the top of the almonds will help create the traditional triangular shape. Brush the almonds with lightly beaten egg. Allow to dry out overnight.

Preheat the oven to 300°F (160°C/gas 2). Bake one sheet at a time, in the upper third of the oven until golden – about 15 minutes. They should just colour, but still be soft in the centre. Allow to cool on the board or baking sheet before storing.

FRANKFURTER BRENTEN

Frankfurt Printed Baked Marzipan

Makes 30–45, according to size

Printed with small decorative wooden moulds, marzipan dough is converted into charming lightly browned cookies dusted with sugar in this traditional Frankfurt speciality. While Brenten are normally very small, 1 × 1¾ inch (2·5 × 4cm), you can use any small wooden moulds or a carved rolling pin – the kind used for Springerle and available in speciality cookware shops. In this case, the size of your Brenten will be determined by your moulds. If you don't have wooden moulds, however, you can still make the cookies without moulding them, cutting them out in the dimensions given above and baking as described in the recipe.

If moulding the cookies, to ensure that the pattern keeps its sharp relief, allow them to dry out on a baking sheet for 24 hours. Once baked and cooled, they can be stored in an airtight tin for up to one month.

NOTE: If buying prepared marzipan, find some that is relatively soft, indicating freshness, and off-white in colour. If it is hard, you might need to use an extra egg white to get it to a consistency that can be rolled out and printed.

1 lb (450g) marzipan, bought or made
  according to the recipe on p. 97
4 oz (125g) icing sugar, sieved
1 no. 3 egg white, lightly beaten
2 tbsp flour, sieved
rose water as needed

To finish

granulated sugar

See the notes under Basic Marzipan, p. 98, on the treatment of baking sheets for baked marzipan. Line a board or baking sheets accordingly and set aside.

Break the marzipan into pieces in a mixing bowl. Add the sifted icing sugar, lightly beaten egg white and flour. Knead together, adding a few drops of rose water or small amounts of sugar, as needed, to make a smooth firm mass that can be rolled out. Dust a pastry board lightly with icing sugar. Roll the marzipan out into a rectangle ⅜ inch (1cm) thick. Dust the moulds (or rolling pin) and the surface of the marzipan with icing sugar. Press the moulds well into the dough, re-dusting the moulds as needed. Brush excess sugar from the dough with a dry pastry brush. Use a sharp knife or plain pastry wheel to cut out the printed biscuits.

Sprinkle each Brenten lightly with granulated sugar. Place on the prepared baking sheets, leaving ¾ inch (2cm) between. Allow them to dry out for 24 hours.

Preheat the oven to 280°F (145°C/gas 1½). Bake one sheet at a time, in the upper third of the oven until golden – approximately 15 to 20 minutes. Cool on the board or baking sheet for several minutes; transfer to a wire rack to finish cooling.

3

BUTTER BISCUITS
Butterplätzchen

Traditionally baked both at home and commercially at Christmas, as well as throughout the year for coffee- or tea-time, butter biscuits are a favourite in all three countries, though especially in Austria where butter plays an important culinary role. The ratio of butter to flour in Austrian biscuits is generally high – often they are of equal weight and sometimes there is more butter than flour. Because such doughs are especially difficult to work with, Austrian butter biscuits require greater skill than most. Although many of the familiar Austrian selection, such as Vanillekipferl (vanilla crescents) and Spitzbuben (jam-filled rounds) are baked in Germany and Switzerland, the butter content is frequently reduced in the recipes used in those countries.

The pliability of rich butter biscuit dough makes it especially versatile in the number of ways it can be shaped: moulded into rods (Mandelstifte), balls (Gewürznüsse), crescents (Vanillekipferl) and pretzels (Butterbrezeln); piped into initials (Spritzgebäck) or spiralled tongues (Hobelspäne); rolled and cut out with plain or decorative cutters (Mailänderli); or formed into logs and sliced (Heidesand).

One thing butter biscuits have in common, for the most part, in all three countries is that they are generally very small – tiny mouthfuls, perfectly executed. With this in mind, I have kept most of the biscuits in these recipes relatively small and have attempted to give as many technical hints as possible for producing a perfectly finished biscuit. Because these are a visual as well as an edible art form, the finishing is important and well worth the effort.

With all but the piped and spooned biscuits, it is important to allow sufficient time for the dough to chill properly, before it is shaped or rolled out. Otherwise it will become too greasy to use and the biscuits will be hard. Any time the dough becomes too soft, simply refrigerate it for fifteen minutes or a little longer, and then proceed. For biscuits that have been shaped, I have usually given instructions for refrigerating them before they are baked. This will help prevent excessive spreading. Additionally, I have found that for thicker shaped biscuits, such as crescents and Ss, it is better not to butter the baking sheet, as the extra butter encourages spreading. For all the other butter biscuits, however, you must butter and flour the baking sheets in advance, rubbing softened butter on a piece of paper towel, spreading it thoroughly over the baking sheet, dusting it well with flour, then shaking off the excess.

The method I use for flaking butter in the basic rubbed-in dough – using a cheese grater instead of a knife – is one I also use for pastry-making and have found to be especially fast and easy. When making a rubbed-in dough, however, it is important to observe the instructions for having the butter well chilled so that it will grate easily. If your butter has been left out and is somewhat soft, try putting it in the freezer for ten to fifteen minutes.

Knead together any scraps left over from cut-out biscuits, wrap them well and refrigerate them for fifteen to thirty minutes before rolling them out again so that they aren't greasy.

For biscuits made with dough that has not been glazed, it is traditional to allow them to colour only barely around the edge and otherwise remain pale yellow. Because butter biscuits colour rapidly once they are cooked, it is important to watch them carefully.

While most biscuits are removed immediately with a metal spatula to wire racks to cool, if one is particularly thick and/or delicate, I would suggest loosening it with a metal spatula first, but not removing it immediately so that the cooling process gives it a chance to firm and it will be less likely to break when it is moved.

For storing at room temperature, I recommend, conservatively, one week's storage for unspiced butter biscuits and ten days for those that are spiced. They can certainly be eaten two weeks after they have been baked, but I find that the delicious butter taste has gone by then. If they are to be stored for a longer period they should be well wrapped and frozen. Thawing time is no more than thirty minutes, and usually much less.

For additional hints on rolling out dough or pastry, see Baking Tips, p. 31.

BASIC RUBBED-IN DOUGH

(Süsser Mürbeteig)

10 oz (300g) plain flour
⅛ tsp salt
4 oz (125g) castor sugar
8 oz (225g) butter, well chilled
grated rind of 1 lemon
2 large egg yolks
1 tsp vanilla extract

Sift the flour and salt together into a large mixing bowl. Add the sugar. Coat the butter with flour from the bowl to make it easier to handle and grate it directly into the flour, using the coarse blades of a cheese grater. As the butter is grated, occasionally mix in the flakes with the flour, using your fingertips, before grating more. Add the grated lemon rind. Using two round-bladed knives, cut the butter into the flour until the texture resembles oatmeal. Shake the bowl, which will cause any larger pieces of butter to rise to the surface. Pick up the mixture with your fingertips and quickly rub any larger bits of butter into the flour, letting it fall back in the bowl. Continue until the butter is well blended but not greasy – 40 to 60 seconds.

Mix the egg yolks lightly with a fork and combine with the vanilla. Using the fork, mix the egg into the flour mixture until well distributed. Then, using your hand, work the dough together into a ball. Knead the dough lightly on a floured board until it forms a cohesive mass – no more than 1 minute. Pat the dough into a flat round, or a log if so specified in the recipe. Wrap it tightly in plastic cling film and refrigerate for at least 1 hour or overnight before using. Use as directed in the recipe.

NOTE: If the dough has been refrigerated for a long time, and is especially hard, allow it to soften at room temperature for about 10 minutes. Hit it several times with a rolling pin to help soften it, then pull it back into a flat round before rolling it out.

BUTTERBREZELN

Buttery Pretzels

Makes about 70

Of the butter biscuits found in Germany and Austria, the pretzel shape, copied from the salt-strewn yeast dough pretzels sold in market stalls and at fairs, makes one of the most charming biscuits. The shape itself has a long history. Thought to have once been a symbol of the solar cycle, it was used by early Christians in the Roman Empire to make a Lenten flour/salt/water pretzel, the crossed arms symbolizing Christianity. Called *bracellae*, 'little arms', the shape travelled north and became known as Brezel (pretzel).

As biscuits, pretzels come in many variations: the dough enriched with egg yolks (Eigelbbrezeln); with hazelnuts (Haselnussbrezeln); or iced with vanilla icing (Vanillebrezeln); lemon icing (Zitronenbrezeln); rum icing (Punschbrezeln); or chocolate (Schokoladenbrezeln. They are equally attractive simply dusted with icing sugar while still warm.

1 recipe basic rubbed-in dough (p. 111)
icing sugar, or one of the icings that follow

Prepare the basic rubbed-in dough as described in the previous recipe and, before it is chilled roll it into two logs, 1½ inches (4cm) in diameter. Wrap them tightly in plastic cling film and chill for 1 hour or until firm.

Cut the logs into ¼ inch (6mm) slices. Form each slice into a log shape, then roll it back and forth on a pastry board until it is 6 inches (16cm) long. The strip should be approximately ¼ inch (6mm) in diameter. Use the first strip as a measure for the rest so that the pretzels will be uniform in size.

To shape the pretzels, bend the arms around to form an oval, then cross one arm over the other, resting them on top of the strand which constitutes the top of the pretzel. Arrange the pretzels about 1 inch (2·5cm) apart on unbuttered baking sheets and place them in the freezer for 10 minutes or the refrigerator for 30 minutes. Meanwhile, preheat the oven to 350°F (180°C/gas 4).

When well chilled, bake, one sheet at a time, on the middle rack of the oven until pale yellow – approximately 12 to 14 minutes. The pretzels should not be allowed to brown. Remove them to a cooling rack. Keep any unbaked pretzels in the refrigerator.

If you are dusting them with icing sugar, do so while they are still warm, pressing the sugar through a tea strainer or using a dredger. Otherwise, ice with one of the following icings.

VANILLEBREZELN

Vanilla Pretzels

8 oz (225g) icing sugar, sifted
1½ tsp vanilla extract

To make the icing, gradually beat the icing sugar into 4 tbsp water and the vanilla extract, beating for approximately 5 minutes. Place the bowl in a pan of water that has just boiled and beat for another 3 or 4 minutes, or until the icing is warm and the sugar has completely dissolved. The icing should be thin enough to brush easily on the pretzels using a pastry brush. If it is too thin or too thick, adjust the consistency with a little more sugar or water. Brush each pretzel with the icing, getting into the corners with your brush, and leave them on a wire rack to dry before storing. Refrigerate in an airtight tin for up to seven days or freeze for up to three months.

PUNSCHBREZELN

Rum Pretzels

8 oz (225g) icing sugar, sifted
4½ tbsp rum
1–2 drops red food colouring (optional)

Make the icing and ice according to the technique for Vanillebrezeln. If desired, the icing can be tinted with a drop or two of red
food colouring to give it a pale pink tint.

ZITRONENBREZELN

Lemon Pretzels

8 oz (225g) icing sugar, sifted
finely grated rind of 1 lemon
4½ tbsp lemon juice

Make the icing and ice according to the technique for Vanillebrezeln.

SCHOKOLADENBREZELN

Chocolate Pretzels

8 oz (225g) icing sugar, sifted
3 oz (100g) dark, semi-sweet chocolate, broken in small pieces
1 tsp vegetable oil

Make the icing according to the technique for Vanillebrezeln, using
4½ tbsp water. Melt the broken pieces of chocolate with the oil in a
double boiler or in a heatproof soup plate or shallow bowl placed
over a saucepan filled with 2 inches (5cm) of simmering water. Stir
occasionally until the chocolate has melted. Remove from the heat.
Stir the chocolate into the warm icing, adding a few drops more
water, if necessary, to reach a thin coating consistency. Ice and store
as above.

MAILÄNDERLI

Milanese Biscuits

Though not evident from the name, Mailänderli are as Swiss as Lindt chocolate or Emmenthal cheese – at least to the Swiss who bake and consume them with relish. Cut out in thin flowers, stars, hearts and crescents, this traditional favourite differs from other cut-out butter biscuits only in the large amount of sugar used, a factor responsible for their crisp texture.

To make, simply increase the sugar in the basic rubbed-in dough (p. 111), to 8oz (225g). Roll out very thin, cut out as desired, brush with lightly beaten egg and bake at 350°F (180°C/gas 4) until lightly coloured – approximately 12 minutes.

SCHWARZ-WEISS-GEBÄCK

Black-and-white Biscuits

The use of contrasting coloured doughs to make interesting designs is a favourite technique in German baking. Once you have made your basic butter biscuit dough and coloured half of it with cocoa powder, you can choose from one or more of the following designs: chessboard, snail, peacock's eye, pig's ear or marbled rounds, the latter an especially good way to use up scraps of different coloured dough.

The biscuits can be stored in an airtight container for up to one week, or frozen for up to three months.

1 recipe basic rubbed-in dough (p. 111)
2 tbsp cocoa powder

Make up the dough following the instructions in the basic recipe, and divide it in half once it is kneaded. Work 2 tbsp of cocoa powder into one half of the dough, kneading it well until blended evenly. Pat each piece of dough into a flat round. Wrap in plastic cling film and refrigerate for several hours. Form the dough into one of the log shapes described in the recipes below. Wrap the logs in cling film and refrigerate for 1 hour before slicing.

Preheat the oven to 350°F (180°C/gas 4). Slice the logs ¼ inch (6mm) thick and place on buttered and floured baking sheets, 1 inch (2·5cm) apart. Bake, one sheet at a time, in the middle of the oven until lightly coloured – approximately 12 minutes. Refrigerate any unbaked biscuits while the others are baking. Remove to wire racks to cool before storing.

SCHACHBRETT

Chessboard

The following directions use the brown dough as an outside wrapper, but you can also make these biscuits using the reverse colours.

After the brown and white doughs have been refrigerated for several hours, remove them from the refrigerator. On a lightly floured board, roll out one-third of the chocolate dough in a rectangle ½ inch (1·5cm) thick and measuring 2 by 7 inches (5 by 18cm). It is important to use a ruler to measure so that the chessboard pattern is even. Using a piece of cardboard or a ruler as a guide, cut the rectangle lengthwise into four even strips, each ½ inch (1·5cm) wide. If they have stuck to the board, loosen them carefully with a metal spatula and set them aside. Knead any scraps back into the remaining chocolate dough. Roll this dough out on a lightly floured board into a 7 inch (18cm) square. Make sure the dough is not sticking to the board and can be picked up. Use a metal spatula to loosen it if necessary. Trim the edges neatly using a piece of cardboard or a ruler as a guide.

Roll out slightly more than one-third of the light coloured dough into a rectangle ½ inch (1·5cm) thick and measuring 2½ by 7 inches (6 by 18cm). Cut the rectangle lengthwise, as before, this time into five even strips, each ½ inch (1·5cm) wide.

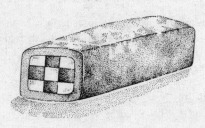

Brush the brown square of dough lightly with water, using a pastry brush, to help make the strips adhere. Measure the square, making a mark in the centre where it measures 3½ inches (9cm). Place a dark strip of dough straight down the centre. Brush the sides of the strip lightly with water. Place a light coloured strip on either side. Brush the tops and sides of the strips lightly with water. Continue in the same fashion with two more layers of three strips: the second layer should have a light strip in the centre with a dark strip on each side of it; the third should be exactly like the first. Continue brushing the sides and tops of the strips lightly with water as new strips are applied. When you have done this you will see a 'chessboard' of nine squares at each end.

Pull the two sides of the wrapper up and fold them around the chessboard. Measure the overlap – it will be approximately ¾ inch (2cm). So that the overlap is no more than ¼ inch (6mm), lay the two sides of the wrapper back on the board and trim off the excess evenly with a sharp knife. Rewrap the chessboard. Brush a little water on the edge where the seam joins and press the dough together well to seal the seam. Smooth out the seam with your finger so it has the same thickness as the rest. Wrap the dough in plastic cling film and chill for 1 hour or until firm. Cut in even ¼ inch (6mm) slices and bake according to the directions given in the master recipe.

You will have quite a bit of light coloured dough and a few scraps of chocolate dough left over. You can either roll them out separately for simple cut-out biscuits, using decorative cutters, or you can partially knead the two colours together to produce a marbled effect, following the instructions for Marmorkeks below.

SCHNECKEN

Snails

Roll out equal-sized rectangles of light and dark dough, each ⅛ inch (3mm) thick. Make sure they do not stick to the board, using a metal spatula to loosen them if necessary. Brush the surface of each lightly with water. Lay one on top of the other – whichever colour is on the bottom will be the colour on the outside edge of the biscuit. Trim the edges so they are perfectly even. If you want small biscuits, roll the dough from the long side of the rectangle into a log. For larger biscuits, begin rolling from one of the short sides of the rectangle until you have a log. At either end you will see a spiral of dark and light dough. Brush the edge with water and press the seam well to seal it. Smooth out the seam with your finger so that it has the same thickness as the rest. Wrap the dough well in plastic cling film and refrigerate for 1 hour or until firm. Cut in even ¼ inch (6mm) slices and bake according to the instructions in the master recipe.

SCHWEINSÖHRCHEN

Pig's Ears

Roll out even-sized rectangles each ⅛ inch (3mm) thick, making sure they do not stick to the board. Brush each with water. Lay one on top of the other. Beginning with the short sides of the rectangle, roll both sides of the dough toward the centre. You should have two rolls of equal size that meet. Brush the seam where they meet with water and press them together well so they stick. Wrap well in plastic cling film and refrigerate for 1 hour or until firm. Cut in ¼ inch (6mm) slices and bake according to the directions in the master recipe.

PFAUENAUGEN

Peacock's Eyes

Using the colour that you want to show on the outside edge, roll that colour dough out into a narrow rectangle, 5 inches (12·5cm) wide and approximately ¼ inch (6mm) thick. Take the dough of the other colour and, using your fists or a rolling pin, beat it into a rectangular or oval shape so that it can be rolled into a log. Using the palms of your hands, roll it back and forth on a lightly floured board to form an even-sized log the same length as the other rectangle of dough. It should be approximately ¾ inch (2cm) in diameter. (If the rectangle is slightly longer, cut it even with the log and use the scraps of dough for cut-out biscuits.) Make sure the rectangle does not stick to the board, loosening it with a metal spatula if necessary. Brush lightly with water. Lay the log of dough down the centre. Pull the rectangle of dough around it. Where the seam joins, there should be no more than a ¼ inch (6mm) overlap. Once you have wrapped it around the log and measured it, lay the overlapping side back on the board and trim the excess off evenly with a sharp knife. Rewrap the log. Brush a little water on the edge where the seam joins and press the dough together well to seal the seam. Smooth out the seam with your finger so it has the same thickness as the rest. Wrap the dough in plastic cling film and chill for 1 hour or until firm. Cut in ¼ inch (6mm) slices and bake according to the directions in the master recipe.

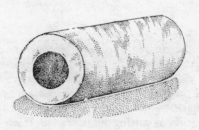

MARMORKEKS

Marbled Rounds

This is a good way to use up scraps of different coloured dough. Otherwise, use equal portions of dark and light coloured dough before they have been refrigerated so they are quite soft. Or, if they have already been refrigerated, leave them at room temperature until they are soft enough to knead. Break each piece of dough into several pieces. Knead all the pieces together, pressing them together with the palm of your hand and folding the dough piece in half. Continue several times until the dough is well streaked. Roll the dough back and forth on a lightly floured board into an even-sized log, approximately 1¼ inches (3cm) in diameter. Wrap the log in plastic cling film and refrigerate for several hours or until very firm. Slice in ¼ inch (6mm) thick rounds and bake according to the instructions in the master recipe.

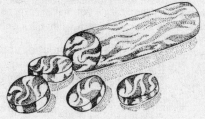

SPITZBUBEN

Jam-filled Butter Biscuits

Makes about 45

These pretty fluted rounds filled with apricot or raspberry jam, found in all German-speaking countries at Christmas time and throughout the year, are characterized by three small holes in the top which reveal the jewel-like filling. There are now round biscuit cutters on the market – use for the lid only – which cut out three holes at the same time as cutting out the round. However, assuming most people won't have this specialized cutter, the holes can be made with small aspic cutters or a thimble. If using aspic cutters, you can make plain round holes or heart- or diamond-shaped holes. The traditional size would be approximately 2 inches (5cm). A thimble will produce a larger hole, so you can either make one hole in a 2 inch (5cm) biscuit, or make three holes in a 3½ inch (8cm) biscuit.

A professional trick to make your biscuits look as beautiful as those at the famous Demel's pastry shop in Vienna is to turn the bases upside down when they are removed from the baking sheet and before they are filled. When sandwiched, the fluted edges of top and bottom then meet perfectly.

1 recipe basic rubbed-in dough (p. 111)

Filling

12 oz (350g) raspberry and/or apricot jam
1 tsp lemon juice (if using apricot jam)

icing sugar, to finish

Equipment

2 inch (5cm) or 3½ inch (9cm) fluted (or plain) round biscuit cutter
small aspic cutter, or thimble

Prepare the basic rubbed-in dough as directed in the recipe. Pat it into a flat round, wrap it, and chill it for 1 hour or until it is firm, or overnight. Butter and flour baking sheets and set them aside.

Roll out the dough ⅛ inch (3mm) thick on a lightly floured board. Cut out the biscuits with a round, preferably fluted cutter. Using a small aspic cutter or thimble, cut out three small holes or one large hole in half of the biscuits: these will be the 'lids'. Place the biscuits about 1 inch (2·5cm) apart on the prepared baking sheets and refrigerate them for 20 minutes or place them in the freezer for 10 minutes. In the meantime, preheat the oven to 350°F (180°C/gas 4).

Bake the biscuits in the centre of the oven, one sheet at a time, until barely coloured around the edges – approximately 12 minutes. Do not allow them to brown. Transfer them to racks to cool. While still warm, dust the lids with sifted icing sugar. Turn the biscuit bases upside down. Keep any unbaked biscuits in the refrigerator while waiting to bake them.

For the filling, you can fill half of them with raspberry jam and the other half with apricot jam. Raspberry jam: bring it to boiling point, but do not allow it to boil or it will lose its bright colour. Spread the jam not quite to the edges on each base while it is still warm. Apricot jam: bring the jam to a full boil with 1 tsp lemon juice and boil for 30 seconds. Then strain through a sieve, pressing down hard on the apricot pieces. If either of the jams becomes too thick and cool, reheat briefly with a few drops of water. Spread the jam not quite to the edges on each base. It should not flow out when the lid is placed on top, but there should be enough so that it is forced up slightly through the holes. Line up the fluted eges (if a fluted cutter was used) when placing the lids on top. Allow the jam to cool. Store carefully so the icing sugar isn't smudged, placing a piece of greaseproof paper or aluminium foil between layers. If necessary, re-dust smudged biscuits with icing sugar.

APRIKOSENAUGEN

Apricot Jam-filled Butter Biscuits

Almost identical to Spitzbuben, Aprikosenaugen, or 'apricot eyes' – found in all German-speaking countries – are characterized by a filling of apricot jam which is revealed through one large 'eye' (unlike Spitzbuben which have three small holes).

Follow the instructions for Spitzbuben, using the apricot filling. For cutters, you will need a 2 inch (5cm), preferably fluted cutter, and a 1¼ inch (3cm) fluted or plain cutter. For the smaller cutter, you can substitute a large metal nozzle from a piping bag which will cut a hole approximately the right size. Cut large holes out of half the biscuits for lids and proceed with the recipe as given.

EIGELBBREZELN

Egg-yolk Pretzels

Makes about 70

Eigelbbrezeln are a practical solution for the baker who has egg yolks left over after making meringues. Because the dough is very rich and softens quickly, it is best to refrigerate it overnight to allow it to become firm enough for shaping. Additional chilling after the pretzels have been shaped will also improve the finished product.

7½ oz (215g) plain flour

3½ oz (100g) icing sugar

grated rind of 1 lemon

icing sugar, to finish

6 oz (175g) butter, well chilled

5 large egg yolks

1 tsp vanilla extract

Sift the flour and icing sugar into a large bowl. Add the grated lemon rind. Coat the butter with flour from the bowl to make it easier to handle and grate directly into the flour, using the coarse blades of a cheese grater. As the butter is grated, occasionally mix in the flakes with the flour, using your fingertips, before grating more. Using two round-bladed knives, cut the butter into the flour until the texture resembles oatmeal. Shake the bowl, which will cause any larger pieces of butter to rise to the surface. Pick up the mixture with your fingertips and quickly rub any larger bits of butter into the flour, letting it fall back in the bowl. Continue until the butter is well blended but not greasy – 40 to 60 seconds.

Mix the egg yolks lightly with a fork and combine with the vanilla. Using the fork, mix the egg into the flour mixture until well distributed. Then, using your hand, work the dough together into a ball. Knead the dough lightly on a floured board until it forms a cohesive mass – no more than 1 minute. Form the dough into two logs, about 1½ inches (4cm) in diameter. Refrigerate, wrapped tightly in plastic cling film, overnight.

The next day, preheat the oven to 350°F (180°C/gas 4) and proceed according to the instructions for shaping and baking Butter-brezeln (p.112). Dust with icing sugar while still warm, or glaze with chocolate as described below.

CHOCOLATE GLAZE

For the chocolate glaze, melt 6 oz (175g) of dark, semi-sweet chocolate broken in pieces with 2 tsp of vegetable oil in a double boiler or in a heatproof soup plate or shallow bowl placed over a pan filled with 2 inches (5cm) of simmering water. Stir the chocolate occasionally until melted. Remove from the saucepan. Using a pastry brush, brush each pretzel evenly with chocolate. If the mixture seems too thick, add a few more drops of vegetable oil. If you feel comfortable doing so, you can also dip each pretzel in the chocolate mixture, holding them carefully with your fingertips. Allow the chocolate-covered pretzels to dry, right side up, on a wire rack before storing.

S-GEBÄCK
Sugared S-shaped Butter Biscuits

Makes about 40

This favourite German biscuit, baked at Christmas time and throughout the year, offers the home baker an opportunity to use up extra egg yolks left over after making meringues. Traditionally, the biscuits are coated with beaten egg white and sprinkled with coarse decorating sugar, available from specialist bakery suppliers. If you can't get coarse sugar, however, you can simply use granulated sugar.

1 recipe Eigelbbrezeln dough (p. 122)

To finish

1 large egg white
decorating sugar, or granulated sugar

Make up the dough as for Eigelbbrezeln. Once it has been kneaded, form it into two logs, about 1½ inches (4cm) in diameter. Refrigerate, wrapped tightly in plastic cling film, overnight.

The next day, preheat the oven to 350°F (180°C/gas 4). Working with one log at a time (the other should stay in the refrigerator), cut each into ⅜ inch (1cm) slices. Form each slice into a log shape and roll it back and forth on a very lightly floured board until you have a roll about ⅜ to ½ inch (1 to 1·5m) in diameter and 4 to 5 inches (10 to 12·5cm) long. Use the first one as a measure for the rest so that they are all the same length. Work with the dough gently but quickly and keep all unused portions in the refrigerator.

Shape the rolls of dough into an S and place on unbuttered baking sheets 1 inch (2·5cm) apart. Beat the egg white with a whisk, rotary or electric beater until it is frothy and lightly thickened. Brush the top and a little of the sides with the white using a pastry brush. Sprinkle each biscuit with a little of the decorating or granulated sugar. Brush off any excess sugar from the baking sheet with a dry pastry brush.

Bake, one sheet at a time, in the middle of the oven until the biscuits are firm and barely coloured – approximately 12 to 15 minutes. Loosen them from the baking sheet immediately using a metal spatula. Allow to firm for about 2 minutes on the baking sheet, then transfer to wire racks to finish cooling before storing. Keep any unbaked biscuits in the refrigerator while waiting to bake them.

SPRITZGEBÄCK

Piped Biscuits

Makes about 60

Soft butter biscuit dough piped or forced through a press in decorative shapes produces a tea time and Christmas time favourite in all German-speaking countries. While the letter S seems to be the most popular pattern, you can use any of the shapes suggested in the recipe. If desired, they can be decorated before baking with a tiny sliver of glacé cherry, red or green. The decorations should be small to correspond with the delicate appearance of the biscuits. However, they need not be decorated at all. An alternative is to dip just the tip of one side of each biscuit in a warm chocolate glaze (no more than one-third of the biscuit), after which they must be dried on a rack before storing.

If you are using a piping bag rather than a biscuit press, it is essential for the dough to be soft enough to force it through the decorative nozzle, but firm enough to hold its shape.

1 recipe basic rubbed-in dough (p. 111), increasing the large egg yolks from 2 to 3
red or green glacé cherries for decoration (optional)

Chocolate glaze

4½ oz (140g) dark, semi-sweet chocolate
2 tsp vegetable oil

Equipment

biscuit press or large piping bag fitted with large star nozzle

Follow the instructions for basic rubbed-in dough. Knead on a lightly floured board until it forms a smooth, soft mass.

Test the consistency of your dough. Place it in a biscuit press or large piping bag fitted with a large star nozzle. If it can be piped easily and hold its shape, use immediately. If it is too firm, leave at room temperature for 10 minutes and test again. If it is too soft, refrigerate for 30 minutes and test again.

Pipe or press the dough on to unbuttered baking sheets, leaving 1 inch (2.5cm) between biscuits. Traditional designs include Ss, wreaths (you can pipe a rosette in the middle), crescents, bars with a rosette at each end, arabesques and, if you like, the initials of your family and friends. At their largest, the biscuits should measure no more than 2½ inches (6cm) since they will spread slightly during baking. If decorating with slivers of glacé cherries, do so now. Once the dough has been piped out, refrigerate the sheets of biscuits for at least 30 minutes before baking. In the meantime, preheat the oven to 350°F (180°C/gas 4).

Bake in the oven, one sheet at a time, until barely coloured – approximately 10 to 12 minutes. They should not be allowed to brown. Using a metal spatula, remove immediately to wire racks to cool. Keep any unbaked biscuits in the refrigerator while waiting to bake them.

Biscuits that have not been decorated with cherries can be dipped in the following chocolate glaze: break the chocolate in pieces and combine with the oil in a double boiler or in a heatproof soup plate or shallow bowl placed over a saucepan filled with 2 inches (5cm) of simmering water. Stir occasionally until the chocolate has melted. Remove from the heat. Test the consistency. Dip the tip of one biscuit in the chocolate. If the chocolate mixture coats too thickly, add a few more drops of vegetable oil until the consistency is correct, being careful not to add too much. Either dip one-third of each biscuit in the chocolate or, if it is easier, use a pastry brush to apply the chocolate. Place on wire racks. Allow the chocolate to set completely, leaving the biscuits to dry in a cool place (not the refrigerator) before storing.

To make chocolate piped biscuits, sift 3 tbsp of cocoa powder with the flour into the mixing bowl before adding the butter and other ingredients. Then, at the end, knead the dough well to blend the cocoa colour evenly throughout.

Alternatively, once you have made up the dough, you can colour half of it, kneading 1½ tbsp of cocoa powder into the dough. When added at the end, the cocoa powder is more difficult to blend evenly; however, the marbled effect which is produced is equally attractive.

GIFT IDEA

For children, you can pipe a giant initial 6 to 7 inches (16 to 18cm) high. Use the largest size star nozzle you have to produce a wider trail of dough. Decorate with glacé cherries or dust with icing sugar while they are still hot. Allow large biscuits to cool on the baking sheet for 2 to 3 minutes so that they are quite firm before moving them to wire racks to cool.

VANILLEKIPFERL

Vanilla Crescents

Makes about 60

One of the most famous Viennese butter biscuits made especially at Christmas time, Vanillekipferl are distinguished by their familiar crescent shape. While tradition says that Viennese bakers were the first to apply this shape to something edible – baking crescent rolls to celebrate victory over the Turks in 1683 – this shape was, in fact, a familiar religious symbol and was used in baking as early as the eighth century at the monastery of St Gallen in Switzerland, where *panis lunatis* (bread of the moon) was made. Regardless of who baked the first crescent, the shape repeats itself throughout the Viennese baking repertoire. The dough for the Vanillekipferl is traditionally made with ground almonds, lots of butter and a small amount of sugar, proportionately, since the biscuits are dusted at the end with icing sugar. While they are generally made with vanilla sugar (which can be made by burying a vanilla pod in 1 lb/450g of sugar in a lidded jar for a week), I have used vanilla extract in the dough recipe since it is more readily available. However, if you have made or can buy vanilla sugar, eliminate the vanilla extract and replace with 1 tbsp vanilla sugar. You can also mix several tablespoons with icing sugar in which the biscuits are rolled at the end. Store in an airtight container in the refrigerator for up to two weeks or freeze, well wrapped, for up to three months.

9½ oz (275g) plain flour
⅛ tsp salt
3 oz (75g) blanched almonds, finely ground (p. 27)
2¼ oz (65g) castor sugar
7 oz (200g) butter
1 tsp vanilla extract (see above)
2 large egg yolks
2 oz (50g) icing sugar, sifted, to finish
2 tbsp vanilla sugar, if available (optional)

Sift the flour and salt together into a large mixing bowl. Add the ground almonds and sugar. Coat the butter with flour from the bowl to make it easier to handle and grate it directly into the flour, using the coarse side of the grater. As the butter is grated, occasionally mix in the flakes with the flour, using your fingertips, before grating more. Using two round-bladed knives, cut the butter into the flour until the texture resembles oatmeal. Shake the bowl, which will cause any larger pieces of butter to rise to the surface. Pick up the mixture with your fingertips and quickly rub any larger bits of butter into the flour, letting it fall back in the bowl. Continue until the butter is well blended but not greasy – 40 to 60 seconds.

Mix the egg yolks lightly with a fork and combine with the vanilla. Using the fork, mix the egg into the flour mixture until well distributed. Then, using your hand, work the dough together into a ball. Knead the dough lightly on a floured board until it forms a cohesive mass – no more than 1 minute. Roll the dough into a smooth log (or two logs, if desired), approximately 1½ inches (4cm) in diameter. Wrap the log in plastic cling film and chill for several hours.

Cut the cylinder of dough into slices ⅜ inch (1cm) thick. Form each slice into a log shape, pressing it together with your fingers, then roll it back and forth on a pastry board, slightly tapering the ends, until it is 3 inches (8cm) long. Bend each gently into a crescent shape. Form the crescents carefully so they are uniform in length and size. As the crescents are shaped, place them at least ¾ inch (2cm) apart on an unbuttered baking sheet, using more sheets as necessary. Refrigerate for 30 minutes before baking to help them keep their shape, keeping unbaked biscuits in the refrigerator while waiting to bake them. In the meantime, preheat the oven to 350°F (180°C/gas 4).

Bake the biscuits one sheet at a time, in the centre of the oven until pale yellow – approximately 12 to 14 minutes. Don't allow them to brown. Remove the crescents carefully to a rack to cool. While still warm, roll them in sifted icing sugar which can be mixed with vanilla sugar, if available. Allow to cool completely before storing.

INGWERPLÄTZCHEN
Ginger Biscuits

Makes about 60

My first job after getting my degree was working for a research institute in Munich which had a large staff of Russian immigrants. Thus I was able to combine two loves – German and Russian – while earning a salary a hair's breadth above subsistence level. Nevertheless, I always found an extra mark each week to treat myself to three delicious biscuits (the purchasing power of my mark) from my favourite bakery in the Theatinerstrasse. My addiction was Ingwergebäck, diminutive buttery mouthfuls filled with moist chunks of ginger. While I never got the Munich recipe, a friend in Frankfurt provided me with this recipe which produces an almost identical biscuit.

8 oz (225g) plain flour, sifted
⅛ tsp salt
1 tsp baking powder
5½ oz (165g) castor sugar
6½ oz (190g) butter, well chilled
1 large egg white, lightly beaten
1 tsp vanilla extract
3 tbsp stem ginger in syrup,
    well drained and finely minced,
    or candied ginger
2 oz (50g) unblanched almonds,
    finely ground

Glaze

1 egg yolk
1 tbsp cream

Equipment

1½ inch (4cm) fluted or plain
    round biscuit cutter

Sift the flour, salt and baking powder together into a large mixing bowl. Add the sugar. Coat the butter with flour from the bowl to make it easier to handle and grate it directly into the flour, using the coarse blades of a cheese grater. As the butter is grated, occasionally mix in the flakes with the flour, using your fingertips, before grating more. Add the lightly beaten egg white, vanilla, minced ginger and ground almonds. Mix the ingredients together with your hands and knead gently on a lightly floured board until well mixed. Pat into a flat round and wrap in plastic cling film. Refrigerate for at least 2 hours or overnight.

Preheat the oven to 350°F (180°C/gas 4). If the dough has been chilled overnight and is too firm, hit it several times with your rolling pin to help soften it, then pull it back into a flat round before rolling. On a lightly floured board, roll out the dough ¼ inch (6mm) thick and cut out with a fluted or plain biscuit cutter. Place the biscuits on buttered and floured baking sheets 1 inch (2·5cm) apart. With a fork, beat the egg yolk together with the cream and brush each biscuit with the glaze. Bake, one sheet at a time, in the middle of the oven until golden – 12 to 15 minutes. Keep any unbaked biscuits in the refrigerator while waiting to bake them. Remove the biscuits with a metal spatula to wire racks and allow to cool completely before storing.

NOTE: If the dough becomes soft while you are cutting out the biscuits, refrigerate each sheet of biscuits for 15 to 20 minutes before baking.

BASIC CREAMED BUTTER DOUGH
(Rührteig)

꧁꧂

8 oz (225g) butter, softened
4 oz (125g) castor sugar
1 tsp vanilla extract
1 large egg
10¾ oz (320g) plain flour
¼ tsp baking powder

Using an electric mixer, cream the butter, sugar and vanilla together until light and fluffy. Add the egg and continue beating until the mixture is smooth. Sift the flour and baking powder together into the butter mixture. Fold the butter mixture into the flour first with a spoon and then with your hands, kneading the dough together until the mixture is cohesive and smooth. Form the dough into a flat round (or a log if called in the recipe). Wrap in plastic cling film and chill for at least 2 hours or overnight. Use as directed.

NOTE: This dough can be rolled out ⅛ inch (3mm) thick on a lightly floured board and used for any small biscuits cut out with decorative cutters (decorate before or after baking as desired). They should be baked, one sheet at a time, in the middle of a preheated 350°F (180°C/gas 4) oven for approximately 10 to 12 minutes, or until just coloured around the edges. When done, remove to a wire rack with a metal spatula to cool before decorating or storing.

MANDELSTIFTE

Almond Sticks

Makes about 45

These delicious German almond biscuits are quick to make and offer a nice contrast to other cut-out and shaped biscuits because of their unusual pencil-like shape and crumbly appearance – the latter is produced by a final coating of egg, ground almonds and sugar.

4 oz (125g) butter, softened
4½ oz (140g) castor sugar
grated rind of 1 lemon
1 tsp vanilla extract
1 pinch of salt
1 pinch of grated nutmeg
1 large egg, lightly beaten
4 oz (125g) unblanched almonds, finely ground (p. 27)
4 oz (125g) plain flour, sifted

To finish

7 oz (200g) unblanched almonds, finely ground
3½ oz (100g) icing sugar, sifted
2 large eggs, lightly beaten

Using an electric mixer, cream the butter, sugar, lemon rind, vanilla, salt and nutmeg together until light and fluffy. Add the egg and continue beating until the mixture is smooth. Fold in the ground almonds and sifted flour first with a large spoon and then with your hands, kneading the dough together until the mixture is cohesive and smooth. Form the dough into a flat rectangle. Wrap in plastic cling film and chill for 2 hours or until firm.

Preheat the oven to 350°F (180°C/gas 4). Divide the dough into four. Roll each piece back and forth into a roll the diameter of a pencil, approximately ⅜ inch (1cm). Cut each roll into 1¾ inch (4·5cm) lengths.

For the coating, mix the ground almonds and icing sugar together on a piece of paper. Beat the eggs lightly with a fork until they are well mixed. Roll each biscuit first in egg, then coat completely in the almond and sugar mixture. Place them on well buttered and floured baking sheets. Refrigerate for at least 30 minutes, keeping any unbaked biscuits in the refrigerator while waiting to bake them.

Bake, one sheet at a time, in the middle of the oven until they are lightly coloured – approximately 15 minutes. Using a metal spatula, remove to wire racks to cool before storing in an airtight tin at room temperature for up to one week, or freezing, well wrapped, for up to three months.

DOMINOSTEINE

Dominoes

Makes about 65

The recipe for these charming dominoes comes from a Frankfurt friend who bakes them at Christmas time. They needn't be reserved just for the holidays, however, and they make an appropriate gift at any time of year. Once glazed with a simple lemon/sugar icing, they are dotted and lined with chocolate.

1 recipe basic creamed butter
  dough (p. 130)

Glaze

8¾ oz (245g) icing sugar
4 tbsp lemon juice
2 oz (50g) dark, semi-sweet chocolate,
  broken in pieces
vegetable oil as needed

Equipment

piping bag with fine writing nozzle

Prepare the dough according to the instructions in the basic recipe, chilling it for at least 2 to 3 hours. On a lightly floured board, roll out the dough ¼ inch (6mm) thick. Using a ruler, cut the dough into rectangles measuring 2½ by 1 inch (6 by 2·5cm). Remove the rectangles to buttered and floured baking sheets, leaving 1 inch (2·5cm) between each, and refrigerate for at least 15 minutes, keeping any unbaked biscuits in the refrigerator while waiting to bake them. Meanwhile, preheat the oven to 350°F (180°C/gas 4).

Before baking, trim any ragged edges neatly with a sharp knife. Bake the biscuits, one sheet at a time, in the middle of the oven until just colouring around the edges – approximately 10 to 12 minutes. Remove with a metal spatula to a wire rack to cool.

When all the biscuits have been baked, make the glaze. Gradually beat the icing sugar into the lemon juice. Beat for 4 minutes. Place the bowl in a pan of hot water and beat for a further 3 or 4 minutes until the icing has warmed and is smooth. Adjust the consistency of the icing with a small amount of water or sugar as needed, so that it will brush easily without being too thick but is not so thin that it is transparent. Brush the surface of each biscuit evenly with the icing, using a pastry brush. Leave the biscuits on a wire rack until the icing is completely set.

You should have some icing left over. Keep it in the pan of hot water while preparing your chocolate. Melt the broken pieces of chocolate in a double boiler or in a heatproof soup plate or shallow bowl placed over 2 inches (5cm) of simmering water. Stir the chocolate occasionally until it has melted. Beat 2 to 3 tbsp of the reserved icing into the chocolate. If the mixture is too thick, thin with a few drops of vegetable oil. Place the chocolate mixture in a piping bag fitted with a fine writing nozzle. When the white icing is completely dry, pipe chocolate dots on the biscuits to resemble dominoes. Pipe a line of chocolate across the middle of each. Work quickly so the mixture does not dry out in the piping bag. Allow to dry completely before storing.

HEIDESAND

Buttery Ice-box Biscuits

Heidesand – butter biscuits made by cutting thin slices from a chilled log of rich dough – is one of the most familiar names in the German biscuit repertoire. While they are always made with butter, sugar and flour, using the same technique, there are several variations: in some, the butter is melted and browned first, giving the biscuits a nut-like flavour, while in others it is simply creamed. There are also variations in finishing. I prefer to roll the chilled log in coarse sugar before slicing it, instead of leaving it plain. This gives the biscuits an attractive brown edge.

The following recipe, using the brown-butter method, is quick to prepare once the butter has cooled.

7 oz (200g) butter	*To finish*
3¼ oz (85g) castor sugar	1 egg, lightly beaten
pinch salt (if using unsalted butter)	3¼ oz (85g) granulated sugar
1 tsp vanilla extract	
8½ oz (240g) plain flour	
1 tsp baking powder	

Heat the butter in a heavy saucepan over low heat, skimming off the froth occasionally, until it turns brown, being careful not to let it burn. Pour it immediately into a bowl and leave at room temperature until it has congealed – approximately 1 hour.

NOTE: You can speed up the process by putting it in the refrigerator and stirring it several times. In this case, however, watch it carefully so it doesn't get too hard. It should be very soft.

Beat the butter together with the sugar, salt (if using) and vanilla extract, using a wooden spoon. Sift the flour and baking powder together over the butter mixture. Fold it in. Work the dough with your hands until you can bring it into a ball and the consistency is smooth. Place the soft dough on a length of greaseproof paper. Wrap the paper around it and roll it back and forth into a log, 1½ inches (4cm) in diameter. Twist the ends of the paper and refrigerate for at least 3 hours or until the dough is very firm.

Preheat the oven to 350°F (180°C/gas 4). Remove the dough from the paper wrapping and brush the surface, excluding the two ends, with lightly beaten egg. Pour the sugar on to a piece of paper. Roll the log in the sugar until it is evenly coated. Cut the log into ¼ inch (6mm) thick rounds. Place them on buttered and floured baking sheets, 1 inch (2·5cm) apart. Bake, one sheet at a time, in the middle of the oven until the edges are lightly browned and the surface is firm – approximately 10 minutes. The centre of the biscuits should remain quite pale. Keep any unbaked biscuits in the refrigerator while waiting to bake them. Remove to a wire rack to cool before storing.

SPEKULATIUS

A Christmas speciality from the Rhineland in Germany, these spicy, crisp biscuits printed with decorative wooden moulds representing animals and figures are also a favourite in Holland where they are called Speculaas. Speculaas are made into figures as much as 2 feet (60cm) tall to be given to children on St Nikolaus Day, 6 December. The smaller German version, given below, is decorated with a few flaked almonds before baking. If you have wooden moulds – there are some available specially for Spekulatius, though any wooden moulds can be used – you will also need a plain pastry wheel and a small, sharp knife to cut out the figures and any of the non-printed areas such as spaces between legs and arms. If you don't have any decorative moulds, you can still make these delicious biscuits, simply cutting them out with biscuit cutters in any shape you choose. As with many spiced biscuits, Spekulatius get spicier with age. See advice on storing on p. 38.

4½ oz (140g) butter, softened
4½ oz (140g) castor sugar,
  or brown sugar
grated rind of 1 lemon
1 egg, lightly beaten
2 oz (50g) blanched almonds,
  ground (p. 27)
1 tsp ground cinnamon
⅛ tsp powdered cloves
⅛ tsp ground cardamom

1 tsp baking powder
8½ oz (240g) plain flour
2½ oz (65g) flaked almonds, to
  decorate

Equipment

decorative Speuklatius or other
  wooden moulds, or biscuit cutters
  plain pastry wheel and small
  sharp knife if using wooden moulds

Cream the softened butter together with the sugar and lemon rind using a wooden spoon. Gradually beat in the lightly beaten egg and ground almonds. Sift the spices and baking powder together with the flour on to the butter mixture, beating them in. Work the mixture with your fingers, gradually drawing it into a ball. Knead the dough briefly. Pat into a flat round and wrap well in plastic cling film. Refrigerate for 2 to 3 hours.

If you are using wooden moulds, dust them lightly with flour. Break off and flatten a piece of dough approximately the size of a mould. Lightly flour the surface of the dough and press it into the mould. Place a damp cloth under the mould to keep it from sliding. Using a rolling pin (preferably one without rotating handles), roll the piece of dough back and forth on the mould to press it well into the crevices. Stand the mould on end and rap it firmly on the counter. Carefully release the dough from the mould. Brush off the excess flour. Cut out the shape neatly, removing any non-printed areas with a small knife. Continue with the remaining dough in the same fashion. Re-knead the scraps, refrigerate and roll out again.

If you are using biscuit cutters, roll out the dough on a lightly floured board ⅛ inch (3mm) thick. Cut out the dough in the desired shapes.

Sprinkle each biscuit with 3 or 4 flaked almonds. Place the biscuits on buttered and floured baking sheets. Refrigerate for at least 30 minutes, keeping each tray in the refrigerator until you are ready to bake it. Preheat the oven to 375°F (190°C/gas 5). Bake in the oven until golden – 10 to 15 minutes, depending on the thickness of the biscuit. If the biscuits are small, remove them with a metal spatula to a wire rack to cool. If they are large, loosen them immediately with a metal spatula and leave them to firm for several minutes on the baking sheet before removing them to a wire rack to cool.

GEWÜRZNÜSSE

Spice Balls

꙳꙳꙳

This recipe for spicy butter biscuit balls comes from Switzerland. They are easy to make and especially enticing with their coating of chopped almonds.

3½ oz (100g) butter, softened	1 tsp vanilla extract
2½ oz (65g) castor sugar	1 tbsp honey
1 large egg yolk, lightly beaten	2 oz (50g) mixed peel, finely minced

5½ oz (165g) plain flour, sifted
½ tsp baking soda
⅛ tsp salt
½ tsp ground cinnamon
½ tsp ground cardamom
¼ tsp powdered cloves
¼ tsp powdered aniseed
¼ tsp grated nutmeg

To finish

1 egg white, lightly beaten with a
    whisk or beater until frothy
4 oz (125g) slivered blanched
    almonds, coarsely chopped

Using a wooden spoon, cream the softened butter together with the sugar. Add the egg yolk gradually, the vanilla and honey and beat briefly to blend evenly. Add the finely minced mixed peel. Sift the flour together with the baking soda, salt and spices on to the butter mixture. Using your fingertips, mix the minced peel around with the loose flour to separate the pieces and prevent it from sticking together. Mix the dry ingredients into the butter. Knead the dough together until the mixture is well blended. Form the dough into a flat round. Wrap in plastic cling film and refrigerate for 2 to 3 hours or overnight.

When well chilled, break off small pieces of dough and form them into balls 1 inch (2·5cm) in diameter. Brush them with lightly beaten egg white and roll them in the coarsely chopped slivered almonds. Place them on buttered and floured baking sheets. Refrigerate for 1 hour, keeping unbaked biscuits in the refrigerator until you are ready to bake them.

Preheat the oven to 350°F (180°C/gas 4). Bake, one sheet at a time, in the middle of the oven until golden – approximately 15 to 20 minutes. Cool on a wire rack when done. Store in an airtight tin at room temperature for ten days or freeze, well wrapped, for up to three months.

HOBELSPÄNE

Spiralled Shavings

Makes about 40

These attractive spiralled biscuits – found in all German-speaking countries – are wound around a wooden spoon handle while still warm, giving them the appearance of wood shavings. It is best to bake no more than five at a time, unless you have someone helping you and lots of wooden spoons, since they must be formed before they cool. They can be stored, with care, in a jar or tin for ten days.

5 oz (150g) butter	*Equipment*
5 oz (150g) castor sugar	pastry bag fitted with a plain
1 tsp vanilla extract	⅜ inch (1 cm) nozzle or tip
3 large eggs	3 to 5 wooden spoons with round handles
5 oz (150g) plain flour, sifted	piping bag with plain ⅜ inch (1cm) nozzle

Preheat the oven to 375°F (190°C/gas 5). Using an electric mixer, cream the butter, sugar and vanilla together until light in colour. Beat in the eggs, one at a time, making sure each is well incorporated before adding the next. Add the sifted flour and fold in with a spoon until well mixed.

Butter and flour the baking sheets. Fit a piping bag with a plain ⅜ inch (1cm) nozzle. Scoop the biscuit mixture into the piping bag with a rubber spatula. Pipe no more than five thin strands approximately ½ inch (1·5cm) wide and 7 inches (18cm) long on the prepared baking sheet, leaving 1½ inches (4cm) between each. Rap the baking sheet firmly on the counter to flatten the biscuits.

Bake in the oven until pale yellow – approximately 5 minutes. Watch them closely as they colour quickly once they are baked. Loosen them with a metal spatula. While still warm, wrap them in a spiral around the handle of a wooden spoon, bottom side (shiny side) facing out, laying each spoon carefully down on the counter while wrapping the rest. They cool quite quickly. When cool, slip carefully off the spoon handle.

NOTE: If they cool too much before you have had a chance to wind them, reheat them for 30 to 60 seconds in the oven. This will soften them enough to wind. Proceed in the same fashion until all the dough is used.

FLORENTINER

Florentines

Found in bakeries in all the German-speaking countries, these delicious almond and candied fruit crisps – obviously borrowed from their southern neighbours – are first baked, then coated underneath with chocolate. Many bakeries make both small (1¼ inches/3cm) and large (3 to 5 inches/8 to 12·5cm) versions, the former being especially suitable for after-dinner coffee. They keep for four to five days if stored in an airtight container in a cool place. However, it is best not to keep them in the refrigerator as this causes them to lose their crisp texture.

Base	*Chocolate glaze*
4 oz (125g) castor sugar	3½ oz (100g) dark, semi-sweet
1 tbsp butter	chocolate, broken in pieces
2½ fl oz (70ml) whipping cream	½ oz (15g) butter
3 tbsp plain flour	2 tsp cocoa powder
4 oz (125g) blanched almonds,	vegetable oil, if needed
slivered	
4 oz (125g) mixed peel, finely minced	

Preheat the oven to 400°F (200°C/gas 6). Mix the sugar, butter, cream and flour together in a saucepan. Stir over a moderate heat until the mixture comes to the boil. Add the remaining base ingredients and continue cooking over a low heat until the mixture thickens. Spoon in small mounds – 1 scant tbsp – on to a buttered and floured baking sheet, leaving plenty of room for the biscuits to expand. Use the back of a spoon dipped in hot water to smooth the mixture.

Bake in the upper part of the oven until the biscuits have caramelized and are golden in colour. Loosen them immediately with a metal spatula. Leave on the baking sheet for several minutes before removing to a wire rack to cool.

When the biscuits are crisp and firm, prepare the glaze. Melt the broken chocolate pieces with the butter in a double boiler or in a heatproof soup plate or shallow bowl placed over a pan filled with 2 inches (5cm) of simmering water. Stir occasionally. When the chocolate has melted, remove from the pan. Stir in the cocoa powder. The mixture should be thin enough to spread evenly. Adjust with a small amount of vegetable oil if it is too thin, or with cocoa powder if it is too thick. Keep the container of chocolate in a pan of hot water to prevent it from becoming too thick. Turn the biscuits upside down. Using a pastry brush, coat the bottoms evenly with the chocolate. When the chocolate is almost cool, use the prongs of a fork to mark wavy or straight lines on the chocolate – the traditional pattern. Allow the chocolate on the biscuits to finish setting in a cool place, but not the refrigerator.

4

YEAST DOUGHS AND FRUIT BREADS
Hefegebäck und Früchtebrote

The recipes in this chapter are guaranteed to give pleasure to the whole household when the wonderful aroma of freshly baked bread pours from the kitchen. The selection I have made includes breads for holidays and special occasions which are generally richer than daily breads, and I have drawn from history. In the pre-Christian tradition bread was not just for sustenance, it was also a symbol of life and fruitful harvest in fertility rites. With the coming of Christianity, these rites were merged into the symbolic elevation in the Eucharist.

Today, many of the fancy breads are drawn from the earliest traditions, in particular the plaited breads baked in different shapes: Zopf, a plain braid; wheels symbolizing the sun; wreaths for eternity; and crescents for the moon. Others are tied more closely to later Christian tradition: Dresdner Christstollen (a rich fruit loaf), and Osterkarpfen (Easter carp). In more recent years, a small number has been assimilated from other cultures – Eier im Nest (Easter egg nests) from Greece and Tauben (doves) from Italy – or have been created by an imaginative baker: Neujahrs-Glücksschweinchen (New Year's 'Good Luck' pigs). Nevertheless, they all have one thing in common: they are baked as a gesture to commemorate and celebrate as well as to savour.

Since bread is a staple, commercial bakers in all German-speaking countries are generally exceptionally skilled. Home-bakers also are for the most part highly competent. While the daily bread is usually bought from the local bakery, it is not uncommon for people to bake speciality breads throughout the year using traditional family recipes: Kugelhopf (an unmoulded raisin-filled round) for Sundays; fruit breads such as Hutzelbrot (dark fruit loaf) and Weihnachtszopf (fruit-filled plait) for Christmas; Speckkuchen (bacon cake) for New Year; and an assortment of fish, wreaths,

Easter egg nests and doves for Easter (Oster-Hefegebäck), to name just a few.

Because most of these breads are made with a rich yeast dough, similar to a brioche dough, in most recipes I have recommended making the dough a day before it is to be baked. Overnight refrigeration makes it much easier to work with and encourages the different shapes to rise up instead of flattening out. While bread-making is a pleasurable task, it's also a time-consuming one, best left for a day when it's no effort for you to stay home (or when the weather is miserable), since the bread must be watched closely during the proving and baking stages and, because of the quantities, will most likely have to be baked in batches.

Many of the fruit-rich breads, especially, have excellent keeping properties if well wrapped and stored in a cool place. The other breads, for the most part, can also be baked ahead when it is convenient, then frozen well wrapped in aluminium foil for up to three months.

BASIC SWEET YEAST DOUGH

(Leichter Hefeteig)

1½ oz (40g) fresh yeast
2 tbsp sugar
2 lb (900g) strong flour
½ pint (275ml) milk
grated rind of 1 lemon
1 tsp salt
2¼ oz (55g) castor sugar
2 large eggs
5 oz (150g) butter, melted

NOTE: If you are using dry yeast, substitute 1½ tbsp dry yeast for the fresh yeast given in the recipe. Dissolve it in 3 fl oz (100ml) warm (90°F/32°C) water and 2 tbsp sugar. Allow to rise in a warm place for about 10 minutes, or until bubbly. Proceed with the recipe as follows, remembering that no additional water need be added.

Crumble the fresh yeast in a small bowl and mash together with 2 tbsp sugar, using a spoon, until the yeast is liquid. Set aside for several minutes. Sift half the flour into a large mixing bowl and sift the other half on to a large piece of paper or into a bowl and set aside.

Make a well in the centre of the flour in the bowl. Heat the milk with 3 fl oz (100ml) water until just warm to the touch – 80°F (27°C). Pour in the well along with the dissolved yeast. Draw in the flour with a wooden spoon, beating well, to make a thick batter. Dust some of the reserved flour over the top, cover with a damp towel, and allow the 'sponge' to rise in a warm place until bubbling and double in bulk – approximately 30 minutes.

Grate the lemon rind into a bowl with the eggs and beat together lightly with the salt and sugar. Add the melted butter which has been allowed to cool. Set aside. When the sponge has risen sufficiently, beat the batter briefly to deflate the mixture. Add the egg and butter mixture, gradually beating in enough of the reserved flour until the dough becomes manageable enough to handle. Knead on a lightly floured board until smooth and shiny, or use an electric kneader, adding more flour if necessary to keep the dough from sticking. You will probably need most or all of the reserved flour. By hand, kneading will take approximately 15 to 20 minutes.

Place the dough in a clean, well-buttered bowl, lightly buttering the surface of the dough, and cover with a damp towel. Allow to rise in a warm place until double in bulk – approximately 1½ hours. Punch the dough down with your fist and knead briefly. Wrap well in plastic cling film, then in a large heavy plastic bag, tightly knotted. Refrigerate overnight, if time permits, for best results. An hour after refrigerating, punch the dough down in the bag – it will have expanded considerably. Use as directed in the recipe, re-kneading briefly.

NOTE: In any of the recipes, if this dough browns too rapidly before the bread tests have been done (i.e. when a wooden skewer inserted in the bread comes out clean), drape a piece of aluminium foil over the bread to keep it from browning further.

WEIHNACHTS-HEFEGEBÄCK

Sweet Yeast Dough Figures
(for Christmas and New Year)

In addition to the fruit-filled Christmas breads included in this chapter, a wide assortment of shapes and figures are made from plain sweet yeast dough for the Christmas holidays, including Santa Claus figures (Weihnachtsmänner), plaited Christmas stars (Geflochtene Weihnachtssterne), Swiss Christmas men (Grittibänzen), and New Year's 'Good Luck' pigs (Neujahrs-Glücksschweinchen). If not to be used within a few days, wrap any of these breads, after baking, in aluminium foil and freeze for up to three months.

WEIHNACHTSMÄNNER

Santa Claus Figures

1 recipe basic sweet yeast dough (p. 141)
1 egg, lightly beaten
whole blanched almonds, split (see p. 27)
currants

Prepare the dough the day before, according to the instructions in the master recipe, re-kneading it briefly before use. Roll out the dough ½ inch (1·5cm) thick. Use a large Santa Claus biscuit cutter or make an 8 inch (20cm) stencil from heavy paper, and cut out medium-sized or large Santa figures. Knead the scraps together and roll a piece of dough back and forth on a board into a long thin roll. Brush the Santa figures with lightly beaten egg. Wind a piece of the roll around its middle for a belt, and other pieces around the bottom of the robe, on the cuffs and hat, to simulate fur. Place a split almond on the top of the hat for a pom-pom and edge the bottom of the robe with split almonds. Use two currants or small pieces of dough for eyes. Cut out a large moustache and beard from scraps of dough. Brush the decorations with beaten egg. Place the Santa figures on buttered baking sheets, leaving 2½ inches (6cm) between each. Leave in a warm place until they have risen noticeably – approximately 20 to 25 minutes. Refrigerate for 15 minutes to help them keep their shape during baking. In the meantime, preheat the oven to 400°F (200°C/gas 6).

Brush the figures once more with beaten egg. Bake in the bottom third of the oven until golden. Cool on wire racks.

GRITTIBÄNZEN

Swiss Christmas Men

Makes 4 or 6

Whimsical Grittibänzen figures are traditionally found in most bread bakeries in German-speaking Switzerland during the Christmas season. They can easily be baked at home using the master recipe for sweet yeast dough and make amusing gifts for children. Instead of the tiny white pipe that is usually placed in the figure's mouth (which would be difficult to find), a twig of evergreen can be placed in his arm.

1 recipe sweet yeast dough (p. 141)
1 egg, lightly beaten
4 to 6 small sprigs of evergreen, to decorate

Prepare the dough the day before, according to the instructions in the master recipe, re-kneading it briefly before use. Roll the dough out into a large rectangle ½ inch (1·5cm) thick. Cut the dough into 4 or 6 rectangles, depending on whether you are making large or medium-sized figures. Leave a small amount of dough to be used for decoration. Using a sharp knife, cut out a round head. Make two slashes on either side of the head and cut away arms. Make one slash up the middle almost to the waist to make the legs. Roll a small piece of dough in a very thin strand. Cut off three small pieces and coil them to form two eyes and a nose. Brush the surface of the figure well with lightly beaten egg and apply the tiny rings to the face. Roll a slightly larger piece of dough into another thin strand twice the height of the figure. Double the rope and loop it around the head and neck of the figure. Twist it two or three times to secure it, like a tie, and trail the ends down the centre of each leg. Trim off even with the feet.

Make a similar strand and tie one piece around the waist for a belt, two small pieces above the feet to simulate the tops of boots, and two others at the wrists to make cuffs. Use a sharp knife to score a smiling mouth and to mark a double-breasted row of three buttons each on either side of the tie. Or make the buttons from dough, pressed in well with the tip of a knife. Tuck one arm behind a hip and raise the other behind the head. Brush all the decorations with

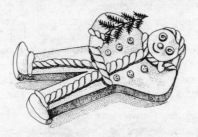

lightly beaten egg. Place the Grittibänzen on buttered baking sheets with 2½ inches (6cm) between each and leave in a warm place until they have risen noticeably – approximately 20 to 25 minutes. Refrigerate for 15 minutes to help them keep their shape during baking. In the meantime, preheat the oven at 400°F (200°C/gas 6).

Brush the figures once more with beaten egg. Bake in the bottom third of the oven until golden – approximately 25 minutes. Cool on wire racks. Place a piece of evergreen in the arm of each.

GEFLOCHTENER WEIHNACHTSSTERN

Plaited Christmas Star

1 recipe basic sweet yeast dough (p. 141)

NOTE: You will need only three-quarters of the amount for this recipe; the remainder can be used for one of the other figures suggested in this section.

1 egg, lightly beaten

Prepare the dough the day before, according to the instructions in the master recipe, re-kneading it briefly before use. Divide the dough to be used into six even pieces. Cut five of the pieces into three strands each. Roll the strands back and forth on a board until they are 10 inches (25cm) long, tapering at one end very thin. You should have fifteen strands.

Plait the strands in threes to make tight plaits. Brush the ends of each with lightly beaten egg and pinch together, pressing the tapered ends under. Each plait will form a point of the star, with the thicker part of the plaits meeting in the centre. Assemble the star, pressing the thick ends together in the centre. Roll the sixth piece of dough until it is approximately 1 inch (2.5cm) in diameter and 20 inches (50cm) long. Starting from the centre, coil it round to form a rosette. Brush the entire surface of the star with lightly beaten egg. Place the rosette in the centre, pressing it down well to seal the seams. Brush the rosette with egg. Place on a buttered baking sheet and leave in a warm place until it has risen noticeably – approximately 30 minutes. In the meantime, preheat the oven to 400°F (200°C/gas 6).

Brush a second time with the beaten egg, making sure it gets well into the crevices. Bake in the bottom third of the oven until golden and until a wooden skewer inserted in the bread comes out clean – approximately 45 minutes. Carefully remove to a rack to cool before eating.

NEUJAHRS-GLÜCKSSCHWEINCHEN

New Year's 'Good Luck' Pigs

Makes 5

In Germany, pigs are a symbol of good luck and make their appearance on cards as well as confections (pink marzipan pigs, for instance) and baked goods (biscuits and breads). These amusing pig faces filled with marzipan make good gifts for children at Christmas time.

1 recipe basic sweet yeast dough (p. 141)
2 eggs, lightly beaten
1 lb (450g) marzipan (p.97), or fresh, ready-made marzipan

Prepare the dough the day before, according to the instructions in the master recipe, re-kneading it briefly before use. Roll out the dough ⅜ inch (1cm) thick. Using a round lid 5 inches (12·5cm) in diameter or a heavy paper stencil as a guide, cut out ten circles. With a biscuit cutter or a glass, cut out five circles 2½ inches (6cm) in diameter. The smaller circles will be the snouts. From the scraps, cut out ten triangles 2½ inches (6cm) long and 1½ inches (4cm) wide. These will be the pigs' ears. Using a small round aspic cutter or thimble, cut out two small circles in the lower part of the small circles (the snouts) to make the nostrils. Roll scraps of dough into small balls, cutting a 'V' with scissors in each to make the eyes. Brush half the large circles with lightly beaten egg. Place a nose almost at the bottom of each circle with the eyes above. Attach a triangular ear on either side, above the eyes, with the tips pointing down and slightly to the side. Brush the decorations with lightly beaten egg.

Roll out the marzipan on a board lightly dusted with icing sugar until it is about ⅜ inch (1cm) thick. Cut out five 4 inch (10cm) circles using a lid or stencil made from heavy paper and a sharp knife. Place a round of marzipan on the five undecorated circles. Brush the edge of the dough with lightly beaten egg. Top with the decorated faces, pressing the edge in well to seal the seam. Place the faces on buttered baking sheets. Leave to rise in a warm place until they have risen noticeably – approximately 20 minutes. Refrigerate for 15 minutes to help them keep their shape during baking. In the meantime, preheat the oven to 400°F (200°C/gas 6).

Brush the faces once more with lightly beaten egg. Bake, one sheet at a time, in the bottom third of the oven until golden – approximately 20 minutes. Remove to a rack to cool before eating.

NOTE: Knead together any scraps that are left over and make another face or use for one of the other figures described in this section.

BIRNBROT

Spicy Pear Bread

Makes 8 loaves 4 by 10 inches (10 by 25cm)

This lovely Christmas bread from Canton Glarus in Switzerland is traditionally made at home and in bakeries in large quantities (as much as twenty loaves) well in advance of the Christmas season, and the extra loaves are consumed during the cold winter months. The wonderfully spicy kirsch-laced filling is made with dried pears (grown in abundance in the region), grapes and nuts mixed with bread dough, and is cleverly concealed in a thin wrapper of plain bread dough. This wrapper helps to keep the bread moist and makes the loaf a great surprise for the uninitiated person who first cuts into it and finds the rich fruit interior. These loaves make ideal Christmas presents and can be kept for two to three months, if well wrapped and stored. They are best made at least two weeks in advance to allow the flavours to ripen.

2 recipes basic sweet yeast dough (p. 141)
2 lb (900g) dried pears, stalked and cored (if necessary)
3 fl oz (100ml) red wine
1 oz (25g) butter
13 oz (375g) sugar
1¼ lb (575g) grapes, preferably seedless, coarsely chopped
4 oz (125g) candied lemon or mixed peel, finely diced
12 oz (350g) walnuts, coarsely chopped
2 oz (50g) ground cinnamon
½ oz (15g) ground cloves
6 fl oz (200ml) kirsch, or rum

2 eggs, lightly beaten, to finish

Prepare the dough the day before, according to the instructions in the master recipe. Also, place the dried pears in a saucepan, cover them with 2 inches (5cm) of water, and leave to soak them overnight.

The next day, pour off all but ¼ pint (150ml) of the water. Add the red wine and butter. Simmer, covered, over a low heat for 20 minutes or until tender, checking occasionally to make sure the pears are not sticking and the liquid has not evaporated. Add a little more water if necessary. When tender, most of the liquid should have evaporated. If not, turn the heat to high and, stirring, cook until you have a fairly thick mixture. The pears should have the consistency of a coarse purée. You should have approximately 3 pints (1.7l) of pears. Mix the pears together with the remaining ingredients. The mixture will be fairly moist.

Cut off one-third of the dough, refrigerating the remainder. Cut this piece into six and place in a bowl with the fruit mixture. Using your hand, knead the fruit and dough together by squeezing it between your fingers until the two are well blended. The mixture will be sticky and moist. The pear filling should be thick enough to hold its shape. Test by spooning a mound on to a plate. If it flattens, add a few tablespoons of flour or as much as is needed to thicken it sufficiently to hold its shape.

Remove the reserved piece of bread dough from the refrigerator. Divide it into four pieces, refrigerating all but one until needed. Roll out each piece on a lightly floured board into a thin rectangle approximately 10 by 16 inches (25 by 40cm). Make sure there are no holes in the rectangle and if there are, re-knead the dough and roll out again. Cut the piece of dough in half, to make two rectangles. Take one-quarter of the fruit/dough filling and divide it between the two rectangles, spooning it lengthwise down the centre of each to within 1½ inches (4cm) of each end. Fold the ends of the rectangle up and the sides over to cover the filling, so that it is like a wrapped parcel. Brush the edges with lightly beaten egg and press them together well to seal the seams.

Butter and flour a baking sheet and carefully place the loaves seam side down, on it, leaving 2½ inches (6cm) between them to allow for expansion. Brush the surface completely with beaten egg. Prick the surface decoratively twelve to fourteen times with the prongs of a fork. Leave the loaves to rise in a warm place until they have risen noticeably – approximately 30 to 45 minutes. In the meantime, preheat the oven to 400°F (200°C/gas 6).

Brush the loaves a second time with beaten egg. Bake in the middle of the oven until golden brown and well risen – approximately 45 to 60 minutes. The loaves will spread slightly because of the moist filling. Cool on racks when done. Wrap tightly in aluminium foil when cool and store in a cool dry place or in the refrigerator for up to two months, or freeze for up to four months. Continue making and baking the remaining loaves in the same fashion, leaving them in the refrigerator before proving (the final rising) until approximately 1 hour before the oven is free.

DREIKÖNIGSKUCHEN

Three Kings' Cake

❧

Makes 2

Twelfth Night, 6 January, is celebrated in many regions of Germany and Switzerland with a wreath or round of rich yeast bread with a single almond or trinket baked inside. Whoever gets the piece with the token is king or queen for the day. The following version, a wreath with eight balls encircling it and topped with a gold foil crown, is typically found in Switzerland.

1 recipe basic sweet yeast dough (p. 141)
1 large, unblanched almond
1 egg, lightly beaten
granulated sugar
decoration: a crown made of gold foil and decorated or not, slightly
    smaller in circumference than the wreath (optional)

Prepare the dough the day before, according to the instructions in the master recipe. The next day, re-knead it briefly before use.

Divide the dough into two to make two wreaths, wrapping and refrigerating the piece not being shaped. For each wreath, cut off one-third of the dough. First roll it out in a long narrow rectangle with a rolling pin to help soften it. Then, using your hands, roll the strip of dough back and forth on a board to form a narrow rope approximately 24 inches (60cm) long. Curve the rope into a perfect circle on a buttered and floured baking sheet. Using your hand, press the rope slightly flat on the surface to make it easier for the balls to stick. Brush the ends of the rope and the surface with lightly beaten egg, pressing the ends together well to seal the seam. Smooth the seam with your fingers. Using the back of a knife, mark eight indentations around the ring at even intervals.

Divide the remaining dough into eight even-sized pieces. On a board or between the palms of your hands, roll each into a perfect ball. Press the unblanched almond into the centre of one of the balls, smoothing over the hole. Place one ball at each marked indentation on the wreath, pressing them in well so they don't fall off. Brush the balls with lightly beaten egg. To prevent the balls from toppling off in the early rising stages, take a piece of aluminium foil and crumple it into a thick round, about 1¼ inches (3cm) high, that will fit in the centre of the ring just touching the balls but well inside the rope base. Butter well the sides that touch the dough. Take another length of aluminium foil and crumple it into a rope approximately 1¼ inches (3cm) high and long enough to wind around the outside of the wreath. As before, it should just touch the balls but not be pressed against the rope base. This is important since you will want to remove the foil supports partway through the baking to allow that part of the dough to brown. Butter well the side of the foil that touches the dough. Leave the wreath in a warm place to rise until double in bulk – approximately 30 to 40 minutes. In the meantime, preheat the oven to 400°F (200°C/gas 6).

Before baking, brush again with lightly beaten egg. Sprinkle each ball lightly with granulated sugar. Bake just below the centre of the oven for about 20 minutes. Remove the outside foil support and, if you can do so with ease, the piece of foil in the centre. If it is difficult to retrieve the centre foil piece, however, leave it until the wreath has finished baking. Bake until the wreath is golden and until a wooden skewer inserted in one of the balls comes out clean – approximately 35 to 45 minutes total baking time. Remove to a wire rack to cool. If the foil is still in the centre, remove it while the dough is still warm. Before serving, if desired, place a decorated gold foil crown in the centre of the wreath.

The second wreath can be shaped and kept in the refrigerator, covered loosely with aluminium foil, until the first wreath has been in the oven for 10 minutes. At that point, remove the second wreath from the refrigerator and allow it to rise, as before. The second wreath can be used to serve extra guests or given as a gift.

OSTER-HEFEGEBÄCK

Easter Breads

While not celebrated with the intensity that it is in the neighbouring Eastern European countries, Easter – which marks the end of the Lenten fast on the church calendar – is marked by bakers in German-speaking countries with an assortment of various rich yeast breads: Bremer Osterklaben (almost identical to Dresdner Christstollen, p. 160); Osterkarpfen (rich yeast dough in a fish shape found in Switzerland); Osterkranz (plaited rich yeast wreath); Eier im Nest (easter egg nests); and Tauben (rich yeast doves), to name just a few.

OSTERKARPFEN

Easter Carp

The fish – an early symbol of Christianity – is a shape seen frequently at Easter time, especially in France where it takes the form of chocolates made in special fish moulds. Swiss bakers, no doubt influenced by this, have used the same shape with yeast bread to make charming glazed fish with almonds for scales, measuring anywhere from 5 to 14 inches (12·5 to 35cm) in length. To make one large or two small fish, use the following quantities.

½ recipe basic sweet yeast dough (p. 141)
1 egg, lightly beaten
2 oz (50g) whole blanched almonds, split (see p. 27)

Prepare the dough the day before according to the instructions in the master recipe. Re-knead it briefly before use.

Roll the dough into a large oval (if one fish is desired), or divide it in two, rolling out two ovals to make two smaller fish. Roll out ¾ inch (2cm) thick. If you are hesitant to cut out a fish free-hand, make a cardboard stencil which should include indentations for fins and tail. Place the stencil on the dough and, using a sharp knife, cut out the fish shape. Brush the fish with lightly beaten egg. Knead together the scraps and roll out. Cut out fins and tail pieces. Score them with parallel lines using the back of a knife. Coil a small rope of dough to make an eye. Form another small crescent of dough for the mouth. Place the pieces of dough on the fish and brush each one with beaten egg. Using a sharp pair of scissors, snip v-shaped gashes at 1 inch (2·5cm) intervals cutting only part-way through the dough on the upper two-thirds of the fish to simulate scales. Press a split almond into each gash, rounded side up, so that it lies flat with two-thirds of the almond showing.

Place the fish on a buttered baking sheet. If there are two, leave 3 inches (8cm) between them to allow for expansion. Cover the fish with a damp cloth and allow to rise in a warm place until double in bulk – approximately 40 minutes. In the meantime, preheat the oven to 400°F (200°C/gas 6).

Brush the entire fish once again with beaten egg. Bake in the bottom third of the oven until golden and risen – approximately 30 to 40 minutes, depending on the size of the fish. Remove to a rack to cool before eating. The fish can be wrapped in aluminium foil and frozen for up to three months.

OSTERKRANZ

Easter Wreath

½ recipe basic sweet rich yeast dough (p. 141)
1 egg, lightly beaten

Prepare the dough the day before, according to the instructions in the master recipe. Re-knead it briefly before use.

Cut off a small piece of dough to be used for decoration. Roll the remainder into a rectangle 12 inches (30cm) long. Cut the rectangle into three even strips. Roll the strips back and forth to round them and extend them another 8 inches (20cm). Brush the ends with lightly beaten egg and press them together. Plait the strands and form into a wreath, pressing the ends of the plait together once the wreath has been formed. Roll out the reserved piece of dough. Using a pastry wheel or a knife, cut out two large leaves and several flower shapes, scoring the leaves and flours with the back of a knife to simulate veins. Brush the wreath well with beaten egg. Apply the leaves in bow-tie fashion where the ends of the plait join. Cover the seam with flowers. Brush the decorations with lightly beaten egg. Place the wreath on a buttered baking sheet. Leave it to rise in a warm place until double in bulk – approximately 40 minutes. In the meantime, preheat the oven to 400°F (200°C or gas 6).

Brush the wreath again thoroughly with beaten egg. Bake in the middle of the oven until golden brown and risen – approximately 30 to 40 minutes. Remove to a rack to cool before eating. If desired, the wreath can be baked in advance, wrapped in aluminium foil, and frozen for up to three months.

EIER IM NEST

Easter Egg Nests

Makes 7

Traditionally found in Greece as well as Italy at Easter time, yeast dough nests with their colourful eggs have migrated north to the German-speaking countries. Hard-boil and dye your Easter eggs in advance. The eggs will not actually be baked in the bread. Instead, aluminium foil eggs are placed on the bread during baking and replaced afterwards by the real eggs.

In Switzerland, an old-fashioned method of dying and decorating the eggs is used which produces a beautiful, more natural colour. To make the dye, cook the skins only from 3 lbs (1·25kg) of Spanish onions (the kind with brownish-yellow skins) in 3 pints (1·7l) of water for 1 hour, partially covering the pan while they simmer. At the same time simmer the eggs (use white eggs) in water for 10 to 12 minutes for eggs at room temperature, the time depending on the size of the eggs. Place them in a pan of cold water when done to stop the cooking.

When the onion skins have simmered for an hour, strain the liquid into a bowl, discarding the skins. Have ready small flowers, especially wild flowers if any are available, grass, or small leaves, an old nylon stocking and a piece of string. Dip whatever flower or green decoration you are using in water and press it against one of the hard-boiled eggs. One pretty flower or leaf can be sufficient. Cut the foot from the stocking to make a small sack. Carefully place the decorated egg in the toe of the stocking without losing any of the decorations. Using a piece of string, tie the egg tightly at the toe of the stocking so it can't move. Lower the egg in the stocking into the hot onion-skin dye, leaving it there from 1 to 5 minutes depending on whether you want a pale or dark tint. Remove the egg from the dye and take it out of the stocking. Remove the decorations which should now appear as white silhouettes on the egg. Repeat with each egg. Reheat the dye if it becomes too cool. Allow the eggs to dry completely. To make them shine, rub them with a piece of bacon fat once they are dry.

NOTE: If you feel ambitious, you can make very complicated designs by tinting the egg briefly the first time, decorated with a large flower or leaf, removing the egg from the dye, redecorating and dying it a second time. This will produce several layers of patterns shadowed over each other.

1 recipe basic sweet yeast dough (p. 141)
7 hard-boiled eggs, dyed in food colouring or in onion-skin dye as above
1 egg, lightly beaten

Prepare the dough the day before, according to the instructions in the master recipe. Re-knead it before use.

Divide the dough into seven even-sized pieces, wrapping and refrigerating those not being used. Taking a little over half of each piece of dough, roll that piece into a small oval approximately 4 inches (10cm) at the widest part and 4½ inches (11·5cms) long. This should give you a rim of approximately 1 inch (2·5cm) or more if an egg is placed in the centre. Press one of the dyed hard-boiled eggs in the centre of each oval. Brush the rim with lightly beaten egg.

Taking the remaining small piece of dough, roll it back and forth to form a narrow rope slightly longer than is needed to go around the circumference of the oval – 14 to 15 inches (35 to 37·5cm). Twist the rope and wind it around the edge of the oval to form a rim or nest. Press it on well and trim the ends. Brush the twisted rope with beaten egg. Press the ends together well. Carefully remove the real egg and make a ball the same size from aluminium foil. Butter the bottom and sides of the foil egg with butter, rest it in the centre of the nest and place the nest on a buttered baking sheet. Continue with the remaining dough, working quickly, leaving at least 2 inches (5cm) between each nest on the baking sheet to allow for expansion. Cover with a damp cloth and leave in a warm place until they have begun to rise noticeably – 10 to 15 minutes. Refrigerate for 15 to 20 minutes before baking. This will help them to keep their shape during baking, without rising too much, so that the foil egg can be easily removed and replaced. In the meantime, preheat the oven to 400°F (200°C/gas 6).

Glaze the dough once more with beaten egg. Bake, one sheet at a time, in the bottom third of the oven until golden – approximately 20 minutes. Remove from the baking sheet to wire racks to cool. Remove the aluminium foil eggs while the dough is still warm. Replace each with a coloured hard-boiled egg.

VARIATION

Before baking, after the nests have been glazed for the last time, you can sprinkle finely chopped mixed peel or coarse decorating sugar sparingly over the glazed rim of each nest.

TAUBEN

Doves

✻❧✻

Like the Easter egg nests, the rich yeast doves traditionally baked in Italy for Easter have crossed the border and are now a regular feature of the Swiss baking repertoire at this time of year.

1 recipe basic sweet yeast dough (p. 141)
1 egg white
4–8 currants or raisins
3 oz (75g) flaked almonds
coarse decorating or granulated sugar

Prepare the dough the day before, according to the instructions in the master recipe. Re-knead it briefly before use. The doves can be prepared in two ways.

Method 1

For a cut-out version, to make four or five medium-sized doves, divide the dough into four, wrapping and refrigerating those portions not being used. Roll the piece of dough into an oval approximately 9 inches (23cm) long and 1 inch (2·5cm) thick. If you are hesitant to cut out a dove free-hand, make a cardboard stencil, giving the dove two wings and making indentations for the beak and tail. Place the stencil on the oval and cut out the dove with a sharp knife. Beat the egg white with a whisk or fork until frothy. Brush the dove completely with the egg white using a pastry brush. Make an eye on the dove using a currant or a raisin. Using the back of a knife, score parallel lines on the wings and tail. Place flaked almonds neatly in overlapping rows on the ends of the wings and tail, beginning at the tip, to simulate feathers. Use them more sparingly in the centre of the wings and tail, extending them slightly further up the outside edges. Brush the almonds carefully with beaten egg.

Place on a buttered baking sheet and leave in a warm place until the dove has begun to rise – about 20 minutes. Refrigerate for 20 minutes. This will help to keep the shape during baking. In the meantime, preheat the oven to 400°F (200°C/gas 6).

Brush the dove once more with egg white and sprinkle with sugar. Bake in the bottom third of the oven until golden and a wooden skewer inserted in the dove comes out clean – approximately 30 minutes. Remove to a rack to cool before eating. Continue with the remaining doves in the same manner.

NOTE: Scraps left over from cutting out the doves can be kneaded together and used to make a fifth dove or one of the knotted doves described below.

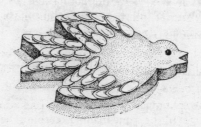

Method 2

In the second method, smaller fatter doves are produced by knotting a rope of dough. Roll the basic sweet yeast dough out into a rectangle 13 inches (33cm) wide and 14 inches (35cm) long. Cut the dough lengthwise in strips 1½ inches (4cm) wide. You should have nine strips. Roll the strips back and forth on the board several times to round them slightly. Tie each strip in a fat knot, slightly off centre, plumping up the knot. The smaller end which should just peek out will be the head. Model it with your fingers shaping it to a beak in the front. Use a pair of scissors to trim a neat, pointed beak. The tail piece should extend out about 2 inches (5cm). Cut several gashes in the tail with the scissors. Use the back of a knife to make parallel lines on the tail piece. Beat an egg white lightly with a wire whisk or fork until frothy. Using a pastry brush, brush the dove with the beaten egg white, getting the glaze well into the crevices.

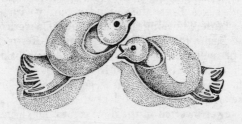

Place a currant on the side of the head for an eye. Place no more than three at a time on a buttered baking sheet. Leave in a warm place until they have risen noticeably – about 15 to 20 minutes. Refrigerate for 15 to 20 minutes before baking to help them keep their shape. In the meantime preheat the oven to 400°F (200°C/gas 6).

Brush the doves once more with the beaten egg white and sprinkle with coarse sugar. Bake in the bottom third of the oven until golden and a wooden skewer inserted in the middle of the dove comes out clean – approximately 25 to 30 minutes.

NOTE: If the heads and tails brown too quickly before the body is baked through, cover them with aluminium foil, leaving the knotted portion exposed.

When done, remove to a wire rack to cool. Continue with the remaining doves in the same manner, keeping the dough refrigerated until it is used.

BASIC RICH SWEET YEAST DOUGH

Schwerer Hefeteig

1½ oz (40g) fresh yeast	2 large eggs
2 tbsp sugar	1 tsp salt
2½ lb (1.1kg) strong flour	4½ oz (140g) castor sugar
12 fl oz (340 ml) milk	12 oz (350g) butter, melted
grated rind of 1 lemon	

NOTE: If using dry yeast, substitute 1½ tbsp dry yeast for the fresh yeast given in the recipe. Dissolve it with the sugar in 4 fl oz (125ml) of warm (90°F/32°C) water. Allow to rise in a warm place for about 10 minutes, or until bubbly. Proceed with the recipe as follows, remembering that no additional water need be added.

Using the above quantities and 4 fl oz (125ml) water, follow the technique for making basic sweet yeast dough (p. 141).

DRESDNER CHRISTSTOLLEN

Dresden Christmas Stollen

Makes 2 large or 4 small loaves

Although different variations are baked in all parts of Germany, the Stollen from Dresden, which generally comprises the richest mixture of butter and dried fruits, is the best known. The traditional shape of Stollen – tapered at each end with a ridge down the centre – is meant to represent the Christ Child in swaddling clothes, thus the name Christstollen. It is a speciality of the Christmas season and because of its good keeping properties, is generally baked well in advance so that it can ripen.

Because it is so rich, it is generally sliced thinly, and is delicious for both breakfast and tea. It can be served at room temperature or slightly warmed (see the instructions at the end of the recipe).

1 recipe basic rich sweet yeast
    dough (p. 159)
8 oz (225g) sultanas
5 oz (150g) currants
2 tbsp rum
2 tsp flour
6 oz (175g) mixed peel, chopped
8 oz (225g) blanched almonds,
    coarsely chopped

To finish
6 oz (175g) butter, melted
castor sugar
icing sugar

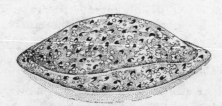

The day before making the Stollen, soak the sultanas and currants in rum, and prepare the dough according to the instructions in the master recipe. Re-knead it briefly before use.

On the day, cut the round of dough into six pieces and place the pieces in a large mixing bowl. If the dough has been refrigerated overnight, cover with a damp towel and allow to come to room temperature for half an hour. Drain the sultanas and currants. Toss them together with a few teaspoons of flour to absorb the moisture and keep them from sticking together. Combine them with the chopped mixed peel and coarsely chopped almonds. Sprinkle some of the fruit and nut mixture over each piece of dough until it is all used up. Knead the dough together with the fruit, first in the mixing bowl and then on a lightly floured board. When they are well blended, divide the dough into two (for large Stollen) or four (for smaller loaves). Roll each piece of dough into a long, flat oval approximately 1 inch (2·5cm) thick, using a rolling pin. Wrap and refrigerate those pieces not being shaped.

With a rolling pin (preferably a long, narrow one), press a firm indentation down the centre of the dough. This will make the Stollen fold more securely. Fold one half of the Stollen over the other, lengthwise. Press the overlapping edge firmly to help seal the seam. Taper the ends neatly to make slightly rounded points. Use your hands to plump a small rounded ridge down the centre: place the side of each hand lengthwise on either side of the visual centre of the Stollen, leaving a space of approximately 2 inches (5cm) between your hands. Press them simultaneously into the soft dough, causing a ridge of dough to protrude slightly. Continue down the length of the Stollen. Place it a buttered baking sheet. If placing more than one on a baking sheet, leave 3 inches (8cm) between them. Brush with some of the melted butter. Allow to rise in a warm place until double in bulk – approximately 45 minutes. In the meantime, preheat the oven to 350°F (180°C/gas 4).

NOTE: Keep any Stollen not being baked with the first batch in the refrigerator. Take it out to rise about 45 minutes before you will have an oven free.

When the Stollen has risen properly, bake, one sheet at a time, in the middle of the oven. After 15 minutes, drape a large piece of aluminium foil loosely over the Stollen, covering the top, sides and ends to keep it light in colour. Bake until lightly coloured and a wooden skewer inserted in the Stollen comes out clean – approximately 50 to 70 minutes, depending on the size.

When the Stollen is done, remove from the oven and brush generously with the remaining melted butter. Allow to cool for 5 minutes on the baking sheet. Dust first with castor sugar, then with icing sugar while the bread is still warm. Transfer to a wire rack to finish cooling.

When well wrapped in several layers of aluminium foil, Stollen will keep in a cool place or in the refrigerator for as long as one month, or it can be frozen after baking for up to three months, and retrieved when needed.

To refresh Stollen that has been refrigerated, slice it thinly, stack the pieces on top of each other and wrap them in aluminium foil. Place in a preheated 375°F (190°C/gas 5) oven and allow to warm through – approximately 10 to 15 minutes.

CHRISTSTOLLEN MIT MARZIPAN

The following Stollen variation is one that was baked by a German bakery in Colorado every Christmas and which I enjoyed as a child.

1 recipe Dresdner Christstollen
1 lb (450g) marzipan (p. 97), or fresh, ready-made marzipan
icing sugar

Prepare the loaves of Stollen as described in the master recipe. Before folding them in half lengthwise, roll out the marzipan on a board lightly dusted with icing sugar. Roll it out slightly shorter than the length of the Stollen and wide enough to cut two or four 2 inch (5cm) strips (depending on whether you are making two or four Stollen). Cut the strips of marzipan to fit down the centre of each loaf. Fold the loaf over the marzipan as described in the master recipe, tucking in any marzipan that protrudes. It should be completely covered. Press the edge down well to seal it. Then proceed as above.

WEIHNACHTSZOPF

Christmas Plait

Makes 2

At Christmas time, the traditional Sunday plaited bread is often made with a slightly richer dough and filled with nuts and fruit. In Germany it would be served, thinly sliced, both at breakfast and as part of a selection of baked goods with afternoon coffee.

1 recipe basic rich sweet yeast dough (p. 159)
4 oz (125g) sultanas
2½ oz (65g) currants
2 tbsp rum
2 tsp flour
5 oz (75g) mixed peel, chopped
6 oz (175g) blanched almonds, coarsely chopped

2 eggs, lightly beaten with a pinch of salt, to finish

The day before baking, soak the sultanas and currants with rum and prepare the dough according to the instructions in the master recipe. Re-knead briefly. Remove dough from refrigerator half an hour before use, covering it with a damp towel.

On the day, drain the sultanas and currants. Toss them together with a few teaspoons of flour to absorb the moisture and keep them from sticking together. Combine them with the chopped mixed peel and coarsely chopped almonds. Cut the round of dough in six pieces. Place the pieces in a large mixing bowl. Sprinkle the fruit and nut mixture over each piece until it is all used up. Knead the dough together with the fruit first in the mixing bowl and then on a lightly floured board. When well blended, divide the dough into two (for two loaves). Taking one piece of dough and divide it into three even pieces. Wrap and refrigerate the piece of dough not being used. Roll each strip back and forth on a board to make long narrow ropes, approximately 14 inches (35cm) long, tapering the ends slightly. Start the plait in the middle, braiding out to each end. Tuck the ends under, pressing them firmly to make sure they stick. Place on a buttered and floured baking sheet and brush the surface well with beaten egg. Allow to rise in a warm place until double in bulk – approximately 1 hour. In the meantime, preheat the oven to 375°F (190°C/gas 5).

NOTE: Unless you have two ovens, you will probably have to bake one loaf at a time. You can plait your second loaf, cover it with aluminium foil and refrigerate it until you place the first one in the oven. Then remove the second plait and leave it in a warm place to rise as before.

When the plait has risen sufficiently, brush once more with beaten egg. Bake just below the centre of the oven until golden brown and a wooden skewer inserted in the bread comes out clean – approximately 1 hour. If the bread is browning too quickly, cover loosely with aluminium foil. Remove to a rack to cool. If desired, sprinkle a little sifted icing sugar just down the centre of the loaf.

If wrapped in several layers of aluminium foil, the plait keeps well in the refrigerator for up to one month or in the freezer for up to three months.

To refresh slices of Weihnachtszopf that have been refrigerated, slice the bread thinly, stack the slices on top of each other and wrap in aluminium foil. Heat in a preheated 375°F (190°C/gas 5) oven until warmed through – approximately 10 to 15 minutes.

HUTZELBROT

Yeast Fruit Bread

Makes 6

Small flat loaves of fruit bread decoratively studded with split blanched almonds and an occasional glacé cherry are traditionally found at Christmas markets, most notably those of Nuremberg and Rothenburg ob der Tauber, as well as commercial bakeries at Christmas time.

The loaves can be baked up to two months in advance and keep well if wrapped in aluminium foil and stored in a cool place.

1 lb (450g) dried pears
1 lb (450g) prunes
8 oz (225g) dried figs
1 oz (25g) fresh yeast
1 tbsp sugar
1 lb 1 oz (475g) bread flour, sifted, plus more as needed
8 fl oz (230ml) soaking liquid drained from the fruit
4 oz (125g) mixed peel, finely chopped
1 lb (450g) sultanas

8 oz (225g) unblanched almonds, coarsely chopped
8 oz (225g) walnuts, coarsely chopped
6½ oz (190g) sugar
½ tsp salt
2 tbsp ground cinnamon
1½ tsps ground cloves
½ tsp allspice
1 tsp powdered anis

split whole blanched almonds and 6 halved glacé cherries, to decorate

NOTE: If using dry yeast, substitute 1 tbsp dry yeast for the fresh yeast given in the recipe. Dissolve it with the sugar in 3 fl oz (100ml) warm (90°F/32°C) water. Allow to rise in a warm place for about 10 minutes or until bubbly. Proceed with the recipe as follows, reducing the liquid used for the sponge to 5 fl oz (145ml).

The day before baking, soak the dried pears in warm water to cover for 1 or 2 hours. Drain them and remove the stems and seeds. Cut into thin strips, place in a saucepan and cover with 3 inches (8cm) of water. Simmer, partially covered, over a medium heat until barely tender – about 15 minutes. While the pears are cooking, remove the pits from the prunes and cut into thin strips. Cut the figs into strips also. When the pears are tender, remove the pan from the heat. Add the prunes and dried figs. There should be at least 1½ inches (4cm) of water covering the fruit. If not, add a little extra hot water. Leave the dried fruit to soak, covered, overnight at room temperature.

The next day, drain the fruit, reserving 8 fl oz (230ml) of the soaking liquid. Cream the fresh yeast with the sugar in a small bowl or cup. Heat the reserved soaking liquid to just warm, about 80°F (27°C). Sift the flour into a large bowl and make a well in the centre. Combine the creamed yeast with the soaking liquid and pour in the well. Beat in some of the flour to make a thick batter – a sponge. Dust extra flour over the sponge, cover the bowl with a damp cloth, and leave to rise in a warm place until risen and bubbly – 20 to 30 minutes. Beat down the sponge with a wooden spoon. Beat the remaining flour into the sponge, adding the drained soaked fruit pieces, the mixed peel, sultanas, almonds, walnuts, sugar, salt and spices. Work the mixture together well for 4 or 5 minutes. If it is still quite sticky, add additional sifted flour in small amounts until the dough no longer sticks to the hands. Knead for several minutes on a lightly floured board until the consistency is smooth. Divide the dough into six pieces. Form each into a somewhat flat narrow loaf 8 inches (20cm) long with rounded ends. Place the loaves on buttered and floured baking sheets, leaving 2¼ inches (6cm) between each to allow for expansion. If you don't have enough oven space to bake all the loaves at one time, refrigerate those that must be baked later, covering them with a damp towel. Take them out to rise shortly before the others are ready to go in the oven.

Cover the loaves that are to be baked first with a damp cloth and leave to rise in a warm place until they have risen noticeably approximately 2 hours. Preheat the oven to 350°F (180°C/gas 4). Decorate just the corners with split blanched almonds, or place the almonds at intervals all around the edge with a halved cherry in the centre. Bake the loaves in the bottom third of the oven until golden – approximately 50 to 70 minutes. Remove the loaves to a wire rack to cool. Allow to cool completely before wrapping in aluminium foil and storing. Proceed with the remaining loaves in the same fashion.

SPECKKUCHEN

Yeast Dough 'Bacon Cake'

Makes 4

In the town of Rothenburg ob der Tauber, Germany, the bakers make this speciality for New Year. The perfect preventive medicine against a hangover on Silvester (New Year's Eve), the bread is traditionally eaten before the merrymaking begins, giving sustenance and a generous coating of bacon fat to an empty stomach. It makes a delicious snack or light luncheon dish served with a green salad.

NOTE: Slab bacon, if it is available, is preferable to pre-sliced bacon as it can be cut in thicker dice and the fat will better penetrate the dough as it bakes. However, pre-sliced bacon can be used. Buy very fatty bacon for best flavour.

½ oz (15g) dry yeast
1 tbsp sugar
2¼ lb (1kg) strong flour, sifted
12 fl oz (340ml) milk
4 oz (125g) butter
3 large eggs
2 tsp salt
1½ lb (675g) fatty streaky bacon (see above), cut in ⅜ inch (1cm) dice

The day before baking, mix the sugar with 6 fl oz (170ml) hot (90°F/32°C) water and sprinkle the yeast over the top. Allow to rise in a warm place for about 10 minutes or until bubbly. In the meantime, sift half the flour into a large mixing bowl, making a well in the centre. Heat the milk to the same temperature as the water. Pour the yeast and milk into the centre of the flour, gradually beating in the flour to make a thick batter-sponge. Dust extra flour over the sponge, cover the bowl with a damp cloth and leave in a warm place until risen and bubbly – approximately 25 minutes.

Melt the butter and allow it to cool slightly. Beat the salt together with the eggs. When the sponge has risen, beat the mixture down. Pour the butter and eggs on to the sponge. Gradually work in the remaining flour. Use just enough flour to prevent the dough from being sticky. Remove to a lightly floured board and knead for 10 minutes by hand or with an electric kneader until smooth and shiny. Wrap tightly in plastic cling film, place in a heavy plastic bag, seal tightly and refrigerate. After an hour, check the dough. Unwrap it and punch it down with your fist. Rewrap it well and return it to the plastic bag, sealing the bag tightly. Leave overnight.

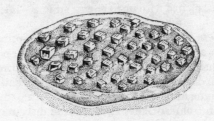

When ready to use, re-knead the dough briefly and divide it into four. Roll out one piece of dough into a 12 inch (30cm) circle, rewrapping and refrigerating the rest until you have room in the oven to bake the other rounds. Lift up the rolled-out dough, holding the outer edge, and rotate it, letting its weight stretch it. Use your fist to stretch out the centre. Roll once more to flatten the circle further. Place on a buttered and floured baking sheet. Stud evenly with a quarter of the diced bacon, pressing it well into the dough. Leave to prove in a warm place – from 15 to 20 minutes – or until it has risen noticeably. In the meantime, preheat the oven to 400°F (200°C/gas 6).

Bake in the oven for 20 to 30 minutes or until golden. Brush the entire surface with the fat that has accumulated around the bacon. Proceed in the same fashion with the other three rounds, cooling them on a wire rack when they are done. The rounds will shrink to approximately 10 inches (25cm).

NOTE: Speckkuchen can also be made in two large rectangles if desired. They are best eaten shortly after they are made or, if baked ahead, they can be wrapped in aluminium foil and warmed in a hot oven.

ZOPF

Rich Yeast Dough Plait

Makes 4

Usually baked at home in Switzerland for Sunday, the baker's day off, plaited bread – ranging from loaves knotted with one strand of dough to those plaited with up to twelve strands – is also a favourite in Austria and Germany where, at Christmas time, extra fruit and nuts are sometimes added; see Weihnachtszopf, p. 162.

Some years ago, a German baker told me that the plaited loaf was baked only on *Allerseelen* (All Souls' Day, 2 November) to commemorate the days when a warrior's wife would have her plait cut off before joining him in the grave.

Frau Gilgen from St Gallen, Switzerland, gave me this recipe – one I'd often sampled with relish in her home – which differs from other rich yeast recipes in this chapter because of the addition of soured cream, which makes the texture especially light.

Because this is not a sweet bread, it is equally good for sandwiches or served at breakfast, warm or toasted, with butter and jam.

¾ oz (20g) dried yeast	4 large eggs, lightly beaten
2 tbsp sugar	5 lbs (2·3kg) bread flour, sifted
1 pint (575ml) milk	plus additional flour as needed
1 lb (450g) unsalted butter	
4 tsp salt	2 eggs, lightly beaten, to glaze
1 pint (575ml) soured cream	

Mix the sugar with 4 fl oz (125ml) warm water and sprinkle the yeast over the top. Allow to double in bulk in a warm place. Heat the milk almost to a simmer with the butter and the salt. Allow to cool for 5 minutes, stirring occasionally. Stir in the soured cream and the lightly beaten eggs. When just warm to the touch, stir in the yeast mixture. Pour the mixture into a large mixing bowl and gradually beat in most of the sifted flour. Remove the dough to a lightly floured board and knead for 10 to 15 minutes by hand until smooth and shiny (or use an electric kneader). Add just enough extra flour to keep the dough from sticking. Place in a buttered bowl. Cover with a hot wet cloth and leave to rise in a warm place until double in bulk.

Divide the dough into four. Plait the loaves as instructed on p. 163. Brush with lightly beaten egg. Place the loaves on buttered baking sheets, leaving 3 inches (8 cm) space between each. Keep the loaves refrigerated until 40 to 50 minutes before there is oven space available. Before baking, leave the plaited loaves in a warm place, draped with a damp towel, until noticeably risen and almost double in bulk – approximately 40 minutes. Preheat the oven to 375°F (190°C/gas 5).

Brush a second time with lightly beaten egg, getting the glaze well into the crevices. Bake, one sheet at a time, just below the centre of the oven until golden and until a wooden skewer inserted in the bread comes out clean – 45 to 60 minutes. Remove to a wire rack to cool. Allow to cool completely before eating.

Zopf can be wrapped in aluminium foil and kept in the refrigerator for up to one week, or frozen well wrapped for up to three months.

KUGELHOPF

Sweet Yeast Round

In the Alsace and in the Black Forest (Schwarzwald) of Germany, Kugelhopf is baked for breakfast on Sundays, the baker's day off, while in Austria, where it is known as Gugelhupf, a richer version is baked – sometimes with yeast, sometimes with baking powder – and served at tea-time (*Jause*). Despite variations in the amount of eggs, butter, and sugar, and in the leavening agent used, Kugelhopf and Gugelhupf have more than shape in common. Traditionally baked in a round, decoratively fluted tin, this enriched yeast bread studded with raisins has long been a measure for judging a home baker's culinary skills. This is one yeast bread that, although available in bakeries, is baked at home as a matter of pride, with each housewife carefully guarding her own special recipe, generally passed on from mother to daughter.

While the Austrian version is a more sophisticated one, richer and slightly more complicated to prepare, I am partial to the simpler German/Alsatian Kugelhopf, probably because I love eating it for breakfast and this version is lighter – suitable for early morning consumption.

Although it is never as good as when freshly baked, Kugelhopf will keep, well wrapped in the refrigerator, for three or four days, or it can be wrapped in aluminium foil and frozen for up to three months. And, if you don't feel like rising at six in the morning to make a freshly baked Kugelhopf for Sunday morning breakfast, it is equally delicious baked in the afternoon and served at tea-time or for an afternoon snack. To refresh Kugelhopf that has been refrigerated, slice it thinly, wrap the slices, stacked, in aluminium foil, and heat them in a preheated 375°F (190°C/gas 5) oven for about 15 minutes or until just warm.

The German/Alsatian recipe given below will make two small (2½ pt/1·4l mould) – or one large (5 pt/2·8l mould) Kugelhopf. If you don't have a proper Kugelhopf mould, available in most speciality cookware shops, you can use any ring mould or Bundt pan. To estimate the size of your mould, use a liquid measuring cup, fill it with water, and see how much water the mould holds.

For the mould

2 oz (50g) melted butter, cooled
2 tsps sugar
½ oz (15g) dry yeast
4 oz (125g) butter, softened
3 oz (75g) sugar
2 large eggs
2 large egg yolks
grated rind of 1 lemon
½ tsp salt
12½ oz (365g) plain flour, sifted,

plus additional flour for kneading
4 fl oz (125ml) milk, scalded
4 oz (125g) raisins

icing sugar, sifted, to finish

Equipment

5 pint (2·8l) Kugelhopf or ring
    mould, or two 2½ pint (1·4l)
    Kugelhopf or ring moulds

Prepare the Kugelhopf mould(s), savarin (ring) mould or Bundt pan by chilling the mould in the freezer for 15 minutes or in the refrigerator for 20 minutes. Brush every part of the mould well with cooled melted butter. Return to the freezer or refrigerator briefly to set the butter. Remove and brush a second time so the mould is heavily coated. Chill until needed.

Mix the sugar with 2 fl oz (60ml) warm (90°F/32°C) water and sprinkle the yeast over the top, leaving it in a warm place for about 10 minutes or until bubbly. Using an electric mixer, beat the butter and sugar together until light and creamy – about 3 minutes. Beat in the eggs and egg yolks, one at a time, beating each well before adding the next. Beat in the lemon rind and salt. Beat in the flour and milk, alternately, and finally the bubbling yeast mixture, beating until all the flour and milk are added. Scrape down the beaters. Finally add the raisins and beat the mixture for several minutes with a wooden spoon. Begin working the sticky dough with your hand, flouring it lightly with up to 1 oz (25g) of flour to keep it from sticking too much to your hand. Work the dough for about 4 minutes.

If using two moulds, divide the dough in two. Spread it evenly around the mould. Cover with a damp towel and leave to rise in a warm place until it has doubled in bulk – approximately 45 minutes.

In the meantime, preheat the oven to 375°F (190°C/gas 5).

Bake just below the centre of the oven. After 25 minutes, check the Kugelhopf. It should be risen, golden and firm; a wooden skewer inserted in the round should come out clean. Baking time will vary considerably according to the depth and thickness of your mould. If not yet ready, return to the oven and test again later.

When done, rap the mould firmly on the counter. Reverse the mould on to a wire rack and rap firmly again to unmould it. Allow the Kugelhopf to cool for several minutes, then sprinkle the top generously with sifted icing sugar. Allow to cool before eating.

5

CAKES AND PASTRIES
Torten und Kuchen

Can anyone resist an exquisite cake or a well-executed tart filled with fresh fruit and custard? *Torten* and *Kuchen* are favourites of mine and I have saved them for last.

In all three countries, cakes and pastries are baked and consumed throughout the year. They are savoured with special relish at the coffee hour, when several different sorts might be sampled – more often than not with a healthy dollop of unsweetened whipped cream (or *Schlag*, as the Austrians call it). For the coffee ritual, it is the custom to dress in one's finery and go to one of the more prominent cafés in town (that is, one which serves good cakes and pastries), which are generally crowded by 4 o'clock.

On Sunday and on any holiday or special occasion, such as birthdays, first communion or confirmation, a special cake or pastry is usually baked and eaten by the family at home.

Multi-tiered wedding cakes as we know them in the English-speaking world are now found only occasionally in German cookery books and rarely seen at weddings. For weddings in Switzerland and Germany, it is customary to buy the most distinctive cake produced by the best bakery in town. In Austria, especially, home bakers often produce elaborate cakes (generally from a special recipe passed down through the family) for country wedding feasts and for Christmas.

In selecting the recipes for this chapter, I have chosen a cross-section of cakes and pastries which includes a few unusual Christmas and New Year specialities, among them Tannenzapfen (pine cone cake) and Preiselbeerenschaumtorte (lingonberry meringue cake). Otherwise, most of these recipes can be baked at any time of year for a special treat, with the exception of a few seasonal fruit tarts and strudels which are of necessity limited to the late summer.

While one cake in this section requires a special mould – Rehrücken, 'saddle of venison' cake – most can be baked in ordinary baking tins or tart tins.

There are numerous complicated preparations in this chapter, among them Zuger Kirschtorte (Zug kirsch cake), Kardinalschnitten ('cardinal' slices), Maroniobersschnitten (chestnut cream slices) and Preiselbeerenschaumtorte. Because they are not easy to make, I have purposely elaborated on the recipes as much as possible so that, despite the time they take to make, they can be produced successfully. For an easier selection, begin with Schönbrunnertorte (chocolate almond cake), Käsekuchen (cheesecake) and Apfelstreuselkuchen (apple crumble cake).

Before using these recipes you might find it useful to look again at the Baking Tips in the opening section of this book. It covers such subjects as lining cake tins and using piping bags. It is important, especially with cakes, to organize all your equipment in advance, pre-weigh your ingredients and preheat your oven. Storing and freezing rules vary in some instances, but for most cakes, unless otherwise stated, these items can be made in advance and kept, loosely covered, in the refrigerator for four to five days or frozen for up to three months. If freezing, allow the cake to freeze overnight before wrapping it carefully in foil, making sure the foil doesn't touch any of the decorations.

SCHÖNBRUNNERTORTE

Schönbrunn Cake

Named after the beautiful summer palace located on the outskirts of Vienna, Schönbrunnertorte is a delicious, flourless chocolate almond cake which is split in half, glazed with redcurrant jelly, and sandwiched together and covered with chocolate butter cream. Much easier to make than most Viennese tortes, it freezes well (for up to three months) or can be refrigerated for up to four days.

softened butter to grease the tin

Cake

3 oz (75g) dark semi-sweet
 chocolate, broken in pieces
4 large egg yolks
4 oz (125g) castor sugar

4½ oz (140g) blanched almonds,
 finely ground (p. 27)
4 large egg whites
pinch of salt

Glaze

8 oz (225g) redcurrant jelly

Icing

4 oz (125g) dark, semi-sweet
   chocolate, broken in pieces
5 oz (150g) butter, softened
4 oz (125g) icing sugar, sifted
1 large egg, lightly beaten
1 tbsp rum

cocoa powder, to finish (optional)
lightly whipped cream, to serve

Equipment

8 inch (20cm) hinged cake tin

Butter the cake tin well with softened butter. Cut out a piece of greaseproof or parchment paper that fits the bottom of the tin perfectly. Butter the paper well. Flour the bottom and sides of the tin, shaking out the excess. Set the tin aside.

Melt the broken chocolate in a double boiler or in a heatproof soup plate or shallow bowl placed over a saucepan filled with 2 inches (5cm) of boiling water. Stir occasionally until the chocolate has melted. Remove from the heat and allow the chocolate to cool.

Preheat the oven to 350°F (180°C/gas 4). Beat the egg yolks and sugar together with a wooden spoon until pale and creamy. Beat in the cooled melted chocolate and finely ground almonds. Using an electric mixer, beat the egg whites with a pinch of salt, beginning on moderate speed until they are frothy. Increase the speed and beat until they are stiff, scraping down the sides of the bowl several times. Stir one-quarter of the stiffly beaten egg whites into the chocolate mixture to lighten it. Pour this mixture on to the remaining egg whites and fold them in carefully with a large metal spoon until no streaks of white remain. Spoon the batter into the prepared cake tin, smoothing it evenly. Bake in the oven until the cake is firm to the touch and has begun shrinking away from the sides of the tin – 30 to 45 minutes. Loosen the cake from the sides of the tin with a knife. Turn out on to a cake rack and remove the piece of paper from the bottom. Allow to cool completely. When cool, use a serrated knife to slice the cake across in half.

For the glaze, heat the redcurrant jelly with 1 tsp of water, stirring continually until it comes to the boil. Strain through a sieve into another bowl or pan. Brush the top of the cake first with the warm glaze; then brush the surface of the bottom half of the cake with the glaze.

For the icing, melt the broken chocolate pieces as before and allow them to cool. Cream the softened butter together with the sifted icing sugar. Beat for at least 5 minutes to dissolve the sugar. Beat in the melted chocolate. Scraping down the sides of the bowl, beat for another 2 minutes. Add the lightly beaten egg and 1 tbsp of rum and beat until smooth. Using a metal spatula, spread one-third of the butter cream on the bottom layer. Cover with the top layer. Spread the top and sides with the remaining butter cream. Dip the spatula in hot water and run it over the top and sides of the cake, redipping it when necessary, to produce a smooth surface. Dust the top of the cake with sifted cocoa powder.

Refrigerate the cake for at least three hours to firm the butter cream before serving. Serve with lightly whipped cream.

FRANKFURTER KRANZ

Rum and Praline Cake

When I first lived in Frankfurt, the old Café Kranzler was still the most fashionable place to meet for a slice of *Kuchen*, a pre-dinner glass of *Sekt* (German champagne), or a delicate post-theatre supper of *Kalbslendchen* (veal fillet) or *Königinpastetchen* (vol-au-vent filled with creamed chicken, tongue and mushrooms). With the construction of Frankfurt's underground went the refined dining area of the old Kranzler. Fortunately, the baking expertise of the Kranzler was preserved, though its walls were not.

On a recent trip, I was delighted to find their doors open once again and their Frankfurter Kranz, my favourite indulgence in that establishment, as delicious as before. A traditional Frankfurt speciality saved for special occasions, Frankfurter Kranz consists of a butter-rich cake baked in a round tin, split in layers which are laced with rum, sandwiched and covered with butter cream and sprinkled with crunchy almond brittle (praline or *Krokant*).

It is best to bake the cake at least a day before you plan to eat it. Once it has been sandwiched and covered with butter cream, it should be refrigerated for at least four hours to firm the butter cream and make it easier to cut. For best appearance, use a plain 9 inch (23cm) round tin or savarin mould rather than a fluted Bundt tin.

2 oz (50g) melted butter, to grease the tin

Cake

6 oz (175g) butter, softened
6½oz (190g) castor sugar
grated rind of 1 lemon
6 large eggs
3½ oz (100g) plain flour
2½ oz (65g) cornflour
1 tbsp baking powder

Syrup

1 tbsp sugar
4 fl oz (125ml) rum

Butter cream

1 lb (450g) butter, softened
10½ oz (315g) icing sugar, sifted
4 large egg yolks
3 tbsp rum

almond brittle (Krokant)

6½ oz (185g) granulated sugar
5½ oz (165g) whole blanched almonds
oil for the baking sheet

glacé cherries, halved, to finish

Equipment

9 inch (23cm) plain round tin, piping
    bag with small or medium star
    nozzle

Prepare a 9 inch (23cm) plain round tin by placing it in the freezer for 15 minutes or in the refrigerator for 20 minutes. While it is chilling, melt 2 oz (50g) of the butter and allow it to cool. Remove the chilled tin and, using a pastry brush, coat the entire inner surface thoroughly with melted butter. Chill for another 10 minutes. Repeat with a second coating of butter. Dust the inside with flour (ideally using a flour dredger). Tip the tin around to coat it thoroughly. Tap out the excess. Set the tin aside.

Preheat the oven to 350°F (180°C/gas 4). For the cake, using an electric mixer, cream the butter, sugar and grated lemon rind together until the mixture is fluffy and light in colour. Beat in the eggs one by one, beating well after each one before adding the next. Scrape down the beaters. Sift the flour, cornflour and baking powder together on to a piece of paper. Sift them a second time on to the butter mixture. Using a large metal spoon, fold the flour carefully into the butter until no visible pockets of flour remain. Spoon the mixture evenly into the prepared tin, smoothing it to make it even. Tap the tin firmly several times on the counter to remove any air pockets.

Bake in the middle of the oven until the cake has risen, is firm to the touch and has begun to pull away slightly from the sides of the tin – approximately 40 minutes. Remove the cake from the oven and allow it to rest for 10 minutes. Loosen the cake from the sides of the tin with a knife. Holding a wire rack firmly against the top of the tin, quickly reverse the cake on to the rack to unmould it. Allow to cool to room temperature. If time allows, wait eight hours or more before slicing the cake. Using a serrated knife, cut the cake across in thirds to make three even layers.

For the syrup, boil 2 fl oz (60ml) water with the sugar for about 30 seconds, stirring until the sugar has dissolved. Remove the pan from the heat and add the rum, mixing it well.

Place the bottom layer of the cake on a serving plate. Pour out half of the syrup mixture into a cup and spoon it slowly and evenly over the bottom of the cake. Reserve the remaining syrup.

Make the *Krokant*. Oil a baking sheet with vegetable oil and set it aside. Place the sugar in a heavy pan and cook over a medium heat, stirring, until the sugar has completely melted. Once it has melted, turn the pan from side to side a few times until the liquid is pale yellow. Add the whole blanched almonds, stirring them to coat them well. Continue stirring until the sugar has turned a caramel colour and the nuts have begun to crackle and give off an aroma. Immediately pour the mixture on to the oiled baking sheet, spreading it out in a thin layer using two forks. Allow it to harden and cool at room temperature. When it is cool, break the *Krokant* into small pieces and pulverize it in a liquidizer or crush it with a mortar and pestle. Spread it out on a piece of aluminium foil and set aside.

For the butter cream, using an electric mixer beat the butter until creamy. Gradually beat in the sifted icing sugar and continue to beat for at least 8 minutes to dissolve the sugar. Add the egg yolks, one at a time, beating well after each addition. Finally add the rum and beat for another minute. You will need about one-third of the butter cream to fill the layers. Spread about one-sixth of the butter cream on the rum-soaked bottom layer of the cake, spreading it evenly with a metal spatula. Place the second cake layer on top. Sprinkle this layer with the remaining rum syrup, spooning it slowly and evenly over the surface. Spread evenly with an equal amount of butter cream. Cover with the top layer. Spoon about 8 tbsp of butter cream into a piping bag fitted with a small or medium star nozzle. Set it aside. Use the remaining butter cream to coat the top and sides of the cake completely. Smooth the icing with a metal spatula dipped in hot water. Sprinkle the reserved pulverized *Krokant* over the top and sides of the cake, pressing it on gently with your hands. Using a dry pastry brush, brush off any *Krokant* that has fallen on the rim of the plate and sprinkle it on top of the cake. Take a small piece of paper towel, twist it and moisten the end. Carefully lower it into the centre hole to pick up any *Krokant* that has fallen on to the plate. Using the butter cream in the piping bag, pipe eight tiny rosettes (or as many as you want) at even intervals on top of the cake. If desired, garnish each rosette with a halved glacé cherry or just a sliver of cherry. Refrigerate for at least four hours to firm the butter cream before slicing.

ZUGER KIRSCHTORTE

Zug Kirsch Cake

Zug may be the smallest canton in Switzerland, but its reputation with pastry-lovers looms large. Its speciality, Zuger Kirschtorte, is a multi-layered pale pink creation of almond meringue, kirsch-soaked sponge and kirsch-flavoured butter cream which together produce an unusual contrast of brittle and moist textures. It is one of Switzerland's greatest cakes.

Inspired by the famous Zug kirsch – a clear unsweetened schnapps distilled from the abundance of special cherries harvested there – it is found in bakery shops throughout Switzerland and is distinguished by the simple presentation typical of Swiss baking: toasted almonds round the sides, a single halved cherry in the centre, the pale pink icing dusted with icing sugar and delicately cross-hatched in a diamond pattern. Its simple appearance, however, is deceptive, as it requires two different cake mixtures and is time-consuming to prepare. However, for a special holiday or birthday, it is well worth the effort. It is best made at least a day ahead to allow the butter cream to firm.

Japonais (almond meringue) layers

2 oz (50g) blanched almonds,
    finely ground (p. 27)
3 large egg whites
2½ oz (65g) castor sugar
1 tbsp plus 1 tsp plain flour, sifted

Sponge

2 oz (50g) plain flour
2 tbsp cornflour
pinch salt
2 large eggs
2¾ oz (70g) castor sugar

Kirsch butter cream

9 oz (250g) butter, softened
5 oz (150g) icing sugar, sifted
2 tbsp kirsch, or to taste
2 egg yolks
2 to 3 drops red food colouring

Syrup

3 tbsp kirsch
1 tbsp icing sugar

Decoration

6 oz (175g) flaked almonds,
  toasted on a baking sheet
  in a hot oven
  and coarsely chopped
1 glacé cherry, halved

Equipment

three 9 inch (23cm) cake tins

Butter three 9 inch (23cm) cake tins. Line the bottoms with a round of greaseproof or parchment paper cut just to fit. Butter the paper. Dust the tins with flour, shaking out the excess. Set aside.

Preheat the oven to 325°F (170°C/gas 3). Make the Japonais (meringue) layers. Grind the almonds in a liquidizer. Set aside. Make the meringue mixture. Beat the egg whites until half stiff using an electric mixer at medium high speed. The egg whites should just hold their shape but not be dry. Beat in the sugar by the tablespoon, beating for at least 20 seconds between each. When all the sugar has been added, beat for another 2 minutes. Add the ground almonds and sifted flour to the meringue. Fold them in carefully with a large metal spoon. Divide the mixture evenly between two prepared cake tins. Bake on the second lowest rack of the oven, with the handle of a wooden spoon propped inside the oven door to keep it slightly ajar, until golden and dry – 40 to 50 minutes. If the bottom of the meringue layers is still moist, remove from the pan, turn upside down, take off the paper, and return to the oven until dry – about 5 minutes. Set aside on a wire rack to cool.

Make the sponge. Preheat the oven to 350°F (180°C/gas 4). Choose a china or glass bowl that will just rest in a saucepan. Pour 2 inches (5cm) of water into the saucepan and bring to the boil. Sift the two flours and salt on to paper. Remove the saucepan from the heat. Place the mixing bowl over the saucepan and add the eggs and the sugar, beating them together with an electric mixer or whisk until the mixture is thick and mousse-like – about 3 minutes with an electric mixer. When ready, the mixture trailed from the beater will hold the shape of the letter M for 3 seconds. Check frequently to prevent over-beating. As soon as it reaches the correct consistency, sift the flour for the second time on to the egg mixture. Fold in carefully with a metal spoon, turning the bowl slightly each time, until no pockets of flour can be seen. Pour into the prepared cake tin. Tap the tin to remove any air bubbles. Bake in the middle of the oven for 15 to 20 minutes, or until golden and the cake has begun to shrink away from the sides of the tin. Loosen the cake from the sides of the tin with a knife. Turn out on to a wire rack to cool, peeling off the paper.

Make the butter cream. Beat the softened butter and icing sugar together until light in colour and creamy – about 4 minutes with an electric mixer. Add the kirsch according to taste, the egg yolks, one at a time, and finally a few drops of red food colouring to tint the icing a pale pink. Beat for at least another 3 minutes to dissolve the sugar completely and to obtain a light creamy icing. Combine the syrup ingredients with 3 tbsp warm water in a small bowl, mixing them well, and set aside.

Assemble the cake. Place four strips of 3 inch (8cm) wide greaseproof paper on a serving plate to form a square slightly larger than the cake. Place one Japonais layer in the middle of the square and spread it with one-quarter of the butter cream mixture. Top with the sponge layer. Prick the sponge with the prongs of a fork. Pour over the syrup mixture, covering the cake evenly. Spread the surface with another quarter of the butter cream. Top with the second Japonais layer, flat side (the bottom side) up. Spread the top and sides of the cake evenly with the remaining butter cream. Warm a metal spatula in hot water and run it across the top of the cake to help spread the icing smoothly.

Coarsely chop the toasted almonds. Press them well into the sides of the cake to cover evenly. Refrigerate the cake for 30 minutes to firm the butter cream slightly. Using a metal spatula dipped in hot water and dried, make diagonal lines on the top of the cake at 1½ inch (4cm) intervals, first in one direction, then in the other, to form a trellis pattern. Re-warm and dry the spatula each time you make a mark, barely pressing it into the icing. Dust the top of the cake with sifted icing sugar. Place a halved glacé cherry in the centre. Remove the paper strips carefully and, using a dry pastry brush, dust off any fallen nuts or sugar.

Refrigerate for at least two hours or overnight. If desired, the cake can be frozen for up to three months, in which case you should again dust the top with icing sugar before serving.

REHRÜCKEN
'Saddle of Venison' Cake

It is not surprising that the Austrians, who are especially fond of game and adept in its preparation, have chosen to honour one of the most popular dishes, saddle of venison, with a chocolate cake made in a special tin shaped like this cut of meat and studded with slivered almonds to simulate the *Speck* (bacon fat) which is used to lard the meat before it is roasted. The cake tin, which resembles a half cylinder with ridges along either side, is generally about a foot long and is sold in many specialist cookery shops outside Austria and Germany. However, if you cannot obtain one, use a 12 by 4 inch (30 by 10cm) loaf tin instead. In this case, eliminate the slivered almond decoration and substitute a row of whole blanched almonds down either side, or a single row of blanched almonds down the centre. The cake itself, made with butter, chocolate, eggs and ground almonds, is flourless and quite delicious – well worth making with or without a Rehrücken tin.

This is an especially festive cake to serve at a dinner party in the autumn when game is in season. It can be made in advance and refrigerated, loosely covered with aluminium foil, for three or four days, or it can be frozen, loosely covered with aluminium foil, for a month or more.

2 oz butter, melted, to grease the tin

Cake

4 oz (125g) dark, semi-sweet chocolate, broken in pieces
5 oz (150g) butter, softened
3 oz (75g) castor sugar
8 large egg yolks
5½ oz (165g) unblanched almonds, finely ground (p. 27)
2½ oz (65g) very fine dried breadcrumbs (pressed through a wire sieve)
8 large egg whites
pinch of salt
2½ oz (65g) castor sugar

Glaze

12 oz (350g) redcurrant jelly

Chocolate icing

8 oz (225g) dark, semi-sweet chocolate, broken in pieces
8 fl oz (230ml) whipping cream
6 oz (175g) slivered almonds, or
2 oz (50g) whole blanched almonds, to finish

Equipment

12 inch (30cm) Rehrücken tin or 12 by 4 inch (30 by 10cm) loaf tin

Place the Rehrücken tin in the freezer for 15 minutes or the refrigerator for 20. Using a pastry brush, brush the chilled tin well with melted butter. Chill and brush a second time, covering all the ridges well. Dust it with granulated sugar and flour, shaking out the excess. If using a loaf tin, prepare it in the same way, lining the bottom with a piece of buttered greaseproof or parchment paper before sugaring and flouring. Set aside.

Melt the broken chocolate in a double boiler or in a heatproof soup plate or shallow bowl placed over a saucepan filled with 2 inches (5cm) of boiling water, stirring occasionally until the chocolate has melted. Remove the chocolate from the heat and allow to cool.

Using an electric mixer, beat the butter until it is creamy. Add the cooled chocolate and 3 oz (75g) of castor sugar and beat the mixture for 2 or 3 minutes until it is smooth. Beat in the egg yolks, one at a time, beating well between each addition. Scrape down the beaters, wash and dry them well for beating the egg whites. Stir in the sieved breadcrumbs and finely ground almonds with a spoon.

Preheat the oven to 350°F (180°C/gas 4). Using an electric mixer at medium high speed, beat the egg whites with a pinch of salt until they are half stiff. The egg whites should just hold their shape but not be dry. Beat in the 2½ oz (65g) of castor sugar by the tablespoon, beating for at least 20 seconds between each. When all the sugar has been added, beat for a further 2 minutes. Using a large metal spoon, fold the stiffly beaten egg whites into the chocolate mixture until no streaks of white are visible. Spoon the cake mixture evenly down the length of the prepared cake tin, smoothing it into the corners and evening the top with a spatula. Tap the tin firmly on the counter several times to remove any air bubbles.

Bake in the middle of the oven until the cake is golden, springs back to the touch and has begun to shrink away from the sides of the tin – approximately 30 minutes. Remove the cake from the oven and allow it to cool for 5 minutes. Don't worry if it sinks slightly. Turn the cake on to a wire rack and allow it to finish cooling. If you are using a loaf tin, remove the piece of paper from the bottom of the cake. Place the wire rack on a clean work surface.

For the redcurrant jelly glaze, heat the jelly in a saucepan with 1 tsp of water, stirring until the jelly comes to the boil. Remove the pan from the heat at once and strain the jelly through a sieve into a bowl. The cake can be glazed either while it is still warm or after it has cooled. Using a pastry brush, brush the entire surface of the cake evenly with the glaze.

To make the icing, melt the broken pieces of chocolate in a saucepan with the cream, stirring continually. Heat until the chocolate has completely melted. Remove the pan from the heat and, stirring occasionally, let it cool to lukewarm. If you wish to accelerate the cooling process, place the saucepan in a bowl or sink filled with cold water which comes two-thirds of the way up the sides of the pan. Stir the icing continually with a wooden spoon until it is lukewarm. (Stir rather than beat or whisk the icing which will lighten its colour.) If the icing is too thick to pour smoothly, add 1 to 2 tbsp warm water, beating it in well. When it is the right temperature and consistency, pour the icing down the centre of the cake, tilting the cake so that the icing runs down the sides. Use a pastry brush dipped in the icing to coat the ends and any part of the cake that is already coated with the icing. Scrape up any icing that has fallen through the wire rack. Place it in a small container and freeze it to be used at a later date. Before the icing has completely set, stud the cake with slivered almonds (if made in a Rehrücken tin). Pressing the almonds upright into the icing, place them in rows about 1 inch (2·5cm) (use about eight slivered almonds per row) at even intervals on the sides and top of the cake. Let the cake cool completely before serving or refrigerate until needed. It can be served with lightly whipped cream.

KARDINALSCHNITTEN
'Cardinal' Slices

Makes 8 to 9 slices

This unusual Viennese cake, made of alternating rows of sponge and meringue, is baked in two layers in a long rectangular shape, then sandwiched with a coffee flavoured whipped cream, or in summer with fresh fruit and whipped cream, before it is cut into finger-width slices. It needs a more complicated preparation than some cakes and is thus best attempted by those with some baking experience. The delicate marriage of textures makes it a favourite dessert for any special dinner. If you use a coffee cream filling, it can be made and filled up to eight hours in advance; and if you are using a fresh fruit and whipped cream filling, the cake layers can be made the day before and filled no more than four hours before it is to be served. Refrigerate until it is needed.

Meringue

4 large egg whites
4¼ oz (130g) castor sugar

Sponge mixture

2 large eggs
3 large egg yolks
2¼ oz (55g) castor sugar
1 tsp vanilla extract
3 oz (75g) plain flour

Filling A (Coffee-flavoured whipped cream)

2 tsp instant coffee granules
12 fl oz (340ml) whipping cream
3 tbsp icing sugar, sifted

Filling B (Whipped cream and fresh berries)

1 pint (575ml) fresh raspberries, blueberries or strawberries, the latter halved or quartered, according to size
4–5 tbsp castor sugar, or to taste
12 fl oz (340ml) whipping cream
sifted icing sugar, to finish

Equipment

1 large baking sheet 13 by 15 inches (33 by 37·5cm) or 2 baking sheets at least 13 inches (33cm) long
piping bag with ¾ inch (2cm) plain nozzle

Butter and flour the baking sheet(s) and set aside. Preheat the oven to 325°F (170°C/gas 3).

For the meringue, beat the egg whites with an electric mixer on a moderately low speed until frothy. Increase the speed and beat until half stiff. The egg whites should softly hold their shape but not be dry. Begin beating in the sugar, a tablespoon at a time, beating for at least 20 seconds between each. When all the sugar has been added, beat the meringue for 3 or 4 minutes longer until the mixture is smooth and glossy. Spoon the meringue into a piping bag fitted with a plain ¾ inch (2cm) nozzle and set aside.

For the sponge mixture, sift the flour once on to a piece of paper and set aside. Choose a crockery or glass mixing bowl that will fit into a saucepan with its base resting well above the bottom of the pan. Bring 2 inches (5cm) of water to the boil in the saucepan and remove the pan from the heat. Set the bowl over the pan, add the eggs and sugar to it and use an electric mixer or whisk to beat the mixture rapidly until it is thick and mousse-like – about 4 minutes. To test the consistency, use the beater to lift a little of the beaten eggs and sugar, then trail the shape of the letter M over the mixture in the bowl. If the shape holds for 3 seconds, the mixture is sufficiently beaten. If the shape dissolves, beat for a further 20 seconds, then test again. Remove the bowl from the pan and beat in the vanilla, beating for 10 seconds. Sift the flour a second time directly on to the whisked egg mixture. Using a metal spoon, fold in the flour carefully, just sufficiently to break up any pockets of flour.

Using a large spoon and a metal spatula, spread half of the sponge mixture on the baking sheet in an even rectangle, approximately 6 by 11 inches (16 by 28cm), not quite reaching the edge of the baking sheet since it will expand slightly. If you are using one large baking sheet, leave space on for the second rectangle. Spread out a second rectangle the same as the first. Smooth and even them with the spatula.

Twist the top of the piping bag tightly and pipe a cylinder of meringue down the centre of each sponge rectangle. Pipe a matching border down each edge on top of (not on the side of) the sponge rectangles. There should be three even ridges of meringue resting on the rectangles. Dust the sponge and meringue well with sifted icing sugar. Bake in the oven, on the rack below centre. If the oven is not big enough to hold two baking sheets at the same level, bake for 6 to 7 minutes, one sheet on the rack below, until the top sheet begins to colour lightly. Reverse the baking sheets. Bake until the sponge mixture is firm – approximately 12 to 14 minutes in all. The meringue should be allowed barely to colour. Immediately after removing from the oven, loosen the bottom of each sponge with a metal spatula to prevent it from sticking. Allow to cool on the baking sheet(s). Cut one layer, which will be the top, across in 1¼ inch (3cm) slices while still warm.

When the cake has cooled completely, make the filling. If you are using Filling A, dissolve the coffee granules in the 1½ tbsp boiling water. Whip the cream with chilled beaters until almost stiff. Add the icing sugar and coffee mixture and beat until stiff. Spread the cream evenly along the length of the uncut sponge base.

If you are using Filling B, sprinkle the sugar over the berries and crush them slightly. Add more sugar to taste. Whip the cream with chilled beaters until stiff. Fold the berries into the cream. Spread the fruit cream evenly along the length of the uncut sponge base.

Using a wide spatula, carefully lift and arrange the cut sponge layer on top. Cut two strips of parchment or greaseproof paper 1½ inches (4cm) wide and several inches longer than the cake. Place them lengthwise at intervals just inside the outside ridges of meringue. Dust the top of the cake with icing sugar. Remove the paper strips carefully. Refrigerate until serving time, at least two hours.

SACHERTORTE

Reputedly the only cake in the world that was ever the subject of a court case, this famous Viennese creation – a rich chocolate sponge cake glazed in apricot and iced in bittersweet chocolate – was first produced in 1832 by Franz Sacher, chef to Metternich. The court issue arose when Demel's, Vienna's most famous pastry shop, and the Sacher Hotel, owned by a branch of the same Sacher family, contested who had the right to call their product the 'genuine' (*echt*) Sachertorte. Demel's case was based on the fact that the shop had bought the right to produce the 'genuine' Sachertorte, stamped with an official seal of bittersweet chocolate, from Edouard Sacher, the grandson of the creator and the last scion of the dynasty. The Hotel Sacher based their case on the family connection with the cake's creator. The most discernible difference between the versions from the two establishments was in the placing of the apricot jam: should it be glazed on top of the cake and then covered with icing, as in Demel's version; or should the cake be split in two and the jam spread between the layers, as in the Hotel Sacher's version? Seven years, and no doubt many samplings later, the courts decided in favour of the Hotel Sacher. Demel's, however, did not sit quietly by. They announced they would simply market their *Torte* as the Ur-Sachertorte, the very first version.

No doubt both establishments have a few tricks that are never disclosed in recipes. The recipe below, however, is certainly closer to the real thing than most Sachertortes I have sampled in other countries. Because Demel's is probably my favourite pastry shop in the world, I have taken the liberty of going against the courts and *not* splitting my cake into two layers. However, if you feel otherwise inclined, you can move your apricot jam from the top of the cake to the middle.

However, from a baker's standpoint apricot glaze has a function other than flavouring. When on top it provides a glassy, smooth surface on which to put the icing. This is especially important in the case of Sachertorte, a cake with a smooth surface and well rounded edges, since the warm icing, worked to exactly the right temperature and consistency, must flow smoothly and rapidly over the cake to give it its flawless chocolate covering. To produce slightly rounded edges on the cake, Viennese bakers' manuals recommend using a special cake tin with rounded edges manufactured specially for the purpose. I have a copper casserole which does this admirably. However, since few people are likely to have such a pan, glazing the tops, edges and sides of the cake well with the hot strained jam helps to produce the rounded edge.

To ensure that the icing is well set, allow it to cool to room temperature first, then leave it overnight in a cool place or not too cold refrigerator before slicing it. In Vienna, it is generally served with a dollop of unsweetened whipped cream which cuts the sweetness and marries wonderfully with the rich chocolate cake.

Sachertorte mixture

6 oz (175g) dark, semi-sweet
   chocolate, broken in pieces
5 oz (150g) butter, softened
4 oz (125g) icing sugar, sifted
6 large egg yolks
6 large egg whites
4 oz (125g) castor sugar
4½ oz (140g) plain flour

Glaze

1 lb (450g) apricot jam
1 tbsp lemon juice

Icing

10 oz (300g) sugar
8 oz (225g) dark, semi-sweet
   chocolate, broken in pieces

12 fl oz (340ml) lightly whipped
   cream, to serve

Equipment

9 inch (23cm) hinged cake tin or
   special cake tin with rounded
   edges (see above)
jam thermometer

Butter the cake tin well with softened butter. Line it with a round of greaseproof or parchment paper that fits perfectly in the bottom. Butter the paper and dust the tin well with flour, shaking out the excess. Set aside.

Place the broken chocolate pieces in a double boiler or in a heat proof soup plate or shallow bowl over a saucepan containing 2 inches (5cm) of simmering water, stirring the chocolate occasionally until it has melted. Remove from the saucepan and allow the chocolate to cool.

Preheat the oven to 350°F (180°C/gas 4). Using an electric mixer, cream the butter with the icing sugar until light in colour – about 2 to 3 minutes. Beat in the egg yolks, one by one, beating well between each. Beat the egg whites until half stiff. They should softly hold their shape but not be dry. Beat in the sugar by the tablespoon, beating for about 20 seconds between each. When all the sugar has been added, beat for a further 2 or 3 minutes to produce a glossy meringue. Using a large metal spoon, fold the meringue into the butter mixture. Sift the flour on to a piece of paper. Sift it a second time on to the butter mixture. Using a large metal spoon, fold it in carefully but thoroughly until no pockets of flour can be seen and the egg whites are well blended. Spoon the mixture into the prepared cake tin, smoothing the mixture evenly into the corners of the tin. Tap the tin several times on the counter to knock out any air pockets.

Bake in the middle of the oven until the cake is firm to the touch and has begun to shrink away from the sides of the tin – approximately 50 minutes. Loosen the cake from the sides of the tin with a knife. Turn the cake on to a wire rack to cool and remove the paper from the bottom.

When the cake is cool, heat the apricot jam with 1 tbsp of lemon juice and allow to boil for 30 seconds. Strain the jam through a sieve, pressing well against the apricot pieces. Using a pastry brush, brush the top, edges and sides of the cake thoroughly and evenly with the apricot glaze, making sure the cake is completely covered. Allow the glaze to cool and set.

Meanwhile, make the icing. Heat the sugar and chocolate, with 4 fl oz (125ml) water in a heavy saucepan, stirring constantly until the mixture comes to the boil. Stop stirring. Attach a jam thermometer to the side of the pan and use a wet pastry brush to brush down any sugar crystals that cling to the sides of the pan. When the mixture reaches 225°F (105°C), remove the pan from the heat. Stir the icing with a wooden spoon constantly, bringing the hot chocolate up from the bottom to help cool the mixture evenly. After stirring for approximately 1 minute, test the icing. Pour a small amount on to a marble slab or clean work surface and work it with a metal scraper or spatula. When ready it will set quickly with a smooth surface. If it takes more than a few seconds to set, keep stirring to cool the icing a little more and test again. If the icing appears granular, it has been overheated. To correct, add a few tablespoons of boiling water to the icing and return it to the heat briefly until the mixture is boiling and smooth. Then proceed as before. When the icing has reached the correct temperature, place the wire rack with the cake over a marble slab or clean work surface. Pour all the icing at once directly on to the centre of the cake, letting it flow in a steady stream and tilting the cake quickly if necessary to coax the icing over an uncovered side. You must work quickly before the icing sets. Once the icing has been poured on the cake, do not try to pour any remaining icing on a second time or use a brush or spatula to smooth it. This will mar the glassy surface of the icing which will have already begun to set. Allow the cake to rest until the icing has dried completely. Scrape up any icing that has overflowed and freeze (it will keep for up to three months; dilute with a little water when reheating it). Store the cake in a cool place overnight before slicing. It keeps well for up to five days. Serve with a bowl of unsweetened lightly whipped cream passed separately.

MARONIOBERSSCHNITTEN

Chestnut Cream Slices

In all the German-speaking countries and many others too in winter, street vendors with charcoal-fired braziers attract customers with the familiar cry, '*Heisse Maroni!*', 'Hot chestnuts'.

In both Austria and Switzerland, these same chestnuts make their way into many delicious winter desserts. The recipe below is a Viennese speciality which combines layers of delicious Sachertorte mixture cut in four strips, partially soaked in rum syrup, sandwiched with chocolate cream, covered with whipped cream (*Obers*) and heavily sprinkled with sieved sweetened chestnut purée (Kastanienreis).

This recipe makes two two-layered rectangular cakes or, if a more elaborate cake is desired, one four-layered cake, using the variation noted at the end of the recipe. The cake and chocolate cream (Parisercreme) can be made and assembled with syrup two or three days in advance. However, for the best appearance, it is advisable to finish the cake with whipped cream and chestnut purée on the day it is to be served, and then to chill it for several hours.

1 recipe Sachertorte mixture (p. 186)

Parisercreme

8 fl oz (230ml) whipping cream
8 oz (225g) dark, semi-sweet
   chocolate, broken in pieces

Rum syrup

2 oz (50g) sugar
3 fl oz (100ml) rum

To finish

1 pint (575ml) whipping cream
4 tbsp icing sugar, sifted
1 tsp vanilla extract

1 pint (575ml) sieved Kastanienreis,
   measured after it has been sieved
   (p. 191)

Equipment

1 baking sheet with sides, 10 by
   13 inches (25 by 33cm)
piping bag with rosette nozzle

Prepare the baking sheet by buttering it well. Cut out a piece of greaseproof or parchment paper 4 inches (10cm) larger than the baking sheet and make a 3 inch (8cm) diagonal cut at each corner. Place on the baking sheet, adjusting the corners so the paper stands up on the sides and the corners overlap neatly. If the sides of the pan are less than 2 inches (5cm) high, clip the overlapping corner points of paper with paper clips. This will secure the corners so that the sides stand up straight and high enough to hold the mixture. Butter and flour the paper, tapping out the excess flour.

Prepare the Sachertorte mixture, following the recipe on p. 186. Preheat the oven to 350°F (180°C/gas 4). Pour the batter on to the prepared baking sheet, easing it into the corners and smoothing it with a metal spatula. Bake in the oven until the cake springs back to the touch – approximately 20 minutes. Prepare a clean towel or a sheet of aluminium foil slightly longer than the baking sheet and sprinkled with sugar. When the cake is done, turn it out quickly on to the prepared towel or foil. When cool, cut off the crusty edges. Cut the cake across in four even strips, approximately 3 inches (8cm) wide. (This recipe will make two two-layered cakes.) Place two strips down on a flat surface to serve as bases.

Make the Parisercreme filling. Heat the cream in a saucepan with the pieces of chocolate and stir over a low heat until the chocolate has melted. Place the saucepan in a pan of cold water and stir until cool, changing the water and adding ice cubes to speed up the process. Using an electric mixer, beat the cream until it is thick enough to spread. Divide the cream and spread evenly on the two cake bases. Place a second layer of cake on top of each base. Prick the top layers with the prongs of a fork.

Make the rum syrup. Heat the sugar in 3 fl oz (100ml) water and boil until the sugar has dissolved. Off the heat, add the rum. Pour the mixture over the top cake layers slowly, dividing it evenly between both. If poured slowly, they should absorb it all. Use a metal spatula to smooth the chocolate cream filling on the sides if it isn't even with the cake layers.

Beat the whipping cream until it begins to thicken. Gradually beat in the sifted icing sugar until the cream is thick enough to hold its shape if piped. Set aside a cup of the whipped cream and spoon it into a piping bag fitted with a star nozzle. Refrigerate until needed. Spread the remaining cream evenly over the sides and top of each cake, leaving the ends free.

Make the Kastanienreis as directed in the recipe on p. 191. Press the mixture, a small amount at a time, through a coarse metal sieve over a piece of greaseproof paper using a wooden spoon. Sprinkle it lavishly over the cream, both top and sides. Using the cream in the piping bag, pipe small single rosettes down the centre of the cake – there should be one for each slice, estimating each slice to be approximately 1¼ inches (3cm) thick. If any Kastanienreis is left over, it can be frozen and used for decoration when needed.

VARIATION

If desired you can make a four-layered cake using the same quantities. Spread the chocolate cream between three layers – they will be slightly thinner layers – and soak the second and third layers with rum syrup, leaving the bottom and top as they are. Since you will want to slice this cake more thinly, simply pipe a decorative frill of cream down each side or the centre, rather than attempting to pipe a rosette for each slice.

KASTANIENREIS

Chestnut Purée (for decoration)

2 lb (900g) chestnuts in their shells (makes 1¼ lb/575g shelled)
icing sugar (see below)
rum
vanilla extract

In a saucepan, cover the chestnuts with 3 inches (8cm) water. Simmer, partially covered, for 45 minutes. Remove one chestnut and cut it in half. The flesh should be soft and completely cooked through. If necessary, cook slightly longer – 15 to 30 minutes – and test again. When they are ready, drain the chestnuts. Cut them in half and, with a small spoon, scoop out the flesh into a bowl. Purée the chestnuts in a food processor or food mill. Weigh the chestnut purée. You will need 4 oz (125g) of icing sugar for 1 lb (450g) of purée. Use 2 to 3 tbsp of rum and 1 tsp of vanilla extract per pound.

Once the purée has been weighed, mix it with the sugar, rum and vanilla. If necessary, add a little extra sugar to make a firm mass. Knead together well. To use as a decoration, press it through a coarse wire sieve, a bit at a time, using a wooden spoon. Alternatively, you can press it through a food mill. Use to garnish cakes or as called for in the recipe. If you need only a small portion, sieve only that amount and wrap and freeze the remainder.

NOTE: You can buy tins of puréed chestnuts from most delicatessens. If it is unsweetened, add sugar as above and flavour with 2 to 3 tbsp of rum and 1 tsp of vanilla extract per pound. Proceed as the recipe above.

BAUMKUCHEN

'Tree' Cake

From Vienna to Berlin, a few specialist bakeries exhibit a treat prominently in their windows, tempting *aficionados* to enter and discover whether or not they have, at last, found the definitive Baumkuchen. A metre or more in height before greedy customers have reduced it, Baumkuchen is so called because of the concentric rings, like those of an ageing tree, which appear on a cross-section of the cake, and because of its tree-like shape, characterized by indentations which resemble the shaft of a screw. Unlike most cakes, Baumkuchen is grilled, not baked, on a rotating rod which turns horizontally in front of a red-hot grill plate. Each time a coating caramelizes, the baker applies a new layer of rich mixture – the process which produces the concentric rings. When the mixture runs out, he presses a long wooden 'comb' into the soft 'tree', giving it the characteristic indentations, before glazing it first with apricot and then with a clear or chocolate icing. It is then stood on end and proudly transferred to the baker's window.

A typical recipe in a bakers' manual calls for, in addition to flavourings: 4½ lb butter; 48 egg yolks; 56 egg whites; 4 lb sugar; 1 lb ground almonds; 2 lb 10 oz mixed cornflour and plain flour. For anyone familiar with baking, it is obvious that the proportion of flour to butter, eggs and sugar is extremely low – accounting for the richness of the cake.

Often brought by guests invited to a German or Austrian home, 'rings' of Baumkuchen are a welcome gift. It is generally eaten at the coffee hour, cut in paper-thin slices, though there is no need to confine its consumption to 4 o'clock in the afternoon.

Unfortunately it is impossible to duplicate this great cake in all its glory at home, but the following recipe from Vienna applies a similar technique and mixture to a baking-tin version which can be made using a conventional grill.

BAUMKUCHENSCHNITTEN

'Tree' Cake Squares

※※✿※

Makes about 100 slices

This home-baked version of Baumkuchen is made layer upon layer in a square cake tin under a hot grill. Then it is cut into narrow strips, glazed with chocolate and cut again into bite-sized pieces. It is perfect for a special after-dinner treat with coffee or as part of a tea-time selection.

Base ingredients

7 oz (200g) butter, softened
   and cut in pieces
5½ oz (165g) marzipan, broken
   in pieces
3½ oz (100g) icing sugar, sifted
3 oz (75g) cornflour, sifted
1 tsp vanilla extract
pinch of salt
grated rind of 1 lemon
6 large egg yolks

Additions

6 large egg whites
4 oz (125g) sugar
3 oz (75g) plain flour

To finish

12 oz (350g) dark, semi-sweet
   chocolate, broken in small pieces
2 tsp vegetable oil

Equipment

square metal baking tin 9 by
   9 inches (23 by 23cm)

Butter the baking tin, sides and bottom. Line the bottom with a piece of buttered greaseproof or parchment paper, cut to size. Flour the tin, shaking out the excess flour. Set aside.

If you have a food processor, you can process all the base ingredients in the machine, first creaming the butter and marzipan together well before adding the rest. The egg yolks should be added one at a time. Process until smooth.

Otherwise, cream the butter with an electric beater or wooden spoon until light and smooth. Crumble the marzipan, add to the butter and beat for a few seconds. Add the icing sugar, cornflour, vanilla, salt and lemon rind. Add one egg yolk at a time, beating it in well before adding the next. When all the yolks have been added and the mixture is smooth, set it aside. If you have used an electric beater, wash and dry the beaters well.

In a non-aluminium bowl, beat the egg whites at moderate speed until frothy. Increase the speed and beat until half stiff. The egg whites should just hold their shape but not be dry. Begin adding the 4 oz (125g) of sugar by the tablespoon, beating for at least 20 seconds between each. When all the sugar has been added, beat for a further 2 minutes. Using a large metal spoon or a rubber spatula, fold the meringue into the butter and egg yolk mixture, only partially folding it in. Sift the flour over the top and fold the flour and egg white in carefully until no more pockets of flour and clumps of meringue are evident.

Preheat your grill. Adjust the grill rack to the lowest level. Spoon the thinnest possible layer of mixture into the paper-lined baking tin. Use a pastry brush to brush the mixture into the corners, covering the paper completely. Place under the grill and cook until golden – 1 to 2 minutes, the amount of time depending on the intensity of your grill. Brush the entire surface with another thin coating of mixture, as before, and again place under the grill. Continue in this fashion until all the mixture has been used. Cool the cake completely before loosening the sides with a knife and unmoulding it on to a work surface. Peel off the paper and set it aside.

Heat the broken chocolate pieces with the vegetable oil in a double boiler or in a heavy pan over low heat. Stir occasionally until the chocolate has melted. Place the pan of chocolate in a pan filled with several inches of hot water.

Return the cake to an upright position and brush the top – the least attractive side – with an even coating of chocolate. This will eventually be the bottom of the cake. If the chocolate seems to be too thick, add a few more drops of vegetable oil, enough to thin it sufficiently so that it can be brushed on easily. Allow the chocolate to cool and set completely. Turn the cake over, chocolate side down. Cut the cake into narrow strips, 1½ inches (4cm) wide. You should have six strips. Brush the sides and top of each strip with chocolate, leaving the ends free. If the chocolate becomes too cool, and thus too thick, replace the water in the outside pan with boiling water and stir the chocolate until it has warmed and is fluid. When the chocolate on the strips has set, cut into ½ inch (1·5cm) slices if using immediately or within the next few days. If you wish to store the Baumkuchenschnitten, leave the strips uncut and slice them as needed. If well wrapped, the strips can be kept in the refrigerator for several weeks, or frozen and thawed as needed.

Before slicing, bring the strips to room temperature. For neat slices, heat a sharp knife in hot water before each cut.

NOTE: If you prefer to serve the cake as a dessert rather than as an accompaniment to tea or after-dinner coffee, you can glaze the top of the cake as described in the basic recipe. Then, when cooled, turn the cake over and cut it in half rather than in six strips. Glaze the top and sides as before, leaving the ends free if you want the layers to show, or coating them if you prefer. To serve, cut in ½ inch (1·5cm) slices and pass a bowl of lightly whipped cream separately.

TANNENZAPFEN

Pine-cone Sponge Cake with Butter Cream

A special Swiss dessert for Christmas, this giant pine-cone cake is studded with toasted split almonds and garnished with a branch of evergreen. It is made by cutting a thin sheet of sponge cake into four cone-shaped layers of graduating size, sandwiching and covering them with mocha butter cream, and inserting toasted split blanched almonds over the surface to simulate the scales of a pine-cone.

You will need a 12 by 16 inch (30 by 40cm) baking sheet with a rim and several pieces of paper to make the cone stencils. When making the stencils, fold the pieces of paper in half before cutting so that the cone is symmetrical. In total, you will have four stencils: one large cone which will be the layer second from the bottom; two equal-sized medium cones which will go on either side of the large cone; and one small cone which will go on top. The large cone should measure 10 inches (25cm) long from tip to end, and 5 inches (12·5cm) across at its widest part. The two medium-sized cones should measure 9 inches (23cm) long and 4 inches (10cm) across. The smallest cone should measure 8 inches (20cm) long and 3 inches (8cm) across. The ends of the cones can be perfectly straight though the corners should be slightly rounded.

If the cake is made in advance and frozen, place in the refrigerator ten hours before it is needed, then dust lightly with icing sugar before serving.

Cake

2 oz (50g) plain flour
3 large eggs
1 large egg yolk
3¼ oz (85g) castor sugar
½ tsp vanilla extract
1 oz (25g) butter, melted and cooled
7 oz (200g) whole blanched
    almonds, split (see p.27)

Butter cream

2 tsp instant coffee granules
12 oz (350g) butter, softened
7 oz (200g) icing sugar, sifted
3 large egg yolks

To finish

icing sugar, sifted
twig of evergreen
satin or silver ribbon for a bow
    (optional)

Equipment

paper stencils (see diagram)
baking sheet with rim 12 by
    16 inches (30 by 40cm)

Butter the baking sheet well with soft butter. Cut out a piece of greaseproof or parchment paper the exact size of the bottom and place in the tin. Butter it well. Dust the tin with flour, shaking out the excess. Set aside.

Preheat the oven to 325°F (170°C/gas 3). For the cake, sift the flour once on to a piece of greaseproof paper and set aside. Choose a crockery mixing bowl that will fit into a saucepan with its base resting well above the bottom of the pan. Bring 2 inches (5cm) of water to the boil in the saucepan and remove the pan from the heat. Set the bowl over the pan, put the eggs and sugar into it, and use an electric hand mixer or whisk to beat the mixture rapidly until it is thick and mousse-like – about 4 minutes. To test the consistency, use the beater to lift a little of the mixture and trail the shape of the letter M over the mixture in the bowl. If the shape holds for 3 seconds, the mixture is sufficiently beaten. If the shape dissolves, beat for a further 20 seconds and then test again. Remove the bowl from the pan and beat in the vanilla for 10 seconds. Sift the flour a second time directly on to the whisked egg mixture. Using a metal spoon, fold in the flour carefully. Half-way through the folding, pour on the cooled melted butter and continue folding until the butter is blended and no pockets of flour remain.

Spoon the mixture on to the prepared baking sheet. Using a spatula, spread it evenly to the edges and into the corners. Bake in the middle of the oven until golden and the cake springs back to the touch – about 13 minutes.

While the cake is baking, lay out a clean tea towel or cloth slightly larger than the baking sheet and sprinkle it evenly with granulated or castor sugar – this will help to keep the cake from sticking to it. Remove the cake from the oven and reverse it quickly on to the prepared cloth. Remove the tin. Peel off the piece of paper from the bottom of the cake. Trim off the crusty edges of the cake on all sides with a long knife. Arrange the paper stencils on the cake so that all of them fit. (If you have difficulty fitting one of the stencils, one of the medium-sized cones can be cut out in two pieces and later sandwiched together with a little butter cream.) Using a sharp knife, cut out all the cone shapes and set them aside.

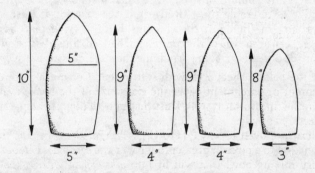

Split the blanched almonds as directed on p. 27. Place them in a single layer on a baking sheet. Bake in the middle of a preheated oven, 425°F (220°C/gas 7) until lightly browned – about 5 to 7 minutes. Watch them carefully as they colour rapidly. Remove the baking sheet from the oven and leave the almonds to cool.

To make the butter cream, dissolve the instant coffee in 2 tbsp of boiling water. Set aside.

Using an electric mixer, beat the butter until it is well creamed. Gradually beat in the sifted icing sugar. Continue beating for at least 8 minutes to dissolve the sugar completely. Beat in the egg yolks, one by one, beating each well before adding the next. Beat in the dissolved coffee and beat for another minute, scraping down the sides of the bowl and blending the coffee thoroughly.

Place a medium-sized cone layer on a serving plate. Set aside one half of the butter cream icing. Spread the remaining icing evenly on all but the smallest layer. Place the largest cone on top of the one already on the serving plate. Place the second medium-sized cone on top of that. Cover with the un-iced small cone. Spread the top, sides and end of the cone with the remaining butter cream icing, smoothing it into the ridges to give the cone a rounded appearance. Dip a metal spatula in hot water and use it to smooth the surface of the icing completely.

Beginning at the point of the cone, insert toasted split almonds, curved side out, pointed end showing so that they lie almost flat. Continue over the top and sides of the cone, completely covering the cake and slightly overlapping the almonds so that they resemble the scales of a real cone. Taper the almonds at the top so they meet approximately in the centre.

Dust a tiny amount of sifted icing sugar just down the centre of the cone to resemble snow. Refrigerate the cake for at least four hours or overnight to firm the icing. Just before serving, place a twig of evergreen at the top of the cone and, if desired, finish with a small bow made of festive ribbon, arranging the streamers decoratively.

PREISELBEERENSCHAUMTORTE

Lingonberry Meringue Cake

This decorative meringue-covered cake from Vienna is made up of rum-soaked layers of Victoria sponge coated with lingonberry preserves. Lingonberries are small red berries resembling red currants or small cranberries; they are fuller flavoured than the latter and thinner skinned than either. Because they are especially tart, they harmonize well with the sweet meringue. While good-quality raspberry jam can be substituted, lingonberries produce a greater contrast in flavour and are readily available in specialist food shops, imported from Germany, Sweden and Eastern Europe.

Because of its spectacular appearance – it has a meringue coating decorated with tiny meringue cups filled with crimson lingonberries and toasted flaked almonds – this cake makes an impressive finish to a special dinner.

Because it takes several hours and a certain amount of patience to prepare, I have worked out the recipe so that it can be made up to two weeks in advance and frozen. The Italian meringue (meringue made with a boiled sugar syrup) holds up perfectly in the freezer. Allow to cool completely before freezing. The cake can be placed in the refrigerator on the day of the dinner and if there is any left over it will keep well, refrigerated.

If freezing, or refrigerating it for more than a day, place five toothpicks or wooden skewers in the top of the cake to stick up well above the meringue cups. Then drape the cake loosely with aluminium foil resting on the wooden picks so it doesn't touch the meringue. Do not place the lingonberry garnish in the tiny cups until just before serving so that there is no danger of the juice 'bleeding'.

A hinged cake tin is called for since, when placed under the cake, the base facilitates moving it from wire rack to baking sheet to serving plate – a task which would otherwise be extremely difficult owing to the weight and size of the cake. It is important to cool it on the baking sheet before attempting to move it. Then loosen the meringue from the baking sheet, using a sharp knife. If you bake the meringue-coated cake on a rimless baking sheet or on the underside of a baking sheet, as recommended in the recipe, you can then slide it easily to a serving plate.

Because it is so rich, it should be served in relatively thin slices – these quantities make up to sixteen servings.

Cake

8 oz (225g) butter, cut in pieces and softened
8 oz (225g) castor sugar
1 tsp vanilla extract
4 large eggs, at room temperature
8 oz (225g) plain flour
1½ tsp baking powder
3 tbsp milk

Syrup

4 tbsp sugar
4 fl oz (125ml) rum

Filling

1¼ lb (575g) lingonberry preserve, or raspberry jam (reserve one-fifth of this amount for garnish)

Meringue

7 large egg whites
(approximately 8 fl oz/230ml),
at room temperature
pinch of salt
4 oz (125g) castor sugar

Meringue syrup

10 oz (300g) granulated sugar

Garnish

2 oz (50g) flaked almonds, to
garnish

12 fl oz (340ml) whipping cream,
to serve
10 oz (300g) lingonberry preserves
to be passed separately (optional)

Equipment

9 inch (23cm) hinged cake tin
1 rimless baking sheet, or the underside of a baking sheet with rim
piping bag fitted with plain ⅜ inch
(1cm) nozzle
jam thermometer

Butter the cake tin. Line it with a round of parchment or greaseproof paper the same size as the bottom. Butter the paper and flour the tin, knocking out the excess flour. Set aside.

Preheat the oven to 350°F (180°C/gas 4). Using an electric mixer, cream the butter and sugar together until light and fluffy. Beat in the vanilla extract. Add one egg at a time, beating well before adding the next. This is necessary to keep the mixture from curdling. Sift the flour and baking powder together. Pour the flour mixture on to the cake mixture and fold it in thoroughly using a large metal spoon. Add the milk and fold it into the mixture. Pour the mixture into the prepared cake tin and spread it evenly with a spatula. Tap the cake tin firmly several times on the counter to knock out any air bubbles. Bake the cake in the oven until golden and the cake springs back to the touch – approximately 35 minutes. Loosen the edges of the cake with a sharp knife. Unmould it on to a cake rack to cool, peeling off the paper. When cool, cut the cake in two slices. Remove the bottom from the hinged tin, wash and dry it, and place it under the bottom half of the cake. Place this in turn on a wire rack.

For the syrup, place the sugar in 4 fl oz (125ml) water and bring to the boil, stirring for 2 minutes. Remove from the heat and add the rum. Prick the surface of the cake base and the top of the lid numerous times with the prongs of a fork. Slowly spoon half of the rum mixture over the base of the cake. Reserve the other half for the lid. Set aside one-fifth of the lingonberry preserve for garnish. Divide the remainder in half. Spread the base of the cake evenly with half of the lingonberries, reaching not quite to the edge. Cover with the top half of the cake. Spoon the remaining syrup slowly over the surface of the cake. Coat it evenly with the remaining lingonberries, reaching not quite to the edge. Set aside.

To make the meringue, place the sugar for the meringue syrup in a heavy-bottomed pan with 3 fl oz (100ml) water. Set aside. Using an electric mixer, beat the egg whites in a large bowl with a pinch of salt. Begin with the mixer on a moderately low speed. When the egg whites are foamy, increase the speed to moderately fast and beat until they hold their shape softly. They should not be dry. Add the 4 oz (125g) of castor sugar by the tablespoon, beating 20 seconds between each. When all the sugar has been added, beat for a further 3 or 4 minutes to make a thick, glossy meringue. Immediately heat the meringue syrup ingredients over a high heat, stirring constantly, until the mixture comes to the boil. Wash down any sugar crystals with a wet pastry brush. Allow the syrup to boil until it reaches the hard ball stage, 248°F (120°C) on a jam thermometer. Pour the hot syrup in a slow steady stream on to the meringue, beating all the time. Beat at high speed until the meringue is cool – approximately 4 minutes. Coat the sides of the cake evenly with a thick layer of meringue, being careful not to mix in any of the lingonberries. Dip a metal spatula in hot water repeatedly and smooth the sides evenly. Place the remaining meringue in a piping bag fitted with a plain ⅜ inch (1cm) nozzle. Beginning on the outside edge of the top, pipe a spiralling circle into the centre of the cake, completely covering the lingonberries. If it isn't perfect, don't worry since it spreads slightly when baked and the flaked almonds cover up mistakes. On the sides, pipe straight up and down waves all the way around the cake. Pipe them as if you were hand-writing an uninterrupted chain of 'U's', reaching up to the top edge of the cake and curving back down to the bottom. Continue the up and down motion to cover the outside of the cake.

Preheat the oven to 450°F (230°C/gas 8). On top of the cake, mark off eight evenly spaced points. Pipe eight small cups, approximately 1¼ inches (3cm) in diameter, going around in a double circle so the cups will be deep enough to hold the final lingonberry garnish. Placing them on one at a time, decorate the top of the cake sparingly with flaked almonds. Slide the cake carefully on to a rimless baking sheet or the underside of a baking sheet with a rim. Bake in the oven until the meringue is lightly browned, watching it carefully. If your oven is hotter in the back than the front, turn the cake once before it is browned all over. Remove the cake from the oven and allow to cool to room temperature before moving. When cool, loosen the meringue from the baking sheet carefully with a sharp knife. When you are sure it isn't sticking, slide the cake (including the metal base from the hinged cake tin) on to a serving plate. Refrigerate or freeze according to the instructions in the introduction. Before serving, fill the meringue cups with the reserved lingonberries.

Serve with lightly whipped cream and extra lingonberry preserve passed separately.

KÄSEKUCHEN
Cheesecake

While Käsekuchen, creamy rich cheesecake baked in a hinged cake tin, would normally be considered everyday baking, like Kugelhopf (p. 169) this is one item against which most German home bakers measure each other's skill. For this reason, I feel it merits elevation to the realm of 'speciality baking.'

The recipe I have chosen is especially rich and creamy and is quick and easy to make. So that it can ripen properly, it is best to make it a day in advance. When loosely covered with aluminium foil, it keeps well in the refrigerator for at least five days.

1 oz (25g) butter, softened, for greasing the pan
5 tbsp dried breadcrumbs
1 tsp sugar
½ tsp ground cinnamon
1 lb (450g) Philadelphia cream cheese, softened
5 oz (150g) castor sugar

4 large eggs
8 fl oz (230ml) whipping cream
2 tbsp plain flour, sifted
1 tsp vanilla extract

Equipment
8 inch (20cm) hinged cake tin

Preheat the oven to 350°F (180°C/gas 4). Grease the cake tin well with the softened butter. Combine the breadcrumbs with the sugar and cinnamon and sprinkle over the sides and bottom of the pan, pressing them to make them stick.

Using an electric mixer, beat the cream cheese with the sugar until creamy – about 2 minutes. Add the eggs, one at a time, beating each well before adding the next. Finally beat in the cream, adding it gradually, then the flour and the vanilla extract. When well blended, scrape down the beaters. Pour the mixture into the prepared tin. Bake in the middle of the oven for 45 minutes. Turn off the oven, leaving the cake inside. Prop the handle of a wooden spoon inside the oven door to keep it slightly ajar. Leave the cake in the oven for 1 to 1½ hours, or until cool. Remove and place in the refrigerator until fully chilled, preferably overnight. To serve, carefully loosen the sides of the cake with a knife and remove the sides of the tin.

STRUDEL

Influenced by the Turkish pastry used for *baklava*, the Hungarians were the first to put strudel on the food map, sprinkling their huge paper-thin round of pastry with butter-toasted breadcrumbs and wrapping it around a filling of juicy apples. The art perfected by the Hungarian bakers soon made its way to Vienna where it became a favourite treat at *Jause* (afternoon tea) filled with apples, sour cherries, plums, ground nuts or ground poppy seeds. When filled with curd cheese (Topfenstrudel) or soured cream and milk (Rahmstrudel), it became a more substantial offering to end the evening meal.

The Viennese learned from the Hungarians the importance of using the right flour – one with plenty of gluten – so that the pastry would develop enough elasticity to be stretched to transparent thinness without tearing. For this reason, bread flour high in gluten has been called for in the recipe rather than pastry or plain flour. If making your own pastry, you will need a large table and a clean sheet or cloth to put over it so that the pastry can be easily rolled when finished. If you don't feel ambitious enough to try your own pastry, I have included a method for using sheets of prepared *fila* pastry, the Middle Eastern pastry which you can buy frozen.

Frau Meyer, a good Viennese friend who comes from a long line of accomplished bakers, told me that in recent years few commercial bakers (with the honourable exception of Demel's) make a strudel which surpasses the traditional home-baked item. The missing ingredient? Butter, lots and lots of butter, used both to toast the breadcrumbs and to coat the thin pastry. Following Frau Meyer's advice, the recipes that follow are well fortified with this favourite Austrian ingredient.

To be at its best, strudel should be eaten as soon as it comes out of the oven or at least before it has completely cooled. At this stage, the leaves of pastry are crisp and separate. Once it has steamed and cooled, the pastry becomes soggy. Not that the strudel isn't delicious even then, but the pastry it is no longer so refined.

For fillings, choose from the apple, sour cherry or plum fillings that follow.

BASIC STRUDEL DOUGH

(Strudelteig)

1 large egg, at room temperature, lightly beaten
1 tsp lemon juice
1 oz (25g) melted butter
12 oz (350g) bread flour
½ tsp salt

To finish

2 tbsp vegetable oil
6 oz (175g) melted butter, or as needed

Crumb mixture

8 oz (225g) dried breadcrumbs
6 oz (175g) butter
3 oz (75g) slivered blanched almonds, coarsely chopped

icing sugar, to finish
whipping cream, to serve

Equipment

large table and clean cloth to cover

Before beginning, you will need a large table, approximately 4 by 5 feet (1·2 by 1·5m), and a clean sheet or large cloth to cover it.

To make the dough, mix 6 fl oz (170ml) water with the egg, lemon juice and melted butter in a small mixing bowl. Sift the flour and salt together into a large mixing bowl and make a well in the centre. Pour the liquid ingredients into the well. Using a wooden spoon, gradually beat in the flour until it is all incorporated. The dough will be sticky at this point. Knead the dough on an unfloured board until it is smooth and elastic and comes away from your hands easily – approximately 7 minutes. Pat the dough into a flat round. Brush the surface with vegetable oil. Cover the dough with a mixing bowl and leave to rest at room temperature for 30 to 40 minutes.

While the dough is resting, brown the breadcrumbs in butter in a large frying pan until golden. If they are especially dry, add a little more butter. Lightly roast the almonds on a baking sheet in a preheated 425°F (220°C/gas 7) oven for approximately 5 minutes to give them a roasted flavour, although this is a personal preference and isn't necessary. In any case, chop them coarsely. Set the almonds and browned crumbs aside.

Prepare the filling you have chosen from one of the recipes that follow and set aside.

When the crumbs, almonds, and filling are prepared and the dough has sufficiently rested, prepare to assemble the strudel. Preheat the oven to 400°F (200°C/gas 6). Cover the table with a clean cloth and dust it lightly with flour. Place the dough on the cloth and, using a rolling pin, roll it as thin as possible. It will be quite resistant. When it will stretch no further with the rolling pin, brush the surface of the dough with vegetable oil. This will keep it from sticking together if it folds on top of itself. Lightly flour your hands. Slip them underneath the dough, palms down, and beginning in the middle of the dough, start pulling gently with the back of your hands, then with your thumbs rather than your fingers, always stretching from the middle out to the outer edges. Rotate your hands around the dough to stretch it evenly all over until the thick ends finally drape over the sides of the table and the dough is paper-thin. Work gently and carefully but if the dough tears, don't worry. It won't ruin the strudel. Moistening your fingers, pinch the hole together as best you can and be extra careful when you roll the strudel. When the dough is thin enough, cut off the thick edge all the way around with scissors. (This can be cut into thin noodles and simmered in a pot of soup, if desired.) Brush the surface of the dough evenly with melted butter.

Scatter the browned breadcrumbs and chopped almonds evenly over the surface of the dough, leaving a 2 inch (5cm) rim free all the way around. Spoon the prepared filling in a long loaf shape near the edge of pastry closest to you, leaving a 3 inch (8cm) rim free between the edge and the filling and 3 inches (8cm) free at either end of the filling. Now, pick up the cloth under the strudel beginning at the edge closest to you and use the cloth to roll the strudel, Swiss roll fashion. Tuck the ends of the pastry in neatly, like a parcel. Brush the pastry well with butter. Place on a large buttered baking sheet, curving it around in a horseshoe shape to make it fit.

Bake just below the centre of the oven until crisp and brown, brushing it generously with butter towards the end of the baking. Baking time will be about 35 to 40 minutes. When done, remove from the oven and cool for 5 minutes before dusting with icing sugar. Serve while still warm with lightly whipped cream.

QUICK FILA PASTRY STRUDEL

Most prepared *fila* pastry comes frozen in sheets slightly larger than standard typewriter paper. The instructions given are for sheets 10 to 12 inches (25 to 30cm) wide and 13 to 14 inches (33 to 35cm) long. Occasionally the pastry comes in huge sheets. In this case, you will not need to piece so many sheets together as instructed here.

Cover a large table with a clean cloth. Using six sheets of pastry, make a large rectangle. With the short side of the rectangles facing you, place three rectangles of pastry side by side, with the edges slightly overlapping. Brush the overlap with melted butter to help seal it. Extend the size of the pastry by placing another three sheets of pastry in front of each of the others, end to end, allowing a 1½ inch (4cm) overlap. Again, brush the overlap with melted butter to seal. You should have a large, almost square patchwork of pastry. Then brush the entire surface of the pastry with butter. If the pastry is not terribly thin, you can stop here. If it is thin and if there are any tears, sprinkle the first layer with some of the browned breadcrumbs (if making apple or cherry strudel). Then place another layer of pastry on top, using six sheets, in the same manner as before. Brush this layer with butter. Then proceed as directed in the master recipe.

APFELSTRUDEL

Apple Strudel

1 recipe basic strudel dough (p. 204)

3½ lb (1·6kg) Granny Smith apples, peeled, cored and thinly sliced
grated rind of 2 lemons
juice of 1 lemon
3 oz (75g) sultanas
5 oz (150g) sugar

Prepare the basic strudel dough, browned breadcrumbs and almonds as in the master recipe, scattering the crumbs and almonds over the strudel dough. Squeeze the lemon juice over the apples once they are sliced and mix together with the grated lemon rind and sultanas. Just before filling, mix in the sugar. Fill and bake according to the instructions in the master recipe.

NOTE: I prefer the lemon flavour to dominate in this filling. However, you can add 1½ tsp of cinnamon to the apple mixture. In a version from the Tyrol, showing obvious Italian influence, 3 oz (75g) of pine nuts are added to the apple filling.

KIRSCHENSTRUDEL

Sour Cherry Strudel

1 recipe basic strudel dough (p. 204)
3 lb (1·4 kg) sour cherries, stoned, or tinned sour cherries, well drained
  (decrease the sugar by a half or two-thirds, depending on the sweetness
  of the cherries)
grated rind of 2 lemons
6½ oz (190g) sugar

Prepare the basic strudel dough, browned breadcrumbs and almonds as in the master recipe, scattering the crumbs and almonds over the strudel dough. Stone the cherries and mix them with the grated lemon rind. Instead of spooning all the cherries in one mound, scatter them evenly over the pastry on top of the crumbs and almonds, leaving a 3 inch (8cm) rim free all the way around. Sprinkle the sugar over the cherries. Then roll and bake according to the instructions in the master recipe.

ZWETSCHKENSTRUDEL

Purple Plum Strudel

In the late summer when small purple plums (*Zwetschken*) are on the market, Zwetschkenstrudel makes a delicious change from the more usual apple or sour cherry fillings.

1 recipe basic strudel dough (p. 204), eliminating the slivered almonds
3 lb (1·4kg) purple plums, pitted and quartered
3¼ oz (85g) sugar
1½ tsp ground cinnamon

Prepare the basic strudel dough and browned breadcrumbs, as in the master recipe, eliminating the slivered almonds. Scatter the crumbs over the strudel dough. Mix all the other above ingredients together. Instead of spooning the plums in one mound, scatter them evenly over the pastry on top of the crumbs, leaving a 3 inch (8cm) rim free all the way around. Then roll and bake according to the instructions in the master recipe.

APFELSTREUSELKUCHEN
Apple Crumble Cake

For many years, whenever I've been visiting my friends in Rothenburg ob der Tauber, in Germany, we've always made a Sunday coffee outing to the tiny village of Freudenbach where Annie Gramm, proprietress of the Gasthof Sonnenhof, bakes her delicious Apfelstreuselkuchen. While it is usually considered to be an everyday cake, not worthy of special excursion, Annie's has always been much lighter and more crumbly than anyone else's. We finally asked her her secret. It is to mix the baking powder with the egg before adding it to the butter and flour. Since baking powder is activated as soon as it is mixed with liquid ingredients and since the pastry isn't allowed to rest before baking, the leavening agent goes to work with full force, producing an especially light crumb.

For a filling, Annie cooks the apple mixture first, then spoons it on top of the bottom layer of pastry and covers it with pastry crumbs. She also recommends rhubarb as an excellent filling.

Once you have cooked the filling, this is a very fast and easy cake to prepare.

Apple filling

2 lb (900g) green or yellow cooking apples, peeled, cored and thinly sliced
2¼ oz (55g) sugar, or more to taste
grated rind of 1 lemon
juice of ½ lemon
½ tsp ground cinnamon
2 oz (50g) sultanas
1 oz (25g) butter

Pastry

8 oz (225g) plain flour, sifted
4 oz (125g) chilled butter
1 large egg
3¼ oz (85g) sugar
1½ tsp baking powder

icing sugar, to finish

Equipment

8 inch (20cm) hinged cake tin

For the filling, mix all the ingredients together in a heavy saucepan with 2 fl oz (60ml) water. Cook the mixture, covered, over a medium low heat, stirring occasionally to make sure the apples aren't sticking on the bottom of the pan. If necessary, add a few more drops of water. Cook until the apples are almost puréed but still have some texture – about 15 minutes. If there is too much liquid, turn the heat to high and simmer, uncovered, stirring so the apples don't stick to the pan. When the mixture is quite thick, remove from the heat and cool to room temperature or refrigerate until needed. The filling can be prepared several days in advance.

Preheat the oven to 350°F (180°C/gas 4). For the pastry, flake the chilled butter into a large bowl. Using a fork, mix the egg with the sugar and baking powder in a small bowl or cup. Pour the egg mixture on to the butter, stirring it in slightly just to help separate the flakes. Sift the flour on top of the butter and egg. Using your fingertips, work the flour into the other ingredients to make a crumb-like texture.

Remove a little over half of the crumb mixture and press it into the bottom of a lightly buttered hinged cake tin. Pat it in evenly with lightly floured hands. It should resemble rich pastry, having lost its crumb-like texture. Prick with a fork.

Spoon the cooled apple filling evenly over the pastry. Crumble the remaining mixture over the filling, distributing the crumbs evenly. Bake the cake in the middle of the oven for about 45 minutes, or until risen and golden. Remove from the oven and allow to rest for several minutes before removing from the tin. While still hot, dust with sifted icing sugar. Serve warm or at room temperature with thick unwhipped or lightly whipped cream, if desired.

RHABARBERSTREUSELKUCHEN

Rhubarb Crumble Cake

Using the pastry and basic instructions for Apfelstreuselkuchen, substitute the following rhubarb filling for the apple filling.

1 lb (450g) trimmed washed rhubarb, cut in 1½ inch (4cm) pieces
5 oz (150g) sugar, or more to taste
2 oz (50g) sultanas
2 tbsp rum (optional)

Mix all the filling ingredients except the rum in a heavy saucepan. Cook the mixture, covered, over a medium low heat, stirring occasionally to make sure the rhubarb isn't sticking to the bottom of the pan. If necessary, add a few tablespoons of water. Cook until the rhubarb is tender – 20 to 30 minutes. If there is too much liquid, turn up the heat and simmer the rhubarb, uncovered, stirring all the time, until the mixture is thick. Stir in the rum, if using, and simmer for a further minute. Allow the rhubarb to cool to room temperature or refrigerate before using.

ENGADINER NUSSTORTE

Engadine Nut Cake

Almost like a sweet, this nut cake from the canton of Engadine is one of my favourites and one of Switzerland's truly great pastries. For the uninitiated, however, this cake would probably pass unnoticed in a pastry shop window, as it has a very plain exterior: simple mahogany brown sweet butter pastry on the sides, top and bottom – no decorations, sugar or icing. The filling is euqally unpretentious – nothing more than caramel cream and walnuts. When the cake is at room temperature, the liquid filling solidifies to a soft, nutty toffee.

One cautionary note: make sure to observe the instructions for using a large, deep, heavy-bottomed pan for caramelizing the sugar, and add the cream slowly. Even though heating the cream as instructed reduces the bubbling reaction, once mixed, the cream and caramel always bubble up. If the pan is too shallow, the mixture will run over the top.

This cake is best made at least one day in advance to allow the caramel to firm and the pastry to soften. The cake will then cut neatly. It is the perfect dessert or gift for caramel-loving friends. It is also useful for taking on picnics or long car rides as it is not at all fragile.

Pastry

8 oz (225g) plain flour	grated rind of 1 large or 2 small
⅛ tsp salt	lemons
4 oz (125) butter	1 large egg
4 oz (125g) castor sugar	1 egg yolk

Filling

8 fl oz (230ml) whipping cream
10 oz (300g) icing sugar
8 oz (225g) walnuts, coarsely chopped

1 egg yolk, beaten with 1 tbsp cream,
  to glaze

Equipment

large, deep, heavy-bottomed
  saucepan
8 inch (20cm) hinged cake tin

Butter the sides and bottom of the cake tin and set aside. Make the pastry using the above ingredients, following the technique for basic sweet rich pastry (p. 212).

On a lightly floured board, roll out the dough in a large thin rectangle, approximately 19 inches (47·5cm) long and 12 inches (30cm) wide. Observe the technique for handling pastry under Baking Tips (p. 31). Using the base of the cake tin as a stencil, cut out two circles. Place one on a piece of greaseproof paper that has been laid on a baking sheet and freeze. This will be your lid. With the sides removed, place the other in the bottom of the cake tin. From the remaining dough, cut out a strip 1½ inches (4cm) wide and long enough to extend around the circumference of the tin. You can use two or three strips and piece them together once they are inside the tin. Replace the ring – the sides – on the tin. Run the strip(s) of dough along the sides, joining it with the base by pressing the seam together well. Refrigerate while making the filling.

Heat the cream in a small pan until almost simmering. Cover and remove from the heat. Sift the icing sugar into a large, deep, heavy-bottomed pan and stir constantly over medium low heat. The sugar will first form into small crusty lumps. Keep stirring and they will soon begin to melt. The mixture will be a caramel colour. Stir until the white lumps have dissolved. Remove from the heat. Immediately add the hot cream in a slow stream. The mixture will boil up so add only a small amount at first. Add the chopped walnuts. Stir briefly over a medium heat to dissolve any bits of caramel that have solidified. Cool to room temperature before proceeding. To speed the cooling process, place the pan of caramel in a bowl of very cold water and stir, changing the water if it becomes too warm. In the meantime, preheat the oven to 375°F (190°C/gas 5).

Remove the pastry-lined cake tin from the refrigerator. Spread the cooled filling evenly over the bottom. Remove the lid from the freezer, peeling off the paper, and place on the top of the filling. Use a pastry wheel or small knife to trim the side rim of pastry evenly so that there is a ½ inch (1·5cm) overlap when the pastry is folded over the lid. Mix the egg yolk and cream with a fork to produce the glaze mixture. With a pastry brush, apply the glaze evenly over the lid. Loosen the side rim of pastry with a table knife. Carefully fold it over the lid, smoothing out any seams, and press it carefully into the lid to seal. Brush the overlap with egg glaze. With the prongs of a fork, prick decorative markings at even intervals just inside the overlapping edge. Prick another circle of tiny holes towards the centre. Bake in the oven until a russet gold – approximately 40 to 50 minutes. Allow the cake to cool completely to room temperature and store in a cool place overnight. If it is refrigerated, allow it to come to room temperature before serving. The next day, or when you are serving the cake, run a knife around the edge of the cake tin to release the pastry. Remove the sides of the hinged tin. Loosen the pastry from the bottom of the tin and transfer it to a serving plate.

BASIC SWEET RICH PASTRY
Süsser Mürbeteig

This pastry is suitable for all dessert tarts, especially those with fruit or custard fillings. The sugar helps to produce a crusty pastry without the need for partial (blind) baking, which is normally required of unsweetened pastries when a juicy or liquid filling is used. The amount given is enough for a 10 to 11 inch (25 to 28cm) tart tin.

6 oz (175g) plain flour
⅛ tsp salt
3 oz (75g) butter, well chilled
3 oz (75g) castor sugar
1 tsp grated lemon rind
1 large egg, lightly beaten

Sift the flour and salt together into a large mixing bowl. Coat the butter with flour from the bowl to make it easier to handle and grate it directly onto the flour, using the coarse blades of a cheese grater. As you grate the butter, mix in the flakes with the flour occasionally, using your fingertips, before grating more. Add the sugar and lemon rind. Using two round-bladed knives, cut the butter into the flour until the texture resembles oatmeal. Shake the bowl, which will cause any larger pieces of butter to rise to the surface. Quickly rub any larger bits of butter into the flour with your fingertips, letting it fall back in the bowl. Continue until the butter is well blended but not greasy – 40 to 60 seconds.

Mix the egg lightly with a fork and pour over the flour mixture. Using the fork, mix the egg into the flour mixture until well distributed. Then, using your hand, pull the dough together into a ball. Knead the dough lightly on a floured board until it forms a cohesive mass. Pat it into a flat round. Wrap tightly in cling film and refrigerate for at least 1 hour before using. Use as directed in the recipe.

WÄHEN

Swiss Tarts

In Swiss German, the word *Wähe* means a tart which can be filled with everything from cheese (*Käswähe*) and vegetables *(Gemüsewähe)* to simple egg, cinnamon and sugar *(Zuckerwähe)* or fruits *(Fruchtwähe)*, such as purple plum, apple, apricot or cherry. Most frequently, the cheese, vegetable and fruit tarts are made with a rich shortcrust pastry and baked with a cream custard mixture which sets with the solid ingredient. While rich yeast dough is also sometimes used for Swiss *Wähe* both sweet and savoury, it is more commonly used in German fruit tarts (*Obstkuchen*) which, for the most part, are not baked with custard. The recipes below are based on the typical Swiss technique.

ZWETSCHGENWÄHE

Plum Tart

In the late summer throughout Switzerland when the small purple plums (*Zwetschken*) are harvested, plain and custard-filled plum tarts appear in bakery-shop windows and farmhouse kitchens. In the Jura region, where I've often consumed this great treat, home bakers generally use enormous fluted black steel tart tins, round or oval, which conduct the heat rapidly to produce an especially crusty pastry. Any kind of tart tin can be used, however, to produce this delicious sunburst of plums. It is best eaten the same or next day – warm or at room temperature – and should not be frozen.

1 recipe basic sweet rich pastry
  (p. 212)

2 lb (900g) purple plums,
  stoned and cut in quarters
3 tbsp castor sugar
2 tsp ground cinnamon
1 oz (25g) butter, cut in flakes

Custard

8 fl oz (230ml) whipping cream
1 tsp cornflour
2 large eggs
1 egg yolk
4 tbsp castor sugar

Equipment

10 inch (25cm) tart tin, preferably
  metal

Make the pastry according to the instructions in the master recipe. Wrap well and refrigerate for at least 1 hour.

Preheat the oven to 375°F (190°C/gas 5). On a lightly floured board, roll the dough out into a thin round 3 to 4 inches (8 to 10cm) larger than the tart tin, see p. 32. Lift the pastry round with your rolling pin and lay it over the tin. Press the pastry well into the sides of the tin, easing some of the excess dough down into the fluted sides to reinforce the edge. Prick the bottom with the prongs of a fork. Run your rolling pin across the top of the tart to cut off the excess pastry. Beginning on the outside edge, place the prepared plums in concentric circles on top of the pastry, skin side down. Dust them with the sugar and cinnamon. Flake the butter on top. Bake for 15 minutes in the oven.

Beat the cornflour into 3 tbsp of the cream. Combine the mixture with the remaining custard ingredients, whisking them briefly to combine well. When the tart has been baking for 15 minutes, pour the custard over the top, adding only as much as the tart can hold. Return to the oven to finish baking until the pastry is golden and the custard has set – another 30 to 35 minutes. Serve warm or at room temperature.

FRUCHTWÄHEN

Fruit Tarts

Besides plums, which have such a short season, apples and fresh or dried apricots – available all year round – are used in fruit tarts with a custard topping. Use the recipe and instructions for Zwetschgen-wähe, substituting apples or apricots as follows.

APFELWÄHE

Apple Tart

Follow the recipe for Zwetschgenwähe, substituting 2 lb (900g) of Golden Delicious apples for the plums and adding 3 oz (75g) of finely ground blanched almonds (see p. 27) and the grated rind of 1 lemon to the basic recipe.

Line the tart tin with the pastry, prick the bottom with the prongs of a fork, and sprinkle the bottom with the ground almonds. Peel, core and quarter the apples. Slice them very thin and toss them in a mixing bowl with the sugar, cinnamon and lemon rind. Place them on top of the almonds, arranging the top layer in neat concentric circles. Flake 2 tbsp of butter on top. Bake for 15 minutes before pouring over the custard mixture, baking until the pastry is golden and the custard has set.

APRIKOSENWÄHE

Apricot Tart

Using fresh apricots, stoned and quartered, instead of plums, follow the recipe for Zwetschgenwähe, eliminating the cinnamon and adding the custard after 15 minutes.

INDEX

MORE ABOUT PENGUINS, PELICANS, PEREGRINES AND PUFFINS

For further information about books available from Penguins please write to Dept EP, Penguin Books Ltd, Harmondsworth, Middlesex UB7 0DA.

In the U.S.A.: For a complete list of books available from Penguins in the United States write to Dept DG, Penguin Books, 299 Murray Hill Parkway, East Rutherford, New Jersey 07073.

In Canada: For a complete list of books available from Penguins in Canada write to Penguin Books Canada Ltd, 2801 John Street, Markham, Ontario L3R 1B4.

In Australia: For a complete list of books available from Penguins in Australia write to the Marketing Department, Penguin Books Australia Ltd, P.O. Box 257, Ringwood, Victoria 3134.

In New Zealand: For a complete list of books available from Penguins in New Zealand write to the Marketing Department, Penguin Books (N.Z.) Ltd, Private Bag, Takapuna, Auckland 9.

In India: For a complete list of books available from Penguins in India write to Penguin Overseas Ltd, 706 Eros Apartments, 56 Nehru Place, New Delhi 110019.